GEORGE TIFFIN

ALL
the
BEST
LINES

A HISTORY OF THE MOVIES IN
QUOTES, NOTES ᴬᴺᴰ ANECDOTES

HEAD
ᵒᶠ ZEUS

An Apollo Book

First published in 2013 by Head of Zeus Ltd
This Apollo paperback edition published in 2019 by Head of Zeus Ltd

1 3 5 7 9 10 8 6 4 2

A CIP catalogue record for this book is available
from the British Library.

ISBN (PB) 9781789542653
ISBN (E) 9781781852026

Typeset by Ed Pickford
Printed and bound in the UK by CPI Group Ltd

Head of Zeus Ltd
5–8 Hardwick Street
London EC1V 4RG
WWW.HEADOFZEUS.COM

ALL
the
BEST
LINES

GEORGE TIFFIN is a writer and film-maker who has travelled from Siberia to the Seychelles shooting and directing music videos and commercials. He is the author of the thriller *Mercy Alexander*.

For my parents, who taught me
to look as well as to listen.

CONTENTS

ESSAYS AND FEATURES

INTRODUCTION

Cinema: spectacle, stars and spotlights. And, somewhere in the distant background, the clatter of a typewriter. This book celebrates the shimmer of the silver screen but really pays tribute to the men and women who dreamed up its stories: the screenwriters.

```
Audiences don't know somebody sits down and
writes a picture. They think the actors make it
up as they go along.
```
> Screenwriter Joe Gillis (William Holden)
> *Sunset Boulevard* (1950)

```
A script has to make sense, and life doesn't.
```
> Screenwriter Harry Dawes (Humphrey Bogart)
> *The Barefoot Contessa* (1954)

In the beginning – the early 1890s – moving pictures were such a novelty that crowds would flock just to see footage of a train pulling into a station, a circus performer or a man sneezing. Before long, directors like D. W. Griffith and Sergei Eisenstein had found ways to shape silent scenes into epic narratives with masterpieces like *The Birth of a Nation* (1915) and *Battleship Potemkin* (1925). But as screen stories grew more sophisticated and engaging one crucial aspect was still absent: the voice.

In 1927 technology enabled feature-length presentations to include a synchronized soundtrack and actors were free to speak at last. Many directors resented this shift in power but producers and public alike embraced the change at once. A subtler shift made itself felt, too: scripts were no longer just structural blueprints but carefully constructed documents filled with description and dialogue that needed pace, sparkle and insight.

The film world was not short of literary talent, and many prestigious authors and journalists soon accepted commissions to write for the movies. But the public had grown used to their stars and no producer wanted to splash the face of a screenwriter across a billboard when he could entice his audience with Errol Flynn or Mae West. Even directors' names remained largely absent from posters for the first half of the twentieth century, but the figures behind the scenes could at least take consolation in their pay cheques. Shortly after his arrival in Hollywood Herman J. Mankiewicz cabled playwright Ben Hecht: 'Will you accept $300 per week to work for Paramount? All expenses paid. $300 is peanuts. Millions are to be grabbed out here and your only competition is idiots. Don't let this get around.' Though Mankiewicz and Hecht may be less well known than their novelist contemporaries Hemingway, Fitzgerald and Steinbeck they penned between them enduring classics such as *Citizen Kane*, *It's a Wonderful World*, *The Pride of St Louis*, *Scarface* and *Notorious*.

The power of a screenwriter to bring a story to life – or to kill it – remains controversial to this day. Alfred Hitchcock famously said 'to make a great film you need three things – the script, the script and the script', while an old industry joke told of the ambitious starlet who was so desperate to break into movies that she seduced a screenwriter. Irving Thalberg, one of the most successful impresarios of Hollywood's golden age, was more astute, remarking that 'the most important person in the motion picture process is the writer, and we must do everything in our power to prevent them from ever realizing it'.

When we see Al Pacino as Shylock in *The Merchant of Venice* we understand we are watching a man interpret Shakespeare's words. When we buy tickets to any theatre production we know we are seeing the work of a particular writer: Strindberg's *Miss Julie*,

Beckett's *Waiting for Godot*. But the cinema is a different world. Who wrote *On the Waterfront* or *Apocalypse Now*? Even while lines like 'I coulda been a contender' or 'I love the smell of napalm in the morning' are universally known, few could name their author.

In many cases, the question is complicated by the fact that films frequently have multiple contributors – for story, for dialogue, for individual scenes or even in some cases to tailor lines for a specific actor. Attribution – and remuneration – are often contentious, leading to the suspicion that the business of screenwriting is perfunctory and competitive. Sitting before their typewriter, laptop or iPad no true writer feels this; as this book hopes to show, they want only to deliver something powerful and true which will captivate us after we have bought our ticket and taken our seat in the dark.

Writers have always had a difficult relationship with their paymasters and it remains true that producers are rarely depicted on screen in a flattering light:

> We're only interested in one thing, Bart. Can you tell a story? Can you make us laugh? Can you make us cry? Can you make us want to break out in joyous song? Is that more than one thing? Okay!

> Producer Jack Lipnick (Michael Lerner)
> *Barton Fink* (1991)

> I was just thinking what an interesting concept it is to eliminate the writer from the artistic process. If we could just get rid of these actors and directors, maybe we've got something here.

> Producer Griffin Mill (Tim Robbins)
> *The Player* (1992)

If these portrayals seem unfair we should remember the genuine remark by Joe Pasternak, one of MGM's staff during the 1950s: 'You call this a script? Give me a couple of $5,000-a-week writers and I'll write it myself.' Many of Pasternak's contracted writers would doubtless have enjoyed watching him try – or, failing that, to accept his cheque since $5,000 back then would be the equivalent of nearly $55,000 today.

While novelists and playwrights enjoy authorial independence and are revered for their unique voices, screenwriters have to satisfy many different masters: producers, directors and actors. To deliver a coherent story in the face of their conflicting demands can be frustrating, if not impossible. Joseph L. Mankiewicz, brother of Herman and author of *All About Eve* and *Cleopatra*, remarked ruefully that 'writers are the highest paid secretaries in the world'. William Goldman, responsible for *All the President's Men*, *Marathon Man* and *The Princess Bride*, is more candid: 'Screenwriting is what feminists call "shit-work"; if it's well done, it's ignored. If it's badly done, people call attention to it.' True of many professions, perhaps, but at least Goldman has two Oscars to show that the best work is often rewarded.

If the names of screenwriters do not readily trip from our tongues, the lines they have written remain with us – zingers, catchphrases, stirring speeches, whispers of endearment. Their words echo everywhere and they prove fitting tribute to their creators long after the credits have rolled.

This book contains five hundred excerpts of varying lengths as well as one-liners, poster quotes, opening scenes and familiar favourites to delight and enlighten. Essays throughout the text shed light on how the scripts were written, and on their journeys from page to celluloid. No matter who dreamed up the story or bought the rights to a bestseller, no matter what it cost or who was cast to play a role, somebody sat down to write it. *All The Best Lines* is about those men and women.

AUTHOR'S NOTE

The films represented are grouped not by genre or title but by theme; a listing will be found on the contents page. Within each theme the running order is chronological; ideally this will allow a lively juxtaposition of style and author. The index will, of course, lead you straight to any particular film the book contains.

Many films benefit from the contributions of uncredited writers. Because this book is not primarily a reference work I have tended to identify only the principal authors, except in cases where anecdotal evidence suggests a more important role.

Where the essays mention budgets and fees I have adjusted figures in line with inflation; modern equivalents are shown in square brackets.

THANKS

Many friends and colleagues sent suggestions for the book. I'm grateful to them all, and hope plenty of them will find their favourites included.

I would particularly like to thank everyone who helped make the process of writing the book such a pleasure: Richard Milbank, Clémence Jacquinet, Anthony Cheetham, Rosie Alison, Plum Webber, Katy Price, Emma Duncan, Edward Tiffin, Titan Fiennes Tiffin, Jane Robertson, Rich Carr and Dan Mogford. The full team at Head of Zeus, Kobal / Shutterstock, and Mercy Fiennes Tiffin have also been vital collaborators.

George Tiffin, June 2019

DREAMS

42ND STREET 1933

Dir: Lloyd Bacon. *Scr*: Rian James, James Seymour. Based on a novel by Bradford Ropes. *Cast*: Warner Baxter (Julian Marsh)

The show's star has broken her leg and the producer encourages the chorus girl who takes her place.

> MARSH
>
> Sawyer, you listen to me, and you listen hard.
> Two hundred people, two hundred jobs, two hundred
> thousand dollars, five weeks of grind and blood
> and sweat depend upon you. It's the lives of
> all these people who've worked with you. You've
> got to go on, and you've got to give and give
> and give. They've got to like you. Got to. Do
> you understand? You can't fall down. You can't
> because your future's in it, my future and
> everything all of us have is staked on you. All
> right, now I'm through, but you keep your feet
> on the ground and your head on those shoulders of
> yours and go out, and Sawyer, you're going out a
> youngster but you've got to come back a star!

SNOW WHITE AND THE SEVEN DWARFS 1937

Dir: David Hand and five others. *Scr*: Dorothy Ann Blank, Richard Creedon, Merrill De Maris, Otto Englander, Earl Hurd, Dick Rickard, Ted Sears, Webb Smith. Based on a story by Jacob and Wilhelm Grimm. *Cast*: Moroni Olsen (voice of the Magic Mirror)

> MAGIC MIRROR
>
> Prepare to be amazed beyond all expectations.
> After all, it is what I do.

This was Walt Disney's first full-length animated feature and still ranks twelfth among the highest grossing films of all time. Although the company focuses on mainstream family entertainment, the director Sergei Eisenstein proclaimed Disney's work 'the greatest contribution of the American people to art' and the critic Mark Van Doren called him a 'first-rate artist [who] knows innumerable truths that cannot be taught'.

GONE WITH THE WIND   1939
Dir: Victor Fleming. *Scr*: Sidney Howard. Based on a novel by Margaret Mitchell. *Cast*: Vivien Leigh (Scarlett O'Hara)

```
              SCARLETT
   As God is my witness they're not going to lick
   me. I'm going to live through this and when it's
   all over, I'll never be hungry again. No, nor any
   of my folk. If I have to lie, steal, cheat or
   kill. As God is my witness, I'll never be hungry
   again.
```

THE MALTESE FALCON   1941
Dir: John Huston. *Scr*: John Huston. Based on a novel by Dashiell Hammett. *Cast*: Ward Bond (Detective Tom Polhaus), Humphrey Bogart (Sam Spade)

Polhaus finally has his hands on the Maltese Falcon, a priceless figurine the pursuit of which has caused mayhem and murder galore.

```
              DETECTIVE POLHAUS
   Heavy. What is it?

              SAM SPADE
   The stuff that dreams are made of.
```

The Maltese Falcon was John Huston's directorial debut, but it was the third screen version of Hammett's novel. The film's final line is a tribute to Prospero's closing speech in Shakespeare's *The Tempest*: 'We are such stuff/As dreams are made on.'

FILM NOIR

'People like me like dark pictures – dark and mysterious. Most were B-movies made on the cheap, others were classy models with A-talent. But they all had one thing in common – they lived on the edge, told stories about life on the streets, shady characters, crooked cops, twisted love and bad luck. The French invented a name for these pictures: film noir. Black film, that's what they called them – about a darker side of human nature. About the world as it really was.'

Richard Widmark
Kiss of Death (1947), *Night and the City* (1950),
Pickup on South Street (1953)

Few genres are unique to the movies; novels, plays and musicals had charted the realms of drama, melodrama, tragedy and farce long before celluloid was invented and for a while mainstream cinema seemed content to base itself on these established styles. No medium, however, had ever been able to reach such huge audiences.

By the 1940s cinema-goers in America were buying sixty million tickets a week. Barely able to meet this demand, studios were quite happy to turn out B-movies, projects created to fill theatres and keep their roster of contracted talent busy without requiring the budgets of their bigger pictures. Not surprisingly, these films were less closely supervised and could be made with a greater degree of freedom, which writers and directors were eager to seize, drawing on an unlikely combination of factors to create – almost accidentally – what we now recognize as film noir.

Weary after the Depression and now in the midst of a global war, audiences had grown impatient with wholesome, censor-approved material. The rise of the pulp novel, with racier protagonists and sexier women, showed that the public was ready for stronger stuff and film-makers were quick to recognize the appeal of hard-boiled writers like Raymond Chandler, James M. Cain and Jim Thompson.

If mainstream studios were still reluctant to put big budgets behind such risqué material, directors like Jacques Tourneur and Robert Wise made the most of these new opportunities. The influx of European talent had spread the influence of German expressionist cinema which suited cheap production perfectly; low lighting budgets created stark chiaroscuro moods mirroring shady storylines, while the fragmented visuals conveniently hid flaws in flimsy sets and affordable locations.

John Huston, Otto Preminger and Orson Welles refined the genre with bigger budget pictures such as *The Maltese Falcon* (1941), *Laura* (1944) and *The Lady from Shanghai* (1947); today, noir remains the most influential and imitated of all film styles and lives on in such diverse classics as *Blade Runner* (1982), *Heat* (1995), *L.A. Confidential* (1997) and *Sin City* (2005). The earliest noir quotes still seem as powerfully contemporary today:

JILL: What's the good of living without hope?
ED: It can be done.
I Wake Up Screaming (1941)

Well, well. You're the first woman I've ever met who said yes when she meant yes.
Suspicion (1941)

A woman doesn't care how a guy makes a living, just how he makes love.
Murder My Sweet (1944)

She was a charming middle-aged lady with a face like a bucket of mud. I gave her a drink. She was a gal who'd take a drink if she had to knock you down to get the bottle.
Murder My Sweet (1944)

Personally, Veda's convinced me that alligators have the right idea. They eat their young.
Mildred Pierce (1945)

She was worth a stare, she was trouble.
The Big Sleep (1946)

I can be framed easier than 'Whistler's Mother'.
The Dark Corner (1946)

How I detest the dawn. The grass always looks like it's been left out all night.
The Dark Corner (1946)

LEROY: Is he dead?
CAPTAIN FINLAY: He's been dead for a long time — he just didn't know it.
Crossfire (1947)

ADRIENNE: Do you fall in love with all of your clients?
MARLOWE: Only the ones in skirts.
Lady in the Lake (1947)

KATHIE: Oh Jeff, you ought to have killed me for what I did a minute ago.
JEFF: There's still time.
Out of the Past (1947)

Those gates only open three times. When you come in, when you've served your time, or when you're dead.
Brute Force (1947)

It was the bottom of the barrel, and I was scraping it.
Out of the Past (1947)

I want you to do something. I want you to get yourself out of the bed, and get over to the window and scream as loud as you can. Otherwise you only have another three minutes to live.
Sorry, Wrong Number (1948)

Experience has taught me never to trust a policeman. Just when you think one's all right, he turns legit.
The Asphalt Jungle (1950)

COP: Can I help you?
BIGELOW: I want to report a murder.
COP: Where was this murder committed?
BIGELOW: San Francisco, last night.
COP: Who was murdered?
BIGELOW: I was.
D.O.A. (1950)

I saw the two of you, the way you were looking at each other tonight, like a couple of wild animals. Almost scared me.
Gun Crazy [aka *Deadly is the Female*] (1950)

You'll always be a two-bit cannon. And when they pick you up in the gutter dead, your hand'll be in a drunk's pocket.
Pickup on South Street (1953)

Every extra buck has a meaning all its own.
Pickup on South Street (1953)

MIKE: You're never around when I need you.
VELDA: You never need me when I'm around.
Kiss Me Deadly (1955)

I'd hate to take a bite out of you. You're a cookie full of arsenic.
Sweet Smell of Success (1957)

THE LOST WEEKEND   1947

Dir: Billy Wilder. *Scr*: Billy Wilder, Charles Brackett. Based on a novel by Charles R. Jackson. *Cast*: Ray Milland (Don Birnam)

A struggling writer confesses that he only feels alive when drinking.

> DON
> It shrinks my liver, doesn't it, Nat? It pickles
> my kidneys, yeah. But what it does to the mind?
> It tosses the sandbags overboard so the balloon
> can soar. Suddenly I'm above the ordinary.
> I'm competent. I'm walking a tightrope over
> Niagara Falls. I'm one of the great ones. I'm
> Michelangelo, moulding the beard of Moses. I'm Van
> Gogh painting pure sunlight. I'm Horowitz, playing
> the Emperor Concerto. I'm John Barrymore before
> movies got him by the throat. I'm Jesse James and

```
his two brothers, all three of them. I'm
W. Shakespeare. And out there it's not Third
Avenue any longer. It's the Nile. The Nile, Nat,
and down it moves the barge of Cleopatra.
```

HARVEY   1950

Dir: Henry Koster. *Scr*: Mary Chase, Oscar Brodney. Based on a play by Mary Chase. *Cast*: Josephine Hull (Veta Louise Simmons)

```
          VETA LOUISE
Myrtle Mae, you have a lot to learn and I hope you
never learn it.
```

GENTLEMEN PREFER BLONDES   1953

Dir: Howard Hawks. *Scr*: Charles Lederer. Based on a musical by Joseph Fields and a novel and play by Anita Loos. *Cast*: Marilyn Monroe (Lorelei Lee), Taylor Holmes (Mr Esmond Sr)

```
          ESMOND SR
Have you got the nerve to tell me you don't want
to marry my son for his money?

          LORELEI
It's true.

          ESMOND SR
Then what do you want to marry him for?

          LORELEI
I want to marry him for your money.
```

Monroe frequently demanded time-consuming retakes even after director Howard Hawks was satisfied. When the studio asked Hawks how to speed up the Production, he replied: 'Replace Marilyn, shorten the script and get a new director.'

SABRINA   1954

Dir: Billy Wilder. *Scr*: Billy Wilder, Ernest Lehman, Samuel A. Taylor. Based on a play by Samuel A. Taylor. *Cast*: Audrey Hepburn (Sabrina Fairchild), John Williams (Thomas Fairchild)

Sabrina refuses to let her father stand in the way of her love for David, a millionaire.

> THOMAS
>
> He's still David Larrabee, and you're still the chauffeur's daughter. And you're still reaching for the moon.

> SABRINA
>
> No, Father. The moon is reaching for me.

THE SEARCHERS   1956

Dir: John Ford. *Scr*: Frank S. Nugent. Based on a novel by Alan Le May. *Cast*: Olive Carey (Mrs Jorgensen)

A settler in 1860s Texas contemplates the devastation on both sides as ranchers battle Comanche braves.

> MRS JORGENSEN
>
> Some day this country's gonna be a fine, good place to be. Maybe it needs our bones in the ground before that time can come.

THE SEVENTH SEAL / *Det Sjunde Inseglet*   1957

Dir: Ingmar Bergman. *Scr*: Ingmar Bergman, based on his play. *Cast*: Max von Sydow (Antonius Block)

In a medieval community ravaged by plague, the knight Antonius Block wonders how God can permit such horror.

ANTONIUS

Faith is a torment. It is like loving someone who
is out there in the darkness but never appears, no
matter how loudly you call.

AUNTIE MAME   1958

Dir: Morton DaCosta. *Scr*: Betty Comden, Adolph Green. Based on a novel by
Patrick Dennis and a play by Jerome Lawrence and Robert Edwin Lee. *Cast*:
Rosalind Russell (Mame Dennis)

The wild and unconventional Mame is determined to raise her
nephew with a true zest for life.

AUNTIE MAME

Live! Life is a banquet, and most poor suckers are
starving to death!

THE MATCHMAKER   1958

Dir: Joseph Anthony. *Scr*: John Michael Hayes. Based on a play by Thornton
Wilder. *Cast*: Shirley Booth (Dolly 'Gallagher' Levi)

Dolly, a divorcée–turned–matchmaker, addresses the audience as
she tries to persuade us that adventures lie ahead.

DOLLY

Life's never quite interesting enough, somehow.
You people who come to the movies know that.

PLAN 9 FROM OUTER SPACE   1959

Dir: Edward D. Wood Jr. *Scr*: Edward D. Wood Jr. *Cast*: Criswell (Narrator)

NARRATOR

Greetings, my friends! We are all interested in
the future, for that is where you and I are going
to spend the rest of our lives.

The production was funded by a Baptist church; it took three years to find a distributor who would take it on, only for it to be voted Worst Film of All Time in *The Golden Turkey Awards* (1980).

BREATHLESS / A Bout de souffle   1960

Dir: Jean-Luc Godard. *Scr*: François Truffaut, Jean-Luc Godard, Claude Chabrol. *Cast*: Jean Seberg (Patricia Franchini), Jean-Pierre Melville (Parvulesco)

An aspiring journalist interviews a writer whose answers are always unexpected.

               PATRICIA
What is your greatest ambition in life?

               PARVULESCO
To become immortal. . . and then die.

THE NEW WAVE

Jean-Luc Godard (b. 1930) may be the only director in film history to have won his career break by insulting a producer: Georges de Beauregard was so impressed by Godard's scathing honesty about a recent film that he hired the young press agent to work on a script he was developing. Godard quickly became bored of the project but had read a treatment for another film about a petty criminal by two star directors, François Truffaut and Claude Chabrol. De Beauregard was intrigued, Truffaut and Chabrol liked the idea of Godard directing it, and since the budget was modest they quickly secured funding.

Across the Atlantic, the golden age of Hollywood was waning and studios were relying increasingly on glossy epics and musicals in their fight against the lure of television. In

Europe, a new school of simpler, more realistic film storytelling was gaining popularity: *Breathless* was the picture that fully captured this spirit in a way that was to transform cinematic narrative across the world. It also established the career of Jean Seberg, the young American who played Patricia; on seeing her performance, Truffaut declared her 'the best actress in Europe'.

Godard's production style would have shocked his American counterparts. Working from an ever-changing script, he shot in real locations across Paris, without official permission, with a small crew and portable equipment. In order to accommodate low light levels, cinematographer Raoul Coutard used Ilford HP5 negative intended for stills cameras and forced its development in the laboratory, giving the image a grainy look. This, combined with the fact that the camera itself was light enough to be hand-held, contributed enormously to the rough-and-ready immediacy of the action.

Godard would write or rewrite scenes each morning in an exercise book nobody else was allowed to read and would sometimes only give the actors their lines as they were being filmed to increase the feeling of spontaneity. On the first day of filming, 17 August 1959, the crew only shot for two hours. Thereafter, the schedule essentially followed the amount of material the director needed, or had prepared. Truffaut, whose involvement had enabled the funding, only visited the set twice and Chabrol never appeared at all. Producer de Beauregard worried that the production was proceeding erratically, and on one occasion got into a fist-fight with Godard when he discovered him in a café after the director had called in sick.

The film also broke conventions in the way it edited the footage together, and the frequent 'jump cuts', which made no attempt to match related action or angles, added to the sense of energy and realism. So bold were the innovations that critics coined a new term for the school of pioneering directors:

Nouvelle Vague, or the New Wave. If the writing about this new style was occasionally overwrought – Andrew Sarris claimed the jagged narrative revealed 'the meaninglessness of the time interval between moral decisions' – the legacy of *Breathless* and similar films changed cinema for ever, influencing directors as diverse as Bertolucci, Scorsese, Wenders and Tarantino.

THE LEOPARD / *Il gattopardo* 1963

Dir: Luchino Visconti. *Scr*: Suso Cecchi D'Amico, Pasquale Festa Campanile, Enrico Medioli, Massimo Franciosa, Luchino Visconti. Based on a novel by Giuseppe Tomasi di Lampedusa. *Cast*: Alain Delon (Tancredi Falconeri)

During the upheavals of the nineteenth century in Sicily, the aristocratic Corbera family take stock of the turmoil around them.

> TANCREDI
>
> If we want things to stay as they are, things will have to change.

THE WILD ANGELS 1966

Dir: Roger Corman. *Scr*: Charles B. Griffith, Peter Bogdanovich. *Cast*: Peter Fonda (Heavenly Blues)

A Hell's Angel explains his credo.

> BLUES
>
> We want to be free! We want to be free to do what we want to do! We want to be free to ride. And we want to be free to ride our machines without being hassled by the Man. And we want to get loaded. And we want to have a good time! And that's what we're gonna do. We're gonna have a good time. We're gonna have a party!

Shot three years before *Easy Rider*, Roger Corman's film about motorcycles, rebellion and counter-culture also starred Peter Fonda. The real Hell's Angels, some of whom appeared as extras in the film, temporarily abandoned their anarchic beliefs to sue Corman for $5 million [$38.5 million] for portraying their organization in 'a negative light'.

PLANET OF THE APES   1968

Dir: Franklin J. Schaffner. *Scr*: Michael Wilson, Rod Serling. Based on a novel by Pierre Boulle. *Cast*: Charlton Heston (George Taylor)

> **GEORGE**
> I can't help thinking that somewhere in the
> universe there has to be something better than
> man. Has to be.

Although the actors playing apes were assigned their species randomly they found that even during breaks they congregated in groups according to whether they had been cast as gorillas, chimps or orangutans. Composer Jerry Goldsmith was reputed to have worn a gorilla mask while writing and even conducting the score.

BUTCH CASSIDY AND THE SUNDANCE KID   1969

Dir: George Roy Hill. *Scr*: William Goldman. *Cast*: Paul Newman (Butch Cassidy)

Outlaw Butch Cassidy describes his ambition to his partner in crime.

> **BUTCH**
> I got vision, and the rest of the world wears
> bifocals.

THE PRIME OF MISS JEAN BRODIE   1969

Dir: Ronald Neame. *Scr*: Jay Presson Allen Jay, based on his play. Based on a novel by Muriel Spark. *Cast*: Maggie Smith (Jean Brodie)

A headstrong, visionary teacher intends to mould her pupils as she sees fit.

>   MISS BRODIE
> Little girls, I am in the business of putting
> old heads on young shoulders, and all my
> pupils are the crème de la crème. Give me a
> girl at an impressionable age and she is mine
> for life.

LOVE AND DEATH   1975

Dir: Woody Allen. *Scr*: Woody Allen. *Cast*: Woody Allen (Boris Grushenko), Diane Keaton (Sonja)

During Napoleon's invasion of Russia, Boris, a cowardly intellectual, chats with his cousin Sonya.

>   BORIS
> Nothingness... non-existence... black
> emptiness...
>
>   SONJA
> What did you say?
>
>   BORIS
> Oh, I was just planning my future.

CALIFORNIA SUITE   1978

Dir: Herbert Ross. *Scr*: Neil Simon. *Cast*: Jane Fonda (Hannah Warren)

Hannah argues with her ex-husband about their daughter's future.

HANNAH
You're worse than a hopeless romantic. You're a
hopeful one.

GREYSTOKE: THE LEGEND OF TARZAN   1984

Dir: Hugh Hudson. *Scr*: Robert Towne (as P. H. Vazak), Michael Austin. Based
on a novel by Edgar Rice Burroughs. *Cast*: Ian Holm (Captain Philippe D'Arnot)

Explorers sail to the coast of an uncharted Africa.

D'ARNOT
This is not the world, John. Just the edge of it.

With *Greystoke*, director Hugh Hudson hoped to deliver a faithful
representation of Burroughs' original hero; Academy Award-
winning writer Robert Towne (*Chinatown*, *Reds*) was so unhappy
with Hudson's vision that he asked for his name to be replaced with
that of his sheepdog, P. H. Vazak. The dog was duly nominated for
an Oscar.

DEAD POETS SOCIETY   1989

Dir: Peter Weir. *Scr*: Tom Schulman. *Cast*: Robin Williams (John Keating)

A schoolteacher warns his pupils that life passes all too quickly.

KEATING
Now I would like you to step forward over here
and peruse some of the faces from the past.
You've walked past them many times. I don't think
you've really looked at them. They're not that
different from you, are they? Same haircuts. Full
of hormones, just like you. Invincible, just like
you feel. The world is their oyster. They believe
they're destined for great things, just like many

of you. Their eyes are full of hope, just like
you. Did they wait until it was too late to make
from their lives even one iota of what they were
capable? Because you see, gentlemen, these boys
are now fertilizing daffodils. But if you listen
real close, you can hear them whisper their legacy
to you. Go on, lean in. Listen. Do you hear it?

He whispers:

            KEATING
Carpe... Hear it?

And again:

            KEATING
Carpe. Carpe Diem. Seize the day, boys. Make your
lives extraordinary.

FIELD OF DREAMS   1989

Dir: Phil Alden Robinson. *Scr*: Phil Alden Robinson. Based on a novel by W.P.
Kinsella. *Cast*: Kevin Costner (Ray Kinsella), Dwier Brown (John Kinsella)

Ray Kinsella is visited by the ghost of his father.

            JOHN KINSELLA
Is this heaven?
            RAY KINSELLA
It's Iowa.

NATIONAL LAMPOON'S CHRISTMAS VACATION   1989

Dir: Jeremiah Chechik. *Scr*: John Hughes. *Cast*: Chevy Chase (Clark Griswold)

Clark wants to give his family the best Christmas ever but his plans
are thwarted when his boss cuts his bonus.

            CLARK
Hey! If any of you are looking for any last-minute

gift ideas for me, I have one. I'd like Frank
Shirley, my boss, right here tonight. I want him
brought from his happy holiday slumber over there
on Melody Lane with all the other rich people and
I want him brought right here, with a big ribbon
on his head, and I want to look him straight in
the eye and I want to tell him what a cheap,
lying, no-good, rotten, four-flushing, low-life,
snake-licking, dirt-eating, inbred, overstuffed,
ignorant, blood-sucking, dog-kissing, brainless,
dickless, hopeless, heartless, fat-ass, bug-eyed,
stiff-legged, spotty-lipped, worm-headed sack of
monkey shit he is! Hallelujah!

GAS FOOD LODGING 1992

Dir: Allison Anders. *Scr*: Allison Anders. Based on a novel by Richard Peck. *Cast*:
Donovan Leitch (Darius)

Teenager Darius tries to persuade his date that women are the true
adventurers.

DARIUS
Well, it's like Adam and Eve. He was fine grooving
in paradise, but Eve wanted something scary. She
wanted the fucking edge. She wanted to jump off
cliffs just so she could see what it was like to
fall.

THE SHAWSHANK REDEMPTION 1994

Dir: Frank Darabont. *Scr*: Frank Darabont. Based on a novella by Stephen King.
Cast: Morgan Freeman (Ellis Boyd 'Red' Redding)

A prisoner risks punishment by broadcasting an opera aria over the
workyard loudspeakers.

> RED
>
> I have no idea to this day what those two
> Italian ladies were singing about. Truth is,
> I don't want to know. Some things are best
> left unsaid. I'd like to think they were
> singing about something so beautiful it can't
> be expressed in words, and makes your heart
> ache because of it. I tell you, those voices
> soared higher and farther than anybody in a
> grey place dares to dream. It was like some
> beautiful bird flapped into our drab little
> cage and made those walls dissolve away, and
> for the briefest of moments every last man in
> Shawshank felt free.

Although the film did not prove a hit in cinemas, it has grown hugely in popularity and is now ranked number one in the Internet Movie Database readers' poll. Since one of the inmates keeps a pet crow, the American Humane Association was present during the shoot to make sure it was properly treated; they approved of the bird's conditions but objected to the scene where the inmate feeds it a maggot on the grounds that it was cruel to the bug. Happily, a maggot that had died from natural causes was discovered and used instead.

THE BRIDGES OF MADISON COUNTY   1995

Dir: Clint Eastwood. *Scr*: Richard LaGravenese. Based on a novel by Robert James Waller. *Cast*: Clint Eastwood (Robert Kincaid)

A passionate affair causes a photographer to review his life.

> ROBERT
>
> The old dreams were good dreams; they didn't work
> out, but glad I had them.

IN THE BEGINNING

After the Twentieth Century-Fox searchlight has swept the sky, the MGM lion has roared and (for those of us old enough to remember) Rank's sculpted bodybuilder has beaten the vast gong an expectant hush settles over the audience as we await the first moments of the film. No wonder screenwriters feel the pressure of capturing our attention in the very opening scene, and actors vie for the juiciest lines for us to recite when the lights come up. Here are some of the most captivating opening salvos:

Rosebud...
Citizen Kane (1941)

This is the universe. Big, isn't it?
A Matter of Life and Death (1946)

I never knew the old Vienna before the war, with its Strauss music, its glamour and easy charm — Constantinople suited me better.
The Third Man (1949)

ANTONIUS: Who are you?
DEATH: I am Death.
The Seventh Seal (1957)

Maycomb was a tired old town, even in 1932 when I first knew it. Somehow, it was hotter then. Men's stiff collars wilted by nine in the morning.
To Kill a Mockingbird (1962)

Ladies and gentlemen, welcome to violence, the word and the act.
Faster, Pussycat! Kill! Kill! (1965)

What can you say about a twenty-five-year-old girl who died? That she was beautiful and brilliant? That she loved Mozart and Bach, the Beatles, and me?
Love Story (1969)

I believe in America.
The Godfather (1972)

I am not a bum. I'm a jerk. I once had wealth, power, and the love of a beautiful woman. Now I only have two things: my friends and... uh... my thermos.
The Jerk (1979)

Saigon... Shit. I'm still only in Saigon. Every time I think I'm gonna wake up back in the jungle. When I was home after my first tour, it was worse. I'd wake up and there'd be nothing. I hardly said a word to my wife, until I said 'yes' to a divorce. When I was here, I wanted to be there; when I was there, all I could think of was getting back into the jungle. I'm here a week now, waiting for a mission, getting softer. Every minute I stay in this room, I get weaker, and every minute Charlie squats in the bush, he gets stronger. Each time I looked around the walls moved in a little tighter.
Apocalypse Now (1979)

I was twelve going on thirteen first time I saw a dead human being.
Stand By Me (1986)

Today is a good day to die.
Flatliners (1990)

As far back as I can remember, I always wanted
to be a gangster.
Goodfellas (1990)

Oh, fuck! Fuck!
Four Weddings and a Funeral (1994)

Come to Los Angeles! The sun shines bright,
the beaches are wide and inviting, and the
orange groves stretch as far as the eye can
see. There are jobs aplenty, and land is cheap.
L.A. Confidential (1997)

We were somewhere around Barstow on the edge
of the desert when the drugs began to take
hold.
Fear and Loathing in Las Vegas (1998)

My name is Lester Burnham. This is my
neighbourhood; this is my street; this is my
life. I am forty-two years old; in less than a
year I will be dead. Of course I don't know that
yet, and in a way, I am dead already.
American Beauty (1999)

What came first, the music or the misery?
High Fidelity (2000)

The world has changed. I feel it in the water.
I feel it in the earth. I smell it in the air.
The Lord of the Rings: The Fellowship of the Ring (2001)

> I only ever met one man I wouldn't wanna fight.
> *Million Dollar Baby* (2004)
>
> Are you watching closely?
> *The Prestige* (2006)
>
> There's a hundred thousand streets in this city.
> You don't need to know the route. You give me a
> time and a place, I give you a five-minute window.
> Anything happens in that five minutes and I'm
> yours. No matter what. Anything happens a minute
> either side of that and you're on your own. Do
> you understand?
> *Drive* (2011)

TRAINSPOTTING   1996

Dir: Danny Boyle. *Scr*: John Hodge. Based on a novel by Irvine Welsh. *Cast*:
Ewan McGregor (Mark 'Rent Boy' Renton)

A junkie celebrates the thrill of oblivion.

> RENTON
> Choose life. Choose a job. Choose a career.
> Choose a family. Choose a fucking big television,
> choose washing machines, cars, compact disc
> players and electrical tin openers. Choose good
> health, low cholesterol, and dental insurance.
> Choose fixed interest mortgage repayments.
> Choose a starter home. Choose your friends.
> Choose leisurewear and matching luggage. Choose
> a three-piece suite on hire purchase in a range
> of fucking fabrics. Choose DIY and wondering
> who the fuck you are on Sunday morning. Choose
> sitting on that couch watching mind-numbing,

> spirit-crushing game shows, stuffing fucking junk
> food into your mouth. Choose rotting away at the
> end of it all, pissing your last in a miserable
> home, nothing more than an embarrassment to the
> selfish, fucked-up brats you spawned to replace
> yourselves. Choose your future. Choose life...
> But why would I want to do a thing like that? I
> chose not to choose life. I chose somethin' else.
> And the reasons? There are no reasons. Who needs
> reasons when you've got heroin?

The first twenty minutes of the Edinburgh-set film had to be redubbed for American audiences. Director Danny Boyle had hoped to license the theme music to *Mission: Impossible* for one sequence until he discovered it would have cost three times the production's budget.

THE TALENTED MR RIPLEY   1999

Dir: Anthony Minghella. *Scr*: Anthony Minghella. Based on a novel by Patricia Highsmith. *Cast*: Matt Damon (Tom Ripley)

A New York lavatory attendant passes himself off as a well-to-do Princeton student.

> RIPLEY
> I always thought it would be better to be a fake
> somebody than a real nobody.

THE MATRIX   1999

Dir: Andy Wachowski, Lana Wachowski. *Scr*: Andy Wachowski, Lana Wachowski. *Cast*: Keanu Reeves (Neo), Carrie-Anne Moss (Trinity)

Cyber-warrior Trinity persuades Neo to join forces with the mysterious Orpheus, who leads the fight against the machines that have enslaved humanity.

TRINITY

I know why you're here, Neo. I know what you've been doing... why you hardly sleep, why you live alone, and why night after night you sit by your computer. You're looking for him. I know because I was once looking for the same thing. And when he found me, he told me I wasn't really looking for him. I was looking for an answer. It's the question that drives us, Neo. It's the question that brought you here. You know the question, just as I did.

NEO

What is the Matrix?

TRINITY

The answer is out there, Neo, and it's looking for you, and it will find you if you want it to.

THE SIXTH SENSE   1999

Dir: M. Night Shyamalan. *Scr*: M. Night Shyamalan. *Cast*: Bruce Willis (Dr Malcolm Crowe), Haley Joel Osment (Cole Sear)

A child psychologist tries to help a young boy who is visited by ghosts.

COLE

I see dead people.

MALCOLM

In your dreams?

Cole shakes his head.

MALCOLM

While you're awake?

Cole nods.

> MALCOLM
>
> Dead people like, in graves? In coffins?

> COLE
>
> Walking around like regular people. They don't see
> each other. They only see what they want to see.
> They don't know they're dead.

> MALCOLM
>
> How often do you see them?

> COLE
>
> All the time. They're everywhere.

Director M. Night Shyamalan described the project to his backers as a cross between *The Exorcist* and *Ordinary People*. Toni Collette (playing Cole's mother) was so immersed in the real emotions of the family that she failed to realize the film was a horror story.

BILLY ELLIOT   2000

Dir: Stephen Daldry. *Scr*: Lee Hall. *Cast*: Jamie Bell (Billy Elliot)

A young boy growing up in a tough mining town fights to protect his dream.

> BILLY
>
> I don't want a childhood. I want to be a ballet
> dancer.

I, ROBOT   2004

Dir: Alex Proyas. *Scr*: Jeff Vintar, Akiva Goldsman. Based on short stories by Isaac Asimov. *Cast*: William Smith (Detective Del Spooner), Alan Tudyk (Sonny)

Detective Spooner questions Sonny, a robot, reluctant to believe it is capable of independent thought.

SPOONER

Human beings have dreams. Even dogs have dreams,
but not you — you're just a machine. An imitation
of life. Can a robot write a symphony? Can a robot
turn a canvas into a beautiful masterpiece?

SONNY

Can you?

THE DEPARTED   2006

Dir: Martin Scorsese. *Scr*: William Monahan. *Cast*: Jack Nicholson (Frank
Costello)

Frank Costello, a Boston mobster, explains his power over the
community.

COSTELLO

I don't want to be a product of my environment.
I want my environment to be a product of me.

When Martin Scorsese received a Director's Guild of America award
for the film, he claimed: 'this is the first movie I have ever done
with a plot'. Jack Nicholson relished the opportunity to play Frank
Costello, describing his character as 'the pure incarnation of evil'.
With Scorsese's approval he improvised much of his performance,
including the scene in a porn theatre where he startles Matt Damon
by pretending to ejaculate on him with a dildo.

SEX AND THE CITY   2008

Dir: Michael Patrick King. *Scr*: Michael Patrick King. *Cast*: Sarah Jessica Parker
(Carrie Bradshaw)

Carrie sets the scene for the romantic adventures of her group of
friends.

> **CARRIE**
> We were perfectly happy until we decided to live
> happily ever after.

The note given to Carrie, letting her have the wedding dress, was written by Vivienne Westwood.

THE ROAD   2009

Dir: John Hillcoat. *Scr*: Joe Penhall. Based on a novel by Cormac McCarthy. *Cast*: Viggo Mortensen (The Man)

A father tries to find a place of safety for his son in a hostile post-apocalyptic world.

> **THE MAN**
> I told the boy when you dream about bad things
> happening, it means you're still fighting and
> you're still alive. It's when you start to dream
> about good things that you should start to worry.

ALICE IN WONDERLAND   2010

Dir: Tim Burton. *Scr*: Linda Woolverton. Based on books by Lewis Carroll. *Cast*: Mia Wasikowska (Alice), Johnny Depp (Mad Hatter)

> **ALICE**
> This is impossible.

> **MAD HATTER**
> Only if you believe it is.

The closest reference to this dialogue in Lewis Carroll's novel seems to be Alice's remark that 'Sometimes I've believed as many as six impossible things before breakfast.'

Dir: Christopher Nolan. *Scr*: Jonathan Nolan, Christopher Nolan. *Cast*: Matthew McConaughey (Cooper)

A team of explorers travel through a wormhole in space in an attempt to ensure humanity's survival.

              COOPER
 Mankind was born on Earth. It was never meant to
 die here.

FRIENDS

THE BRIDE OF FRANKENSTEIN   1935

Dir: James Whale. *Scr*: William Hurlbut, John L. Balderston. Based on a novel by Mary Shelley. *Cast*: Boris Karloff (The Monster)

>   THE MONSTER
>   Alone, bad. Friend, good.

Boris Karloff's costume for the monster was so hot that he sweated off 10kg over the course of the shoot. The actor was so famous at the time that his screen credit was simply his surname.

THE PHILADELPHIA STORY   1940

Dir: George Cukor. *Scr*: Donald Ogden Stewart. Based on a play by Philip Barry. *Cast*: Katharine Hepburn (Tracy Lord), James Stewart (Macaulay 'Mike' Connor)

Tracy Lord needs to get married; tabloid reporter Macaulay Connor chivalrously offers his hand.

>   MACAULAY
>   It can't be anything like love, can it?
>
>   TRACY
>   No, no, it can't be.
>
>   MACAULAY
>   Would it be inconvenient?
>
>   TRACY
>   Terribly.

George Cukor was a tactful director of actors and a generous, loyal colleague. During the filming of Cukor's *Camille* (1936), Greta Garbo was confused to notice the same actor taking several different background roles in various scenes. She asked Cukor: 'Who is that big man, and what part is he playing?' The director replied: 'His name is Rex Evans, and he's playing the part of a friend who needs a job.' Evans eventually appeared in ten Cukor pictures.

Despite his renown as a difficult artist who resisted creative discussions with his actors, Cukor candidly confessed: 'Give me a good script, and I'll be a hundred times better.'

ALL ABOUT EVE 1950

Dir: Joseph L. Mankiewicz. *Scr*: Joseph L. Mankiewicz. Based on a story by Mary Orr. *Cast*: Gregory Ratoff (Max Fabian)

An ambitious Broadway producer kids himself – and his colleagues – about his motives.

>   MAX
> Let the rest of the world beat their brains out
> for a buck. It's friends that count. And I got
> friends.

THE KILLING 1956

Dir: Stanley Kubrick. *Scr*: Stanley Kubrick, Jim Thompson. Based on a novel by Lionel White. *Cast*: Sterling Hayden (Johnny Clay), Tito Vuolo (Joe Piano)

Johnny plans a racetrack heist with his accomplice Joe.

>   JOHNNY
> A friend of mine will be stopping by tomorrow to
> drop something off for me. He's a cop.

>   JOE
> A cop? That's a funny kind of a friend.

>   JOHNNY
> Well, he's a funny kind of a cop.

The film tells the story of the robbery from multiple points of view, but the producers forced Kubrick to cut a more linear version; the result was even more confusing, so they relented and the original edit was restored. When they insisted on a narrator to clarify the plot, Kubrick wrote a voice-over that was full of deliberate errors. The film's style proved a huge influence on later non-linear movies like *Reservoir Dogs* (1992) and *Magnolia* (1999).

BUTCH CASSIDY AND THE SUNDANCE KID   1969

Dir: George Roy Hill. *Scr*: William Goldman. *Cast*: Robert Redford (The Sundance Kid), Paul Newman (Butch Cassidy)

Butch and Sundance are sharing a cabin – and a friendship – with Etta.

> SUNDANCE KID
> Hey, what are you doing?

> BUTCH CASSIDY
> Stealing your woman.

Sundance thinks about it.

> SUNDANCE KID
> Take her.

He sighs.

> SUNDANCE KID
> Take her.

> BUTCH CASSIDY
> Well, you're a romantic bastard, I'll give you that.

NOBODY KNOWS ANYTHING

William Goldman (b. 1931) is the screenwriter's screenwriter, responsible for *All the President's Men* (1976), *A Bridge Too Far* (1977), *Marathon Man* (1976) and *The Princess Bride*

(1987). Originally a successful novelist, he spent over a decade researching the idea for his first major screenplay – 'The Sundance Kid and Butch Cassidy'. He sold it as a 'spec' (speculative or uncommissioned) script for $400,000 [$2.75 million] and soon attracted Steve McQueen and Paul Newman for the lead roles. When McQueen dropped out and Robert Redford was approached, the title's names were fortuitously reversed since Redford was a virtual unknown. The film put both Goldman and Redford firmly on the map, winning four Oscars in 1971; it also garnered nine BAFTA awards, a record that still stands.

Goldman's delightful and self-deprecating memoir, *Adventures in the Screen Trade* (1983), is not a formal writing guide but contains plenty of wisdom about the process and pitfalls of delivering a script. It is unafraid to deal with Hollywood in the same way Hollywood frequently deals with its writers:

'Directors – even though we all know from the media's portrayal of them that they are men and women of wisdom and artistic vision, masters of the subtle use of symbolism – are more often than not a bunch of insecure assholes.'

'Understand this: all the sleaze you've heard about Hollywood? All the illiterate scumbags who scuttle down the corridors of power? They are there, all right, and worse than you can imagine.'

Goldman reserves particular scorn for the industry's belief that it can predict the public's taste and therefore has the right to dictate all creative decisions. The most famous line from the book is now well established as a salutary warning to all film-makers: 'Nobody knows anything.'

HAROLD AND MAUDE 1971

Dir: Hal Ashby. *Scr*: Colin Higgins. *Cast*: Bud Cort (Harold Parker Chasen),
Ruth Gordon (Dame Marjorie 'Maude' Chardin)

Introspective teenager Harold finds an inspiring friend in seventy-
nine-year-old Maude after meeting her at a funeral.

> HAROLD
>
> You sure have a way with people.

> MAUDE
>
> Well, they're my species!

RAIDERS OF THE LOST ARK 1981

Dir: Steven Spielberg. *Scr*: Lawrence Kasdan, George Lucas, Philip Kaufman.
Cast: Harrison Ford (Indiana Jones), Karen Allen (Marion Ravenwood)

Two ex-lovers cross paths in a remote bar in Nepal.

> MARION
>
> You're not the man I knew ten years ago.

> INDIANA
>
> It's not the years, honey. It's the mileage.

The unforgettable remark was improvised on set by Ford himself.
Harrison Ford did a good deal of the stunt work himself, including
being dragged behind a speeding truck. He sustained several bruised
ribs but when asked if he considered the shot dangerous, replied:
'No. If it really was . . . they would have filmed more of the movie
first.'

The sound effects proved an easier assignment: fist-fights were
dubbed with the recording of a baseball bat pounding a pile of
leather jackets, and the opening of the stone ark was suggested by
sliding the lid of a lavatory cistern.

ON GOLDEN POND   1981

Dir: Mark Rydell. Ernest Thompson, based on his play. *Cast*: Katharine Hepburn (Ethel Thayer), Henry Fonda (Norman Thayer Jr)

> ETHEL
>
> You're my knight in shining armour. Don't you
> forget it. You're gonna get back up on that horse
> and I'm gonna be right behind you holding on tight
> and away we're gonna go, go, go.

> NORMAN
>
> I don't like horses.

She kisses him.

> NORMAN
>
> You are a pretty old dame, aren't you? What are
> you doing with a dotty old son of a bitch like me?

> ETHEL
>
> Well, I haven't the vaguest idea.

TOOTSIE   1982

Dir: Sydney Pollack. *Scr*: Larry Gelbart, Murray Schisgal, Don McGuire. *Cast*: Dustin Hoffman (Michael Dorsey/Dorothy Michaels), Teri Garr (Sandy Lester)

Michael hopes he can still work with Sandy after they split up.

> MICHAEL
>
> Friends?

> SANDY
>
> No, we are not friends. I don't take this shit
> from friends. Only lovers.

Sydney Pollack was rare among producer/directors in also being an accomplished actor, studying with Sanford Meisner at The

Neighborhood Playhouse School of the Theatre before beginning a parallel career behind the camera. After he had taken the lead role in *Tootsie*, Dustin Hoffman refused to proceed unless Pollack himself played his agent. Pollack appeared in forty productions including *The Player, Eyes Wide Shut* and *Michael Clayton*, and directed thirty-six films, notably *They Shoot Horses, Don't They?, Jeremiah Johnson, Three Days of the Condor, The Firm* and *Out of Africa*.

Hoffman decided to give his female character a Southern accent as he felt it helped him play the voice in a more feminine register; several of the crew said of Hoffman in drag that he was 'much nicer as a woman'.

DO THE RIGHT THING   1989

Dir: Spike Lee. *Scr*: Spike Lee. *Cast*: Giancarlo Esposito (Buggin' Out), Spike Lee (Mookie)

Two friends greet each other on the streets of New York's Brooklyn.

                    BUGGIN' OUT
    You the man.

                    MOOKIE
    No, you the man.

                    BUGGIN' OUT
    You the man.

                    MOOKIE
    No, you the man.

                    BUGGIN' OUT
    No. I'm just a struggling black man trying to keep
    my dick hard in a cruel and harsh world.

Barack Obama has said this was the movie he and his wife went to see on their first date.

Dir: Robert Zemeckis. *Scr*: Eric Roth. Based on a novel by Winston Groom. *Cast*: Tom Hanks (Forrest Gump)

Forrest celebrates his love for Jenny, his best friend from high school.

```
                    FORREST GUMP
    Me and Jenny goes together like peas and carrots.
```

'DON'T NEVER LET NOBODY MAKE A MOVIE OF YOUR LIFE'S STORY'

Thus begins *Gump & Co.*, the novel Winston Groom wrote following *Forrest Gump*. Frustrated by the way the team who adapted his book twisted the story and censored both language and sex, Groom was further angered when the film received six Oscars but none of the winners thought to mention the original writer in their speeches.

This is a familiar tale in the world of adaptations, although producers who buy the rights to books justify themselves by saying that they are doing the authors a favour; in the case of *Forrest Gump*, the novel sold 30,000 copies on its original appearance but the reprint to accompany the film sold 1.7 million across the world.

In the case of those whose reputations are already established and whose bank balances are perfectly healthy, the arrangement can still be depressing. P. L. Travers, creator of *Mary Poppins*, had a contract with Disney which was supposed to safeguard her much-loved character but the 'script approval' she was promised did little to deflect the changes executives wanted to the book. Travers thought Poppins had been made far less strict than she intended and she hated the animated sequences; what she made of Dick Van Dyke's mangled cockney accent sadly goes unrecorded. Relations between author and studio had become so strained by the time the film was finished that Travers had to beg the producers for a ticket for the première and spent much of the screening in tears. Needless to say, she refused to sell Disney the rights to the rest of the series.

Anthony Burgess was not a man given to tears but his response to the furore surrounding Kubrick's screen version of *A Clockwork Orange* shocked him profoundly. 'The book I am best known for, or only known for, is a novel I am prepared to repudiate: written a quarter of a century ago, a jeu d'esprit knocked off for money in three weeks, it became known as the raw material for a film which seemed to glorify sex and violence. The film made it easy for readers of the book to misunderstand what it was about, and the misunderstanding will pursue me till I die. I should not have written the book because of this danger of misinterpretation.'

Nor was this the only time Kubrick came under fire. Stephen King has had no fewer than thirty-five of his books turned into films, including *The Shawshank Redemption*, *Carrie*, *Misery* and *The Green Mile*, but he felt the director's treatment of *The Shining* was a particular disappointment. 'I'd admired Kubrick for a long time and had great expectations for the project, but I was deeply disappointed in the end result... Kubrick just couldn't grasp the sheer inhuman evil of the Overlook Hotel. So he looked, instead, for evil in the characters and made the film into a domestic tragedy with only vaguely supernatural overtones. That was the basic flaw: because he couldn't believe, he couldn't make the film believable to others.'

Bret Easton Ellis makes a similar complaint: 'I think the problem with *American Psycho* was that it was conceived as a novel, as a literary work with a very unreliable narrator at the centre of it, and the medium of film demands answers... You can be as ambiguous as you want with a movie, but it doesn't

> matter – we're still looking at it. It's still being answered for us visually. I don't think [the story] is particularly more interesting if you knew that he did it, or think that it all happens in his head. I think the answer to that question makes the book infinitely less interesting.'
>
> Graham Greene, put it more succinctly: 'Hollywood made a bad film of nearly every book I did.'

WAKING NED   1998

Dir: Kirk Jones. *Scr*: Kirk Jones. *Cast*: Ian Bannen (Jackie O'Shea)

Speaking at Ned's funeral, Jackie reminds the townsfolk of the pleasures of friendship.

                         JACKIE
    The words that are spoken at a funeral are spoken
    too late for the man who is dead. What a wonderful
    thing it would be to visit your own funeral. To
    sit at the front and hear what was said, maybe
    say a few things yourself. Michael and I grew old
    together. But at times, when we laughed, we grew
    young. If he was here now, if he could hear what
    I say, I'd congratulate him on being a great man
    and thank him for being a friend.

TOY STORY 2   1999

Dir: John Lasseter, Ash Brannon, Lee Unkrich. *Scr*: John Lasseter, Pete Docter, Ash Brannon, Andrew Stanton, Rita Hsiao, Doug Chamberlin, Chris Webb. *Cast*: Joan Cusack (Jessie, the Yodelling Cowgirl)

A toy laments the truth that her owner is growing older.

                         JESSIE
    You never forget kids like Emily or Andy, but they
    forget you.

Dir: Cameron Crowe. *Scr*: Cameron Crowe. *Cast*: Kate Hudson (Penny Lane),
Patrick Fugit (William Miller)

A young music journalist on tour with a band strikes up a friendship
with one of their groupies.

               PENNY

How old are you?

              WILLIAM

Eighteen.

               PENNY

Me too! How old are we really?

              WILLIAM

Seventeen.

               PENNY

Me too!

              WILLIAM

Actually, I'm sixteen.

               PENNY

Me too. Isn't it funny? The truth just sounds
different.

              WILLIAM

I'm fifteen.

The film features over fifty songs from the 1960s and 1970s and the
music licensing budget alone was $3.5 million [$5.2 million].

The actors in the band *Stillwater* rehearsed for six weeks to establish
a convincing musical rapport; Peter Frampton gave Billy Crudup
guitar coaching, although his actual performances were recorded by
Pearl Jam's Mike McCready. Production was complicated by the

fact that the young actor Patrick Fugit's voice broke and he grew three inches during filming.

TOGETHER / *Tillsammans*   2000
Dir: Lukas Moodysson. *Scr*: Lukas Moodysson. *Cast*: Sten Ljunggren (Birger)

A lonely alcoholic calls a plumber who worked for him recently.

> **BIRGER**
> I unscrewed it so you'd come here to fix it and we could talk some more.

I AM SAM   2001
Dir: Jessie Nelson. *Scr*: Kristine Johnson, Jessie Nelson. *Cast*: Michelle Pfeiffer (Rita Harrison Williams), Sean Penn (Sam Dawson)

Mentally challenged Sam persuades Rita, a lawyer, to help him regain custody of his daughter.

> **RITA**
> I just don't know what to call you: retarded, mentally retarded, mentally handicapped, mentally disabled, intellectually handicapped, intellectually disabled, developmentally disabled...

> **SAM**
> You can call me Sam.

HARRY POTTER AND THE PHILOSOPHER'S STONE   2001
Dir: Chris Columbus. *Scr*: Steve Kloves. Based on a novel by J. K. Rowling. *Cast*: Richard Harris (Albus Dumbledore)

The headmaster of a school for magicians addresses his pupils.

DUMBLEDORE

It takes a great deal of bravery to stand up to
your enemies, but a great deal more to stand up
to your friends.

DIVINE SECRETS OF THE YA-YA SISTERHOOD 2002

Dir: Callie Khouri. *Scr*: Mark Andrus, Callie Khouri. Based on a novel by
Rebecca Wells. *Cast*: James Garner (Shepard 'Shep' Walker), Sandra Bullock
(Siddalee 'Sidda' Walker)

Shep helps his daughter Sidda come to terms with the difficulties of
her childhood.

SHEP

The road to hell is paved with good intentions.

SIDDA

Well, what about the road back? What's that paved
with?

SHEP

Humility.

THE LORD OF THE RINGS: THE RETURN OF
THE KING 2003

Dir: Peter Jackson. *Scr*: Peter Jackson, Fran Walsh, Philippa Boyens. Based on a
novel by J. R. R. Tolkien. *Cast*: Elijah Wood (Frodo Baggins)

Frodo and Sam have vanquished their enemies but realize they will
be unable to return home as the world around them destroys itself.

FRODO

I'm glad to be with you, Samwise Gamgee... here
at the end of all things.

The filming of the trilogy had a huge impact on the film and tourist industries in New Zealand. One hundred thousand people turned out for the première in Wellington – almost a quarter of the population.

ALMOST...

Imagine *Brokeback Mountain* directed by Joel Schumacher (*The Phantom of the Opera, 8mm*) and starring Mark Wahlberg (*Boogie Nights*) and Joaquin Phoenix (*Gladiator*). How about *The Shawshank Redemption* with Rob Reiner at the helm (*Spinal Tap, Stand By Me*) and Kevin Costner as Andy Dufresne? Or *Forrest Gump* in the hands of Terry Gilliam (*Fear and Loathing in Las Vegas, Jabberwocky*) with John Travolta as Forrest and Tupac Shakur as Bubba? Well, it nearly happened: all of the above were considered for, or expressed an interest in, the roles.

Hardly any projects are conceived and put into production by a fixed director with an actor already attached, and the complexity of scheduling key players further complicates matters. Few directors have so many other projects ready to go that they can afford to bide their time; Spielberg took ten years to persuade Daniel Day-Lewis to play Lincoln in his 2012 biopic. Conversely, when enough key players are in place and a production is slated to start the final pieces of the puzzle have to be found urgently. Kevin Spacey was cast as the killer in *Se7en* only two days before filming began.

One of the most unlikely combinations would surely have been the Beatles' version of *The Lord of the Rings*, not least since they asked Stanley Kubrick to direct it. Even so, when Peter Jackson got the green light for his adaptation, he faced perhaps the greatest casting challenge of his career. A large number of key characters are iconic figures whose presence would need to carry audiences across nine hours split into three films, and whose actors would need to commit to many years of production, re-shoots and dubbing. It seems almost impossible to imagine the result now without Ian McKellen, Christopher Lee and Viggo Mortensen, but it is amusing to bear in mind that the cast might have read as follows:

- Gimli the Dwarf: Bill Bailey
- Elrond, the Elf Lord: David Bowie
- Aragorn: Russell Crowe
- Frodo: Jake Gyllenhaal
- Arwen: Uma Thurman
- Boromir: Bruce Willis
- Saruman: Tim Curry
- Gandalf: Sean Connery

Connery turned the offer down, claiming that he didn't understand the script and hated the idea of spending three years in New Zealand.

Other alternative universes might have given us:

- Shirley MacLaine as Maria and Yul Brynner as Captain von Trapp in *The Sound of Music* (1965)
- Harrison Ford as Benjamin and Ingrid Bergman as Mrs Robinson in *The Graduate* (1967)
- Sissy Spacek as Princess Leia and Bill Murray as Han Solo in *Star Wars* (1977)
- Muhammad Ali as Superman in *Superman* (1978)
- Dustin Hoffman as Deckard in *Blade Runner* (1982)
- Christopher Reeve as Edward and Sarah Jessica Parker as Vivian in *Pretty Woman* (1990)

- Daniel Day-Lewis as Vincent and Jennifer Aniston as Mia in *Pulp Fiction* (1994)
- Macaulay Culkin as Jack and Angelina Jolie as Rose in *Titanic* (1997)
- Will Smith as Neo in *The Matrix* (1999)
- Robin Williams as Hagrid in the *Harry Potter* series (2001–2011)

GRAN TORINO   2008

Dir: Clint Eastwood. *Scr*: Nick Schenk, Dave Johannson. *Cast*: John Carroll Lynch (Barber Martin), Clint Eastwood (Walt Kowalski)

An elderly man visits the barber who has cut his hair all his life.

> MARTIN
>
> There. You finally look like a human being again. You shouldn't wait so long between haircuts, you cheap son of a bitch.

> WALT
>
> Yeah. I'm surprised you're still around. I was always hoping you'd die off and they got someone in here that knew what the hell they were doing. Instead, you're just hanging around like the doo-wop dago you are.

> MARTIN
>
> That'll be ten bucks, Walt.

> WALT
>
> Ten bucks? Jesus Christ, Marty. What are you, half Jew or somethin'? You keep raising the damn prices all the time

MARTIN

It's been ten bucks for the last five years, you
hard-nosed Polack son of a bitch.

WALT

Yeah, well, keep the change.

MARTIN

See you in three weeks, prick.

WALT

Not if I see you first, dipshit.

THE DANISH GIRL   2015

Dir: Tom Hooper. *Scr*: Lucinda Coxon, based on a book by David Ebershoff.
Cast: Matthias Schoenaerts (Hans Axgil)

When Einar Wegener rejects his birth gender to become Lili, Hans
embraces the change.

HANS

I've only liked a handful of people in my life,
and you've been two of them.

ENEMIES

DUCK SOUP 1933

Dir: Leo McCarey. *Scr*: Bert Kalmar, Harry Ruby, Arthur Sheekman, Nat Perrin.
Cast: Groucho Marx (Rufus T. Firefly)

Wisecracking Rufus T. Firefly is introduced to the gorgeous dancer Vera Marcal.

> RUFUS T. FIREFLY
> I could dance with you until the cows come home.
> On second thoughts, I'd rather dance with the cows
> till you come home.

GONE WITH THE WIND 1939

Dir: Victor Fleming. *Scr*: Sidney Howard. Based on a novel by Margaret Mitchell.
Cast: Vivien Leigh (Scarlett O'Hara), Clark Gable (Rhett Butler)

Desperate not to be abandoned, Scarlett asks Rhett what will become of her once he is gone.

> SCARLETT
> Where shall I go? What shall I do?

> RHETT
> Frankly, my dear, I don't give a damn.

Rhett's final line – 'Frankly, my dear, I don't give a damn' – was recently voted the greatest ever movie quote by the American Film Institute. The Motion Picture Production Code frowned on profanity and suggested the following substitutes: 'Frankly, my dear, I just don't care'; or 'it makes my gorge rise'; or 'my indifference is boundless'; or 'I don't give a hoot'; or 'nothing could interest me less'. At the last moment the Code was amended specifically to let the line stand on the tenuous grounds that it was taken from a 'literary work'.

Astonishingly, the author's first suggestion for the casting of her male hero was Groucho Marx.

THE SHOP AROUND THE CORNER 1940

Dir: Ernst Lubitsch. *Scr*: Samson Raphaelson. Based on a play by Miklós László.
Cast: James Stewart (Alfred Kralik), Margaret Sullavan (Klara Novak)

Two shop assistants detest each other, only to fall in love as anonymous pen-pals.

> ALFRED
>
> There might be a lot we don't know about each
> other. You know, people seldom go to the
> trouble of scratching the surface of things
> to find the inner truth.

> KLARA
>
> Well, I really wouldn't care to scratch your
> surface, Mr Kralik, because I know exactly
> what I'd find. Instead of a heart, a handbag.
> Instead of a soul, a suitcase. And instead of
> an intellect, a cigarette lighter... which
> doesn't work.

CASABLANCA 1942

Dir: Michael Curtiz. *Scr*: Julius J. Epstein, Philip G. Epstein, Howard Koch.
Based on a play by Murray Burnett, Joan Alison. *Cast*: Claude Rains (Captain
Louis Renault), Humphrey Bogart (Rick Blaine)

Captain Renault, a corrupt official with loyalties to the Nazis, is suspicious of Rick's presence in neutral Casablanca.

> CAPTAIN RENAULT
>
> I have often speculated on why you don't return
> to America. Did you abscond with the church funds?
> Run off with a senator's wife? I like to think you
> killed a man. It's the romantic in me.

> RICK
>
> It was a combination of all three.

>   CAPTAIN RENAULT
> What in heaven's name brought you to Casablanca?
>
>   RICK
> My health. I came to Casablanca for the waters.
>
>   CAPTAIN RENAULT
> The waters? What waters? We're in the desert.
>
>   RICK
> I was misinformed.

Warner Brothers originally hoped Ronald Reagan would play the part of Rick, but director Michael Curtiz wanted someone tougher. When the producers approached George Raft (*Scarface*, *Each Dawn I Die*) for the role to play alongside Ingrid Bergman, he replied: 'Whoever heard of Casablanca?', adding 'I don't want to star opposite an unknown Swedish broad.'

John Gielgud worked with Bergman on *Murder on the Orient Express*, and lamented: 'Poor Ingrid – she speaks five languages and can't act in any of them.'

THE MAN WHO CAME TO DINNER   1942

Dir: William Keighley. *Scr*: Julius J. Epstein, Philip G. Epstein. Based on a play by George S. Kaufman, Moss Hart. *Cast*: Mary Wickes (Nurse Preen)

Nurse Preen has had enough of her patient's selfishness and bullying.

>   NURSE PREEN
> I am not only walking out on this case, Mr
> Whiteside, I am leaving the nursing profession.
> I became a nurse because all my life, ever since
> I was a little girl, I was filled with the idea
> of serving a suffering humanity. After one month
> with you, Mr Whiteside, I am going to work in
> a munitions factory. From now on anything I can
> do to help exterminate the human race will fill

me with the greatest of pleasure. If Florence
Nightingale had ever nursed you, Mr Whiteside,
she would have married Jack the Ripper instead
of founding the Red Cross.

TO BE OR NOT TO BE 1942

Dir: Ernst Lubitsch. *Scr*: Edwin Justus Mayer. Based on a story by Melchior
Lengyel. *Cast*: Jack Benny (Joseph Tura), Stanley Ridges (Professor Alexander
Siletsky)

Polish actor Joseph Tura pretends to be German Colonel Ehrhardt
in order to win the confidence of Nazi agent Siletsky.

TURA
I can't tell you how delighted we are to have you
here.

PROFESSOR SILETSKY
May I say, my dear Colonel, that it's good to
breathe the air of the Gestapo again. You know,
you're quite famous in London, Colonel. They call
you 'Concentration Camp Ehrhardt'.

TURA
Ha ha. Yes, yes... we do the concentrating and the
Poles do the camping.

LAURA 1944

Dir: Otto Preminger. *Scr*: Jay Dratler, Samuel Hoffenstein, Elizabeth Reinhardt.
Based on a novel by Vera Caspary. *Cast*: Clifton Webb (Waldo Lydecker)

A newspaper columnist considers his fearsome reputation.

LYDECKER
I don't use a pen. I write with a goose quill
dipped in venom.

Dir: Orson Welles. *Scr*: Orson Welles. Based on a novel by Sherwood King. *Cast*: Everett Sloane (Arthur Bannister)

Arthur tries to evade a killer – his wife – in a carnival hall of mirrors.

> **ARTHUR**
> You'd be foolish to fire that gun. With these
> mirrors, it's difficult to tell. You are aiming
> at me, aren't you? I'm aiming at you, lover. Of
> course, killing you is killing myself. It's the
> same thing. But you know, I'm pretty tired of
> both of us.

Welles only agreed to direct the film to get himself out of a financial jam. His Mercury Theatre company was opening a musical version of *Around the World in 80 Days* in Boston and at the eleventh hour the costumes had been impounded. Urgently in need of $55,000 [$630,000] to release them, Welles cabled producer Harry Cohn and told him about the novel on which *The Lady from Shanghai* was based, promising that if he cabled the cash to Boston within two hours Welles would make the film for him. Cohn agreed on the spot.

ADAM'S RIB   1949

Dir: George Cukor. *Scr*: Ruth Gordon, Garson Kanin. *Cast*: Katharine Hepburn (Amanda Bonner), Judy Holliday (Doris Attinger)

Lawyer Amanda Bonner questions a guilty – and unrepentant – defendant.

> **AMANDA**
> And after you shot your husband... how did you
> feel?

Hungry.

Encouraged by her parents to be ambitious and self-reliant, Katharine Hepburn was known for her outspoken remarks. After shooting *A Bill of Divorcement* (1932), she told her co-star John Barrymore: 'Thank goodness I don't have to act with you any more.' Barrymore reputedly replied: 'I didn't know you ever had, darling.'

WHITE HEAT   1949

Dir: Raoul Walsh. *Scr*: Ivan Goff, Ben Roberts. Based on a story by Virginia Kellogg. *Cast*: Paul Guilfoyle (Roy Parker), James Cagney (Cody Jarrett)

Escaping from jail, Cody Jarrett abducts a prisoner who betrayed him earlier.

PARKER
You wouldn't kill me in cold blood, would you?

JARRETT
No, I'll let you warm up a little.

ALL ABOUT EVE   1950

Dir: Joseph L. Mankiewicz. *Scr*: Joseph L. Mankiewicz. Based on a short story by Mary Orr. *Cast*: Bette Davis (Margo Channing)

Theatre star Margo Channing takes Eve Harrington, an aspiring actress, under her wing. Throwing a party one night, she realizes her protégée's ambitions threaten her own eminence.

MARGO
Fasten your seatbelts — it's going to be a bumpy night.

Dir: Billy Wilder. *Scr*: Charles Brackett, Billy Wilder, D. M. Marshman Jr. *Cast*: Nancy Olson (Betty Schaefer), William Holden (Joe Gillis)

Screenwriter Joe Gillis is not happy to see Betty, the studio reader who turned down his latest script.

```
              BETTY
I've been hoping to run into you.

              JOE
What for? To recover that knife you stuck in my
back?
```

'I AM BIG. IT'S THE PICTURES THAT GOT SMALL'

Sunset Boulevard attracted keen interest even before it started shooting. Because the story portrays a venal industry, egotistical stars and heartless producers, Wilder and co-writer Charles Brackett gave the project the name 'A Can of Beans' to deflect attention. Fearful of interference from censors and the studio itself, they handed them the script piecemeal as the scenes were finished in the hope that the full impact of the story might be softened.

If its depiction of a fading self-obsessed star were not metaphor enough for the decline of the industry, the production itself was filled with delicious ironies and larger-than-life episodes. Gloria Swanson, a legend in her silent days, was willing to play the role of Norma Desmond, but felt herself too grand to audition; director and friend George Cukor was convinced it would be an extraordinary opportunity, and told her: 'If they want you to do ten screen tests, do ten screen tests. If you don't, I will personally shoot you.'

Down-on-his-luck screenwriter Joe Gillis was played by William Holden, whose career had recently suffered a string of flops and a period of heavy drinking; Erich von Stroheim, a top director and actor from the 1920s, was Max, Desmond's butler, driver and projectionist, and on one occasion screens a picture of his in which Swanson actually starred (*Queen Kelly*, 1929). Even the publicity photos of the young Norma Desmond seen throughout her mansion are genuine stills from Swanson's own career.

Wilder persuaded plenty of other industry figures to play cameos, including Buster Keaton and gossip columnist Hedda Hopper. Cecil B. DeMille, the first great American director, also plays himself in a brief but vital role. He agreed to shoot his scene for $10,000 [$105,000] and a Cadillac, but when Wilder called him back later to get a further close-up DeMille demanded the same fee again.

All of the actors deliver lines bitterly appropriate to their own experiences:

```
JOE: Funny how gentle people get with you once
you're dead.
```

```
NORMA: I am big. It's the pictures that got
small.
```

```
CECIL B. DEMILLE: A dozen press agents working
overtime can do terrible things to the human
spirit.
```

Despite the sensitive personal dynamics on set, Wilder remained his mischievous self. On one occasion, William Holden's wife paid a visit to the studio just as Holden was required to kiss actress Nancy Olson passionately. Wilder knew he had a perfectly good performance on the first take but made them repeat it and refused to call 'Cut!' until Mrs

Holden – after several uncomfortable minutes – did so. When Norma Desmond first finds Gillis in her house, she assumes he must be an undertaker who has come to take away her recently deceased pet chimpanzee. Wilder was subsequently asked the meaning of this cryptic encounter and breezily replied: 'Don't you understand? Before Gillis came along, Desmond was fucking the monkey.'

At the end of the film Desmond descends her grand staircase and delivers the famous line 'All right, Mr DeMille, I'm ready for my close-up', mistaking the reporters and policemen for newsreel cameramen and adoring fans. Swanson was so moved by this that when the scene was finished she burst into tears. Wilder remained unimpressed; when interviewers later asked him whether the final dissolve was deliberately ambiguous he replied: 'I have no idea! All I know is that she's meshuggah [crazy], that's all. That's the end.'

The picture was a huge hit, winning three Oscars, and in 1989 was among the first group of films deemed 'culturally, historically, or aesthetically significant' by the Library of Congress.

SINGIN' IN THE RAIN 1952

Dir: Stanley Donen, Gene Kelly. *Scr*: Adolph Green, Betty Comden. *Cast*: Jean Hagen (Lina Lamont), Gene Kelly (Don Lockwood)

Actor Don Lockwood does not return his co-star Lina Lamont's affections.

> LINA
>
> Oh Donny! You couldn't kiss me like that and not mean it just a teensy bit!
>
> DON
>
> Meet the greatest actor in the world! I'd rather kiss a tarantula.

                    LINA
You don't mean that.

                    DON
I don't? Hey Joe, get me a tarantula.

THE QUIET MAN   1952

Dir: John Ford. *Scr*: Frank S. Nugent. Based on a story by Maurice Walsh. *Cast*:
Victor McLaglen ('Red' Will Danaher)

A bullying landowner takes against a man who tries to buy a local
property.

              'RED' WILL DANAHER
He'll regret it to his dying day... if he lives
that long.

BAD DAY AT BLACK ROCK   1955

Dir: John Sturges. *Scr*: Millard Kaufman, Don McGuire. Based on a story by
Howard Breslin. *Cast*: Spencer Tracy (John J. Macreedy), Walter Sande (Café
Proprietor)

A traveller finds himself threatened by the inhabitants of a town
with secrets to hide.

                CAFÉ PROPRIETOR
What'll you have?

                    MACREEDY
What've you got?

                CAFÉ PROPRIETOR
Chilli and beans.

                    MACREEDY
Anything else?

                CAFÉ PROPRIETOR
Chilli without beans.

Dir: Jerome Robbins, Robert Wise. *Scr*: Ernest Lehman, Arthur Laurents. Based on a play by Jerome Robbins, Stephen Sondheim. *Cast*: Natalie Wood (Maria)

Maria confronts the Sharks, a neighbourhood gang who killed her boyfriend.

> MARIA
>
> How do you fire this gun, Chino? By pulling
> this little trigger? How many bullets are left,
> Chino? Enough for you? Or you? All of you! You
> all killed him. And my brother. And Riff. Not
> with bullets and knives — with *hate*. Well, I
> can kill now too because now I have hate. How
> many can I kill, Chino? How many — and still
> have one bullet left for me?

The song 'I Feel Pretty' in the original stage show contains the lyrics 'I feel pretty and witty and bright / And I pity / Any girl who isn't me tonight.' For production reasons the scene could not be shot when it was dark, so the words were changed to 'I feel pretty and witty and gay / And I pity / Any girl who isn't me today.'

CARRY ON CLEO   1964

Dir: Gerald Thomas. *Scr*: Talbot Rothwell. *Cast*: Kenneth Williams (Julius Caesar)

The Emperor Julius Caesar realizes he is surrounded by traitors.

> CAESAR
>
> Infamy, infamy. They've all got it in for me!

The cheeky historical comedy was shot on the sets left behind from the multimillion-dollar production of *Cleopatra* (1963), starring Elizabeth Taylor and Richard Burton. Adding insult to injury, the producers of *Carry on Cleo* also closely copied the epic's poster design – and were promptly sued.

INCLUDE ME OUT

Producer Samuel Goldwyn (1879–1974) was born in Poland as Schmuel Gelbfisz but on arriving in America aged twenty took the name Samuel Goldfish, a simple translation from the original. Although he was responsible for numerous hits (*The Best Years of Our Lives*, *Wuthering Heights*, *Guys and Dolls*) his greatest fame came as a result of his headstrong outbursts and legendary malapropisms.

Some Goldwynisms have been verifiably documented, others misquoted or misattributed, and in some cases even duplicated. When he bought the rights to *The Well of Loneliness* and a colleague warned him that the book was about lesbians, he was said to have replied: 'That's all right, we'll make them Hungarians.' However, the same story circulates about *The Children's Hour*, with Goldwyn suggesting the lesbians became Armenians.

Goldwyn's claim that 'a verbal contract isn't worth the paper it's written on' is delightful but skewed; what he actually said was: 'his verbal contract is worth more than the paper it's written on'. Charlie Chaplin fought to persuade the world that he, not Goldwyn, once said: 'In two words: im-possible.'

Perhaps the true sign of fame is that the myths loom larger than the truths. When he was told that his eponym had been officially listed in a dictionary, he was furious to discover he had a reputation for putting his foot in it and immediately planted another: 'Goldwynisms? They should talk to Jesse Lasky!'

Whether the following are true or not, who could wish to doubt they were ever really uttered?

- Include me out.

- I'm willing to admit that I may not always be right, but I'm never wrong.

- Anyone who goes to a psychiatrist should have his head examined.
- When you're a star, you have to take the bitter with the sour.
- What we need now is some new, fresh clichés.
- I had a monumental idea this morning, but I didn't like it.
- Flashbacks are a thing of the past.
- I don't care if my pictures never make a dime, so long as everyone keeps coming to see them.
- I'll give you a definite maybe.
- I read part of it all the way through.
- Don't talk to me while I'm interrupting.
- Our comedies are not to be laughed at.
- Tell me, how did you love my picture?
- Don't pay any attention to the critics; don't even ignore them.
- Every director bites the hand that lays the golden egg.
- If I could drop dead right now, I'd be the happiest man alive.
- I never put on a pair of shoes until I've worn them five years.
- The scene is dull. Tell him to put more life into his dying.
- Go see it and see for yourself why you shouldn't see it.
- For your information, I would like to ask a question.
- When I want your opinion, I'll give it to you.
- It's more than magnificent; it's mediocre.
- We want a story that starts out with an earthquake and works its way up to a climax.

- Never make forecasts, especially about the future.
- I don't think anyone should write his autobiography until after he's dead.
- I don't want any yes-men around me. I want everyone to tell me the truth – even though it costs him his job.
- We'd do anything for each other; we'd even cut each other's throats for each other.
- We've all passed a lot of water since then.
- The next time I send a damn fool for something, I'll go myself.
- (On William Wyler's films) I made them – Willy only directed them.

On a more charitable note, these statements contain – for all their clumsiness – more than a grain of truth:

- A wide screen just makes a bad film twice as bad.
- When everybody's happy with the rushes (daily footage), the picture's always a stinker.
- God makes stars. I just produce them.
- A producer shouldn't get ulcers; he should give them.
- I am a rebel. I make a picture to please me. If it pleases me, there is a chance it will please others. But it has to please me first.
- Actors think with their hearts. That's why so many of them die broke.
- It's a mistake to remake a great picture because you can never make it better. Better you should find a picture that was done badly and see what can be done to improve it.
- (On actor Fredric March) I'm overpaying him, but he's worth it.

THE PROFESSIONALS   1966

Dir: Richard Brooks. *Scr*: Richard Brooks. Based on a novel by Frank O'Rourke.
Cast: Ralph Bellamy (Joe Grant), Lee Marvin (Henry 'Rico' Fardan)

Rico, a mercenary hired to find Joe's kidnapped wife, realizes Joe has
tried to deceive him.

> JOE
>
> You bastard.

> RICO
>
> Yes, sir. In my case an accident of birth. But
> you, sir, you're a self-made man.

PAPER MOON   1973

Dir: Peter Bogdanovich. *Scr*: Alvin Sargent. Based on a novel by Joe David Brown.
Cast: Ryan O'Neal (Moses Pray), Tatum O'Neal (Addie Loggins)

Nine-year-old Addie travels with conman Moses – whom she
suspects to be her father.

> MOSES
>
> I got scruples too, you know. You know what that
> is? Scruples?

> ADDIE
>
> No, I don't know what it is, but if you got 'em
> it's a sure bet they belong to somebody else.

The film is based on the novel *Addie Pray* by Joe David Brown,
but director Peter Bogdanovich proposed renaming it *Paper Moon*.
Uncertain about his decision, he consulted his great friend Orson
Welles who replied: 'That title is so good, you shouldn't even
make the picture, just release the title!' Tatum O'Neal remains the
youngest-ever Best Actress – at the age of ten – to win an Oscar.

THE WITCHES OF EASTWICK   1987

Dir: George Miller. *Scr*: Michael Cristofer. Based on a novel by John Updike.
Cast: Cher (Alexandra Medford)

Alexandra scorns a lover – secretly, the devil in human form – who
has mistreated her.

> ALEXANDRA
>
> I think – no, I am positive – that you are
> the most unattractive man I have ever met in
> my entire life. You know, in the short time
> we've been together, you have demonstrated
> every loathsome characteristic of the male
> personality and even discovered a few
> new ones. You are physically repulsive,
> intellectually retarded, you're morally
> reprehensible, vulgar, insensitive, selfish,
> stupid, you have no taste, a lousy sense
> of humour and you smell. You're not even
> interesting enough to make me sick. Goodbye,
> Darryl, and thank you for a lovely lunch.

Despite their on-screen magical powers none of the witches could
play tennis, so in their doubles match with the devil the ball was
replaced with a CGI version.

MISSISSIPPI BURNING   1988

Dir: Alan Parker. *Scr*: Chris Gerolmo. *Cast*: Gene Hackman (Rupert Anderson)

An FBI agent warns his partner not to underestimate the racism of
the South.

> RUPERT
>
> When I was a little boy there was an old negro
> farmer lived down the road from us, name of

Monroe. And he was, uh — well, I guess he was just a little luckier than my daddy was. He bought himself a mule. That was a big deal around that town. Now, my daddy hated that mule, 'cause his friends were always kiddin' him about oh, they saw Monroe out plowin' with his new mule, and Monroe was gonna rent another field now they had a mule. And one morning that mule just showed up dead. They poisoned the water. And after that there was never any mention about that mule around my daddy. It just never came up. So one time, we were drivin' down the road and we passed Monroe's place and we saw it was empty. He'd just packed up and left, I guess. Gone up north, or somethin'. I looked over at my daddy's face and I knew he'd done it. And he saw that I knew. He was ashamed. I guess he was ashamed. He looked at me and he said: 'If you ain't better than a nigger, son, who are you better than?' He was an old man just so full of hate that he didn't know that bein' poor was what was killin' him.

Hackman felt the brief but brutal clip of his performance shown at the 1989 Oscars was taken out of context, and vowed he would no longer make violent films. That decision prevented him from accepting a role in *The Silence of the Lambs* (1991) and almost cost him the part of the sheriff in *Unforgiven* (1992). Clint Eastwood finally persuaded him to sign on, and his performance won him his second Oscar.

Many of the extras used during the shoot were actual members of the Ku Klux Klan.

POINT BREAK   1991

Dir: Kathryn Bigelow. *Scr*: W. Peter Iliff, Rick King. *Cast*: John C. McGinley
(Ben Harp), Keanu Reeves (Johnny Utah)

>   BEN
> You're a real blue flame special, aren't you, son?
> Young, dumb and full of come, I know. What I don't
> know is how you got assigned here. Guess we must
> just have ourselves an asshole shortage, huh?
>
>   JOHNNY
> Not so far.

25TH HOUR   2002

Dir: Spike Lee. *Scr*: David Benioff, based on his novel. *Cast*: Edward Norton
(Monty Brogan)

When Monty, a drug dealer sentenced to seven years in prison,
glimpses his reflection in a restroom mirror, he sees the graffiti:
'Fuck You'.

>   MONTY
> Yeah, fuck you too. Fuck me? Fuck you. Fuck
> you and this whole city and everyone in it.
> Fuck the panhandlers, grubbing for money,
> and smiling at me behind my back. Fuck the
> squeegee men dirtying up the clean windshield
> of my car — get a fucking job! Fuck the Sikhs
> and the Pakistanis bombing down the avenues
> in decrepit cabs, curry steaming out their
> pores stinking up my day. Terrorists in
> fucking training. Slow the fuck down! Fuck
> the Chelsea boys with their waxed chests and
> pumped-up biceps. Going down on each other in

my parks and on my piers, jingling their dicks
on my Channel 35. Fuck the Korean grocers
with their pyramids of overpriced fruit and
their tulips and roses wrapped in plastic.
Ten years in the country, still no speaky
English? Fuck the Russians in Brighton Beach.
Mobster thugs sitting in cafés, sipping tea
in little glasses, sugar cubes between their
teeth. Wheelin' and dealin' and scheming.
Go back where you fucking came from! Fuck
the black-hatted Hassidim, strolling up and
down 47th Street in their dirty gabardine
with their dandruff. Selling South African
apartheid diamonds! Fuck the Wall Street
brokers. Self-styled masters of the universe.
Michael Douglas, Gordon Gekko wannabe mother
fuckers, figuring out new ways to rob hard-
working people blind. Send those Enron
assholes to jail for fucking life! You think
Bush and Cheney didn't know about that shit?
Give me a fucking break! Tyco! Worldcom! Fuck
the Puerto Ricans. Twenty to a car, swelling
up the welfare rolls, worst fuckin' parade
in the city. And don't even get me started
on the Dominicans, 'cause they make the
Puerto Ricans look good. Fuck the Bensonhurst
Italians with their pomaded hair, their nylon
warm-up suits, their St Anthony medallions,
swinging their Jason Giambi Louisville Slugger
baseball bats, trying to audition for *The
Sopranos*. Fuck the Upper East Side wives with
their Hermès scarves and their fifty-dollar
Balducci artichokes. Overfed faces getting
pulled and lifted and stretched, all taut and

shiny. You're not fooling anybody, sweetheart!
Fuck the uptown brothers. They never pass the
ball, they don't want to play defence, they
take five steps on every lay-up to the hoop.
And then they want to turn around and blame
everything on the white man. Slavery ended
one hundred and thirty-seven years ago. Move
the fuck on! Fuck the corrupt cops with their
anus-violating plungers and their 41 shots,
standing behind a blue wall of silence. You
betray our trust! Fuck the priests who put
their hands down some innocent child's pants.
Fuck the church that protects them, delivering
us into evil. And while you're at it, fuck
J.C.! He got off easy! A day on the cross, a
weekend in hell, and all the hallelujahs of
the legioned angels for eternity! Try seven
years in fuckin' Otisville, J.! Fuck Osama
Bin Laden, al-Qaeda, and backward-ass cave-
dwelling fundamentalist assholes everywhere.
On the names of innocent thousands murdered,
I pray you spend the rest of eternity with
your seventy-two whores roasting in a jet-fuel
fire in hell. You towel-headed camel jockeys
can kiss my royal Irish ass! Fuck Jacob
Elinsky. Whining malcontent. Fuck Francis
Xavier Slaughtery my best friend, judging me
while he stares at my girlfriend's ass. Fuck
Naturelle Riviera, I gave her my trust and she
stabbed me in the back, sold me up the river,
fucking bitch. Fuck my father with his endless
grief, standing behind that bar sipping on
club sodas, selling whiskey to firemen, and

cheering the Bronx Bombers. Fuck this whole
city and everyone in it.

THE DARK KNIGHT   2008

Dir: Christopher Nolan. *Scr*: Jonathan Nolan, Christopher Nolan, David S.
Goyer. *Cast*: Heath Ledger (The Joker)

Realizing that Batman has spared his life, the Joker taunts his rival
that their battle will never be over.

> ### THE JOKER
>
> You just couldn't let me go, could you? This
> is what happens when an unstoppable force meets
> an immovable object. You truly are incorruptible,
> aren't you? You won't kill me out of some
> misplaced sense of self-righteousness. And I
> won't kill you because you're just too much
> fun. I think you and I are destined to do this
> forever.

THE SOCIAL NETWORK   2010

Dir: David Fincher. *Scr*: Aaron Sorkin. Based on a book by Ben Mezrich. *Cast*:
Rooney Mara (Erica Albright)

Erica ends her relationship with Mark Zuckerberg, founder of
Facebook.

> ### ERICA
>
> You are probably going to be a very successful
> computer person. But you're going to go through
> life thinking that girls don't like you because
> you're a nerd. And I want you to know, from the
> bottom of my heart, that that won't be true.
> It'll be because you're an asshole.

Mark Zuckerberg was initially reluctant to see a film which painted such an uncompromising portrait of his company's meteoric success. When he did watch it, he is reported to have said that it was 'interesting', and that the film-makers got his clothes right.

EX MACHINA   2014

Dir: Alex Garland. *Scr*: Alex Garland. *Cast*: Alicia Vikander (Ava)

The first perfect android not only looks human, but expresses human feelings.

>   AVA
> Isn't it strange, to create something that hates
> you?

PARTNERS

TROUBLE IN PARADISE   1932

Dir: Ernst Lubitsch. *Scr*: Samson Raphaelson, Grover Jones. Based on a play by Aladár László. *Cast*: Kay Francis (Madame Mariette Colet)

A millionairess brushes off an eager suitor.

> MARIETTE
> No, no, François, I tell you, no. You see,
> François, marriage is a beautiful mistake which
> two people make together.

HIS GIRL FRIDAY   1940

Dir: Howard Hawks. *Scr*: Charles Lederer. Based on a play by Ben Hecht and Charles MacArthur. *Cast*: Cary Grant (Walter Burns)

> WALTER
> You've got an old-fashioned idea divorce is
> something that lasts forever, 'Till death do
> us part'. Why, divorce doesn't mean anything
> nowadays, Hildy, just a few words mumbled over
> you by a judge.

Most movie speeches are delivered at roughly 90 words a minute. Here, the dialogue is so zippy the average is 240.

THE LADY EVE   1941

Dir: Preston Sturges. *Scr*: Preston Sturges. Based on a story by Monckton Hoffe. *Cast*: Charles Coburn (Colonel Harrington)

Colonel Harrington encourages his daughter, also a confidence trickster.

> COLONEL HARRINGTON
> Let us be crooked, but never common.

DOUBLE INDEMNITY 1944

Dir: Billy Wilder. *Scr*: Billy Wilder, Raymond Chandler. Based on a novella by James M. Cain. *Cast*: Edward G. Robinson (Barton Keyes)

An insurance claims adjuster suspects murder in a case he has paid out on, little knowing one of his own salesmen is the killer.

> BARTON
>
> It's beginning to come apart at the seams already. Murder's never perfect. Always comes apart sooner or later, and when two people are involved it's usually sooner. Now we know the Dietrichson dame is in it and somebody else. Pretty soon, we'll know who that somebody else is. He'll show. He's got to show. Sometime, somewhere, they've got to meet. Their emotions are all kicked up. Whether it's love or hate doesn't matter — they can't keep away from each other. They may think it's twice as safe because there's two of them, but it isn't twice as safe. It's ten times twice as dangerous. They've committed a murder! And it's not like taking a trolley ride together where they can get off at different stops. They're stuck with each other and they got to ride all the way to the end of the line, and it's a one-way trip — and the last stop is the cemetery.

DETOUR 1945

Dir: Edgar G. Ulmer. *Scr*: Martin Goldsmith. *Cast*: Ann Savage (Vera)

Two strangers join forces to claim a dead man's inheritance.

> VERA
>
> Shut up — you're making noises like a husband.

Detour was the first B-movie – and the first *film noir* – to be included in the Library of Congress's register of films deemed 'culturally, historically or aesthetically' significant.

NOTORIOUS   1946

Dir: Alfred Hitchcock. *Scr*: Ben Hecht. *Cast*: Ingrid Bergman (Alicia Huberman), Cary Grant (T. R. Devlin)

A spymaster suspects his female agent is a romantic at heart.

                         ALICIA
        This fog gets me.

                         DEVLIN
        That's your hair in your eyes.

After working with Hitchcock, Ingrid Bergman said: 'I'd like to know more about his relationships with women. No, on second thoughts, I wouldn't.'

THE SHAKESPEARE OF HOLLYWOOD

Lured to Hollywood by his friend Herman Mankiewicz in 1926, Ben Hecht (1894–1964) won his first Oscar within a year for the screenplay of *Underworld* (*Paying the Penalty*). He won again for *The Scoundrel* in 1935, and as Hollywood's most famous and best-paid scribe wrote or contributed to *Scarface* (1932), *Gone with the Wind* (1939), *Notorious* (1946), *Gilda* (1946) and *Wuthering Heights* (1939).

Often spoken of as the 'Shakespeare of Hollywood', he personified the media's view of the hard-boiled, hard-drinking wordsmith and was famed for delivering drafts in as little as two weeks. In 'Elegy for Wonderland', published in *Esquire* magazine in 1959, he wrote:

'Most of my script-writing friends – I never had more than a handful – took eagerly to the bottle or the analyst's couch, filled their extravagant ménages with threats of suicide, hurled themselves into hysterical amours. And some of them actually died in their forties and fifties. Among these were the witty Herman Mankiewicz and F. Scott Fitzgerald, the fine novelist.'

Hecht also penned several Broadway hits, including *The Front Page* (1928), and the fact that this parallel career gave him independent fame may have prompted his diatribes against the film studios who set little store by the notion of authorship:

'The factors that laid low so whooping and puissant an empire as the old Hollywood are many. I can think of a score, including the barbarian hordes of television. But there is one that stands out for me in the post-mortem . . . The factor had to do with the basis of movie-making: "Who shall be in charge of telling the story?" The answer Hollywood figured out for this question was what doomed it. It figured out that writers were not to be in charge of creating stories. Instead, a curious tribe of inarticulate Pooh-Bahs called supervisors and, later, producers were summoned out of literary nowhere and given a thousand sceptres. It was like switching the roles of teacher and pupil in the fifth grade. The result is now history. An industry based on writing had to collapse when the writer was given an errand-boy status.'

He was also bitterly sarcastic about Hollywood's prim morality:

'Two generations of Americans have been informed nightly that a woman who betrayed her husband (or a husband a wife) could never find happiness; that sex was no fun without a mother-in-law and a rubber plant around; that women who fornicated just for pleasure ended up as harlots or washerwomen; that any man who was sexually active in his youth later lost the one girl he truly loved; that a man who indulged in sharp practices to get ahead in the world ended in poverty and with even his own children turning on him; that any man who broke the laws, man's or God's, must always die, or go to jail, or become a monk, or restore the money he stole before wandering off into the desert... For forty years the movies have drummed away on the American character. They have fed it naïveté and bunkum in doses never before administered to any people. They have slapped into the American mind more human misinformation in one evening than the Dark Ages could muster in a decade. One basic plot only has appeared daily in their fifteen thousand theatres – the triumph of virtue and the overthrow of wickedness.'

We can only wonder whether his astonishing earnings made his complicity in this intellectual decline more – or less – painful:

'I received from each script, whether written in two weeks or (never more than) eight weeks, from $50,000 to $150,000 [$550,000 to $1.65 million]. I worked also by the week. David O. Selznick once paid me $3,500 [$38,500] a day.'

THE BIG SLEEP 1946

Dir: Howard Hawks. *Scr*: William Faulkner, Leigh Brackett, Jules Furthman. Based on a novel by Raymond Chandler. *Cast*: Lauren Bacall (Vivian Rutledge), Humphrey Bogart (Philip Marlowe)

Vivian is not happy that Marlowe has been called in to investigate her family's affairs.

>   VIVIAN
> I don't like your manners.
>
>   MARLOWE
> And I'm not crazy about yours. I didn't ask
> to see you. I don't mind if you don't like my
> manners, I don't like them myself. They are
> pretty bad. I grieve over them on long winter
> evenings.

Bogart and Bacall first worked together on *To Have and Have Not* where they quickly fell in love. Their return to the studio for *The Big Sleep* effectively destroyed Bogart's marriage to his third wife, Mayo Methot, and his subsequent heavy drinking often rendered him unable to shoot. He wed Bacall shortly after the production wrapped and they subsequently starred together in *Dark Passage* and *Key Largo*.

THE TREASURE OF THE SIERRA MADRE 1948

Dir: John Huston. *Scr*: John Huston. Based on a novel by B. Traven. *Cast*: Walter Huston (Howard)

An old prospector warns of the perils of teamwork when fortunes are at stake.

>   HOWARD
> That's gold, that's what it makes us. Never
> knew a prospector yet that died rich. Make

one fortune, he's sure to blow it in tryin' to
find another. I'm no exception to the rule.
Aw sure, I'm a gnawed old bone now, but say,
don't you guys think the spirit's gone. I'm all
set to shoulder a pickaxe and a shovel anytime
anybody's willin' to share expenses. I'd rather
go by myself. Going it alone's the best way. But
you got to have a stomach for loneliness. Some
guys go nutty with it. On the other hand, goin'
with a partner or two is dangerous. Murderers
always lurkin' about. Partners accusin' each
other of all sorts of crimes. Aw, as long as
there's no find, the noble brotherhood will
last. But when the piles of gold begin to grow,
that's when the trouble starts.

Walter Huston, father of director John Huston, won the Academy
Award for Best Supporting Actor. John won for Best Director: the
first ever father-and-son win.

THE AFRICAN QUEEN   1951

Dir: John Huston. *Scr*: John Huston, James Agee, Peter Viertel, John Collier.
Based on a novel by C. S. Forester. *Cast*: Katharine Hepburn (Rose Sayer)

A Christian missionary and a dissolute river captain are thrown
together in the African jungle.

ROSE
Nature, Mr Allnut, is what we are put in this
world to rise above.

Katharine Hepburn disapproved of the amount of whisky John
Huston and Humphrey Bogart drank on location and made a
great show of sticking to water. Her protest led to a severe bout of
dysentery.

Blue Script: 21-09-11
Pink Script: 12-10-11
Yellow Script: 27-10-11
Green Revisions: 03-11-11
Goldenrod Revisions: 02-12-11
Buff Revisions: 08-12-11
Salmon Revisions: 13-01-12
Violet Revisions: 22-01-12
Tan Revisions: 23-01-12
2nd White Revisions: 26-01-12
2nd Blue Revisions: 05-02-12
2nd Pink Revisions: 18-02-12
2nd Yellow Revisions: 19-02-12
2nd Green Revisions: 06-03-12
2nd Goldenrod Revisions: 21-03-12
2nd Buff Revisions: 10-04-12

SKYFALL

Screenplay by

Neal Purvis & Robert Wade

Revised by

John Logan

LOCKED SHOOTING SCRIPT: August 15, 2011

In the beginning was the word… and then the rewrites.

Hitchcock's three priorities were: *the script, the script and the script.*

Dressed to kill… and licensed to kill.

A kiss is just a kiss…

… but the greatest are timeless.

Heroes do what they must…

… but villains do as they please.

Even monsters get a tea break.

Dir: Billy Wilder. *Scr*: Billy Wilder, Edwin Blum. Based on a play by Donald Bevan, Edmund Trzcinski. *Cast*: Peter Graves (Sergeant Price), William Holden (Sergeant J. J. Sefton)

American airmen held in a German prison camp suspect one of their number is an informant.

> PRICE
>
> Are you questioning me?

> SEFTON
>
> Getting acquainted. I'd like to make one friend in this barracks.

> PRICE
>
> Well, don't bother, Sefton. I don't like you, I never did, and I never will.

> SEFTON
>
> A lot of people say that, and the first thing you know is they get married and live happily ever after.

Director Wilder kept the identity of the informant a secret from the cast so their genuine suspicions would influence their performances.

GUYS AND DOLLS   **1955**

Dir: Joseph L. Mankiewicz. *Scr*: Joseph L. Mankiewicz, Ben Hecht. Based on short stories by Damon Runyon and a libretto by Jo Swerling, Abe Burrows. *Cast*: Marlon Brando (Sky Masterson)

Sky cautions Adelaide to think hard before walking up the aisle with Nathan, an inveterate gambler.

> SKY
>
> No matter who you marry, you wake up married to someone else.

GIANT   1956

Dir: George Stevens. *Scr*: Fred Guiol, Ivan Moffat. Based on a novel by Edna Ferber. *Cast*: Rock Hudson (Jordan 'Bick' Benedict Jr)

Towards the end of his life, Bick Benedict reflects on his enduring friendship with his wife.

> BICK
>
> You want to know something, Leslie? If I live to be ninety, I'm never going to figure you out.

SWEET SMELL OF SUCCESS   1957

Dir: Alexander Mackendrick. *Scr*: Clifford Odets, Ernest Lehman. Based on a novella by Ernest Lehman. *Cast*: Burt Lancaster (J. J. Hunsecker)

A newspaper magnate cautions an embittered press agent.

> J. J. HUNSECKER
>
> Don't remove the gangplank, Sidney — you may want to get back on board.

This film's shoot was filled with macho tensions and at one point the temperamental Burt Lancaster threatened to punch the film's writer, Ernest Lehman. The witty scribe replied: 'Go ahead, I need the money.'

VERTIGO   1958

Dir: Alfred Hitchcock. *Scr*: Alec Coppel, Samuel A. Taylor. Based on a novel by Pierre Boileau, Thomas Narcejac. *Cast*: James Stewart (John 'Scottie' Ferguson), Kim Novak (Madeleine Elster)

> SCOTTIE
>
> Don't you think it's sort of a waste for the two of us to . . .

Wander separately? Ah, but only one is a
wanderer. Two together are always going
somewhere.

A tough call among so many outstanding Hitchcock pictures, *Vertigo* was recently voted the greatest film of all time in the British Film Institute's *Sight and Sound* magazine.

SOME LIKE IT HOT   1959

Dir: Billy Wilder. *Scr*: Billy Wilder, I. A. L. Diamond. Based on a story by Robert Thoeren, Michael Logan. *Cast*: Jack Lemmon (Jerry/'Daphne'), Joe E. Brown (Osgood Fielding III)

Jerry, a jazz musician, disguises himself as a woman to escape his mobster pursuers but finds he has attracted the attentions of an amorous millionaire.

JERRY

Oh no you don't! Osgood, I'm gonna level with
you. We can't get married at all.

OSGOOD

Why not?

JERRY

Well, in the first place, I'm not a natural
blonde.

OSGOOD

Doesn't matter.

JERRY

I smoke! I smoke all the time!

OSGOOD

I don't care.

                    JERRY

Well, I have a terrible past. For three years
now, I've been living with a saxophone player.

                    OSGOOD

I forgive you.

                    JERRY

I can never have children!

                    OSGOOD

We can adopt some.

                    JERRY

But you don't understand, Osgood! Ohh...

*Jerry gives up and pulls off his wig. His voice is
deeper now.*

                    JERRY

  I'm a *man*!

Osgood just smiles uncomprehendingly.

                    OSGOOD

Well, nobody's perfect!

There was no love lost between Billy Wilder and Marilyn Monroe
on set; as the director described the shoot, 'We were in mid-flight
and there was a nut on the plane.' The star required forty-seven
takes to get 'It's me, Sugar' correct, instead saying either 'Sugar, it's
me' or 'It's Sugar, me'. After take 30, Wilder had the line written
on a blackboard. On another occasion, Monroe had to search some
drawers before saying 'Where's the bourbon?' After forty attempts,
including 'Where's the whiskey?', 'Where's the bottle?' or 'Where's
the bonbon?', Wilder wrote the line inside one of the drawers. Even
so Monroe could never seem to find the drawer containing the
prompt, so Wilder had it written in every drawer.

'I JUST WANT TO BE WONDERFUL'

All stars wax and wane but none, male or female, has achieved the enduring fame of Marilyn Monroe (born Norma Jeane Mortenson, 1926–62). Although she appeared in classic films including *Gentlemen Prefer Blondes* (1953), *The Seven Year Itch* (1955) and *Some Like It Hot* (1959), she has far outlived the pictures themselves and the bittersweet story of her own life remains her true legacy.

Discovered in 1945 by army photographers during a wartime propaganda photo shoot at the factory where she was working, she signed with the Blue Book modelling agency where her first assignment paid $5 [$72]. Over the coming years she changed her stage name so frequently that when she gave her first autograph as Marilyn Monroe she had to ask a friend how to spell it. Within a matter of years she was *Playboy*'s first ever 'Sweetheart of the Month'; forty years after her death, *People* magazine still voted her 'Sexiest Woman of the Century'.

While she was universally adored by the public, her reputation among her peers was less flattering and her habit of turning up late for work infuriated directors and co-stars. Billy Wilder said: 'She has breasts of granite and a mind like a Gruyère cheese.' Otto Preminger claimed: 'She's a vacuum with nipples' and Tony Curtis complained: 'It's like kissing Hitler.'

Her suicide at the age of thirty-six from an overdose of sedatives caused huge controversy as her recent affair with John F. Kennedy had become widely known; rumours quickly spread that her death was in fact ordered by the government to protect the president's image. Startling inconsistencies in the investigation itself and destruction of key evidence were subsequently revealed but no murder charges were ever filed.

The inquest was periodically reviewed and on each occasion a verdict of suicide was returned, but the idea of a murderous conspiracy was reignited in 1972 when the home where she died was refurbished and contractors discovered a standard-issue FBI eavesdropping system in every room.

It is widely accepted now that Monroe was a depressive and that the conflict between her desire for fame and the pressures it brought exacerbated her condition. As she said herself:

- I want to be a big star more than anything. It's something precious.

- I'm not interested in money, I just want to be wonderful.

- My problem is that I drive myself... I'm trying to become an artist, and to be true, and sometimes I feel I'm on the verge of craziness, I'm just trying to get the truest part of myself out, and it's very hard. There are times when I think, 'All I have to be is true'. But sometimes it doesn't come out so easily. I always have this secret feeling that I'm really a fake or something, a phony.

After *The Seven Year Itch* (1955) she grew tired of disparaging comments about her acting skills and attended Lee Strasberg's New York's Actors Studio where Marlon Brando and other notable actors had studied. Her next film, *Bus Stop* (1956), gained more respectful reviews and the press was equally surprised by her marriage the same year to leading playwright Arthur Miller. Interviews and tributes from her friends in later life emphasized her desire to gain intellectual credibility, citing her love of poetry, a library filled with books on history, philosophy and literature and an IQ (never actually substantiated) of 168.

Even so, Monroe found it hard to shake off the public image

she had already created and the pressures of the industry grew increasingly intolerable. Her later comments are classic cries from the heart:

- My illusions didn't have anything to do with being a fine actress. I knew how third rate I was. I could actually feel my lack of talent, as if it were cheap clothes I was wearing inside. But my God, how I wanted to learn, to change, to improve! No one ever told me I was pretty when I was a little girl. All little girls should be told they're pretty, even if they aren't.

- I knew I belonged to the public and to the world not because I was talented or even beautiful, but because I never had belonged to anything or anyone else.

- I did what they said and all it got me was a lot of abuse. Everyone's just laughing at me. I hate it. Big breasts, big ass, big deal.

- In Hollywood a girl's virtue is much less important than her hairdo. You're judged by how you look, not by what you are. Hollywood's a place where they'll pay you a thousand dollars for a kiss, and fifty cents for your soul. I know, because I turned down the first offer often enough and held out for the fifty.

- Please don't make me a joke. End the interview with what I believe… I want to be an artist, an actress with integrity.

- Dogs never bite me. Just humans.

- People had a habit of looking at me as if I were some kind of mirror instead of a person. They didn't see me, they saw their own lewd thoughts, then they white-masked themselves by calling me the lewd one.

- A sex symbol becomes a thing, I just hate being a thing. But if I'm going to be a symbol of something I'd rather have it [be] sex than some other things we've got symbols of.

- Suicide is a person's privilege. I don't believe it's a sin or a crime, it's your right if you do. Though it doesn't get you anywhere.

Early in the morning of 5 August 1962, Monroe's body was discovered naked in her bed in her Los Angeles home, a telephone in her hand. She left 75 per cent of her estate to Lee Strasberg and the remainder to Marianne Kris, her first psychoanalyst. Even today the licensing of her name and likeness alone nets the Monroe estate about $2 million a year.

THE MANCHURIAN CANDIDATE   1962

Dir: John Frankenheimer. *Scr*: George Axelrod. Based on a novel by Richard Condon. *Cast*: Laurence Harvey (Raymond Shaw)

Raymond, unwittingly brainwashed to be a killer, finds it hard to relax with his lover.

> RAYMOND
> My dear girl, have you ever noticed that the
> human race is divided into two distinct and
> irreconcilable groups: those that walk into rooms
> and automatically turn television sets on, and
> those that walk into rooms and automatically
> turn them off. The trouble is that they end up
> marrying each other.

MARY POPPINS   1964

Dir: Robert Stevenson. *Scr*: Bill Walsh, Don DaGradi. Based on a novel by P. L. Travers. *Cast*: David Tomlinson (George Banks)

On learning that their children have disappeared, George attempts to calm his distraught wife.

> MR BANKS
> Kindly do not attempt to cloud the issue with facts.

TWO FOR THE ROAD   1967

Dir: Stanley Donen. *Scr*: Frederic Raphael. *Cast*: Albert Finney (Mark Wallace), Audrey Hepburn (Joanna Wallace)

A couple on a long journey recall the beginning – and end – of their marriage.

> MARK
> Just wish that you'd stop sniping.

> JOANNA
> I haven't said a word!

> MARK
> Just because you use a silencer doesn't mean you're not a sniper.

CARRY ON UP THE KHYBER   1968

Dir: Gerald Thomas. *Scr*: Talbot Rothwell. *Cast*: Kenneth Williams (The Khasi of Kalabar), Sid James (Sir Sidney Ruff-Diamond)

> KHASI OF KALABAR
> May the benevolence of the god Shivoo bring blessings on your house.

RUFF-DIAMOND
And on yours.

KHASI OF KALABAR
And may his wisdom bring success in all your
undertakings.

RUFF-DIAMOND
And in yours.

KHASI OF KALABAR
And may his radiance light up your life.

RUFF-DIAMOND
And up yours.

Perhaps only the British truly delight in the schoolboy humour of the *Carry On...* movies. Foreign distributors would certainly have had a hard time translating the title: 'Khyber (Pass)' is cockney rhyming slang for arse.

LAST TANGO IN PARIS   1972
Dir: Bernardo Bertolucci. *Scr*: Bernardo Bertolucci, Franco Arcalli, Agnès Varda.
Cast: Marlon Brando (Paul)

Paul mourns his wife's suicide with a mixture of rage and grief.

PAUL
Even if a husband lives two hundred fucking
years, he'll never discover his wife's true
nature. I may be able to understand the secrets
of the universe, but ... I'll never understand
the truth about you. Never.

Brando and his co-star Maria Schneider felt so 'raped' by their roles they never spoke to director Bertolucci again.

THE LAST DETAIL 1973

Dir: Hal Ashby. *Scr*: Robert Towne. Based on a novel by Darryl Ponicsan. *Cast*: Otis Young (Richard 'Mule' Mulhall), Jack Nicholson (Billy 'Badass' Buddusky)

        MULHALL
You ever been married?

        BUDDUSKY
Not so you'd notice.

PAT GARRETT AND BILLY THE KID 1973

Dir: Sam Peckinpah. *Scr*: Rudy Wurlitzer. *Cast*: Richard Jaeckel (Sheriff Kip McKinney), James Coburn (Pat Garrett)

Lawman Pat Garrett persuades the reluctant sheriff Kip McKinney to join him in hunting down Billy the Kid.

        MCKINNEY
I ain't goin'.

        GARRETT
You owe it to me.

        MCKINNEY
I do? For what?

        GARRETT
For not killin' you over at Rosewater, for
gettin' you this job, and not seein' you run
outta this territory, for pullin' you outta that
snowdrift up at Shamus, for cold cockin' you over
at Stillwater Saloon last fall, savin' you from
Rabbit Owens bitin' off your ear, and from just
puttin' up with you for a hell of a lot longer
than I oughta.

Yeah... Well, I hope they spell my name right in
the paper.

Director Peckinpah, always something of a live wire, frequently argued with Kris Kristofferson, who played Billy the Kid. On one occasion the confrontation escalated and Peckinpah only backed off because he feared Kristofferson – a former Army Airborne Ranger – might actually kill him. When the film was released, Peckinpah so despised the way the studio had recut it that he urinated on the screen.

THE JERK   1979

Dir: Carl Reiner. *Scr*: Steve Martin, Carl Gottlieb, Michael Elias *Cast*: Steve Martin (Navin R. Johnson), Bernadette Peters (Marie Kimble Johnson)

NAVIN
Now be totally honest. You do have a boyfriend,
don't you?

MARIE
Kind of.

NAVIN
I know this is our first date, but do you think
the next time you make love to your boyfriend you
could think of me?

MARIE
Well, I haven't made love to him yet.

NAVIN
That's too bad. Do you think it's possible that
someday you could make love with me and think of
him?

MARIE

Who knows? Maybe you and he could make love and you could think of me.

NAVIN

I'd be happy to be in there somewhere.

THE BLUES BROTHERS   1980

Dir: John Landis *Scr*: John Landis, Dan Aykroyd *Cast*: Dan Aykroyd (Elwood Blues), John Belushi (Jake Blues)

ELWOOD

It's 106 miles to Chicago, we got a full tank of gas, half a pack of cigarettes, it's dark... and we're wearing sunglasses.

JAKE

Hit it.

ROUND UP THE USUAL SUSPECTS

Every screenwriter dreams of penning a line which needs no introduction, encapsulates an entire story or just takes root in the popular imagination:

One morning I shot an elephant in my pyjamas. How he got in my pyjamas, I don't know.
Animal Crackers (1930)
Scr: Morrie Ryskind. Based on a play by George S. Kaufman, Morrie Ryskind, Bert Kalmar, Harry Ruby

It's alive! It's alive!
Frankenstein (1931)
Scr: John L. Balderston, Garrett Fort, Francis Edward Faragoh. Based on a story by Mary Shelley and a play by Peggy Webling

Well, here's another nice mess you've gotten me
into!
Sons of the Desert (1933)
Scr: Frank Craven

After all, tomorrow is another day.
Gone with the Wind (1939)
Scr: Sidney Howard. Based on a novel by Margaret Mitchell

Toto, I've got a feeling we're not in Kansas any
more.
The Wizard of Oz (1939)
Scr: Noel Langley, Florence Ryerson and eighteen others

Here's looking at you, kid.
Casablanca (1942)
Scr: Julius J. Epstein, Philip G. Epstein, Howard Koch. Based on a play by
Murray Burnett, Joan Alison

Badges? We ain't got no badges! We don't need
no badges! I don't have to show you any stinking
badges!
The Treasure of Sierra Madre (1948)
Scr: John Huston. Based on a novel by B. Traven

A martini. Shaken, not stirred.
Goldfinger (1964)
Scr: Richard Maibaum, Paul Dehn. Based on a novel by Ian Fleming

What we've got here is a failure to communicate.
Cool Hand Luke (1967)
Scr: Donn Pearce, Frank Pierson. Based on a novel by Donn Pearce

Hello, gorgeous.
Funny Girl (1968)
Scr: Isobel Lennart, based on her play

I'm walking here! I'm walking here!
Midnight Cowboy (1969)
Scr: Waldo Salt. Based on a novel by James Leo Herlihy

Love means never having to say you're sorry.
Love Story (1970)
Scr: Erich Segal, based on his novel

Keep your friends close, but your enemies closer.
The Godfather: Part II (1974)
Scr: Francis Ford Coppola, Mario Puzo. Based on a novel by Mario Puzo

Is it safe?
Marathon Man (1976)
Scr: William Goldman, based on his novel

You talkin' to me?
Taxi Driver (1976)
Scr: Paul Schrader

May the Force be with you.
Star Wars (1977)
Scr: George Lucas

STRIKER: Surely you can't be serious!
RUMACK: I am serious . . . and don't call me Shirley.
Airplane (1980)
Scr: Jim Abrahams, David Zucker, Jerry Zucker

All work and no play makes Jack a dull boy. Here's Johnny!
The Shining (1980)
Scr: Stephen King, Stanley Kubrick. Based on a novel by Stephen King

They're here!
Poltergeist (1982)
Scr: Steven Spielberg, Michael Grais, Mark Victor

E.T. phone home.
E.T. The Extraterrestrial (1982)
Scr: Melissa Mathison

Say hello to my little friend.
Scarface (1983)
Scr: Oliver Stone

Go ahead, make my day.
Sudden Impact (1983)
Scr: Joseph Stinson, Earl E. Smith, Charles B. Pierce. Based on characters created by Harry Julian Fink, Rita M. Fink

I'll be back.
The Terminator (1984)
Scr: James Cameron, Gale Anne Hurd

Game over, man! Game Over!
Aliens (1986)
Scr: James Cameron, David Giler, Walter Hill. Based on characters created by Dan O'Bannon, Ronald Shusett

I feel the need... the need for speed!
Top Gun (1986)
Scr: Jim Cash, Jack Epps Jr.. Based on a magazine article by Ehud Yonay

If you build it, he will come.
Field of Dreams (1989)
Scr: Phil Alden Robinson. Based on a novel by W. P. Kinsella

I'll have what she's having.
When Harry Met Sally (1989)
Scr: Nora Ephron

Hasta la vista, baby.
Terminator 2: Judgment Day (1991)
Scr: James Cameron, William Wisher Jr.

Mama always said life was like a box of
chocolates. You never know what you're gonna get.
Forrest Gump (1994)
Scr: Eric Roth. Based on a novel by Winston Groom

Houston, we have a problem.
Apollo 13 (1995)
Scr: William Broyles Jr., Al Reinert. Based on a book by Jim Lovell, Jeffrey
Kluger

To Infinity and beyond!
Toy Story (1995)
Scr: John Lasseter, Pete Docter, Andrew Stanton, Joe Ranft, Joss Whedon,
Joel Cohen, Alec Sokolow

Show me the money!
Jerry Maguire (1996)
Scr: Cameron Crowe

My precious...
Lord of the Rings, Two Towers (2002)
Scr: Fran Walsh, Philippa Boyens, Stephen Sinclair, Peter Jackson. Based on
a novel by J. R. R. Tolkien

AIRPLANE! 1980

Dir: Jim Abrahams, David Zucker, Jerry Zucker. *Scr*: Jim Abrahams, David Zucker, Jerry Zucker. Based on the film *Zero Hour!* (1957) by Arthur Hailey, Hall Bartlett, John C. Champion. *Cast*: Kareem Abdul-Jabbar (Roger Murdock), Peter Graves (Captain Clarence Oveur), Unknown (Control Tower), Frank Ashmore (Victor Basta)

Airline pilot Clarence Oveur and his flight officers Roger and Victor prepare for take-off.

> ROGER MURDOCK
>
> Flight 2-0-9'er, you are cleared for take-off.

> CAPTAIN OVEUR
>
> Roger!

> ROGER MURDOCK
>
> Huh?

> CONTROL TOWER
>
> L.A. departure frequency 123 point 9'er.

> CAPTAIN OVEUR
>
> Roger!

> ROGER MURDOCK
>
> Huh?

> VICTOR BASTA
>
> Request vector, over.

> CAPTAIN OVEUR
>
> What?

> CONTROL TOWER
>
> Flight 2-0-9'er cleared for vector 324.

> ROGER MURDOCK
>
> We have clearance, Clarence.

                    CAPTAIN OVEUR
Roger, Roger. What's our vector, Victor?

                    CONTROL TOWER
Tower's radio clearance, over!

                    CAPTAIN OVEUR
That's Clarence Oveur. Over.

                    CONTROL TOWER
Over.

                    CAPTAIN OVEUR
Roger.

                    ROGER MURDOCK
Huh?

                    CONTROL TOWER
Roger, over!

                    ROGER MURDOCK
What?

                    CAPTAIN OVEUR
Huh?

                    VICTOR BASTA
Who?

The film parodies many airborne or disaster movies of the time, including *Airport 1975* in which a stewardess is also forced to pilot a plane after both pilots are incapacitated, a girl needs a kidney transplant and one of the passengers is also a singing nun. It includes so many direct references to the unintentionally hilarious *Zero Hour!* ('We have to find someone who can not only fly this plane, but who didn't have fish for dinner') that the producers had to buy the rights to the film to avoid charges of plagiarism.

THE BIG CHILL   1983

Dir: Lawrence Kasdan. *Scr*: Lawrence Kasdan, Barbara Benedek. *Cast*: Mary Kay Place (Meg Jones)

Meg is frustrated she never seems to meet any suitable men.

> MEG
>
> They're either married or gay. And if they're not gay, they've just broken up with the most wonderful woman in the world, or they've just broken up with a bitch who looks exactly like me. They're in transition from a monogamous relationship and they need more space. Or they're tired of space, but they just can't commit. Or they want to commit, but they're afraid to get close. They want to get close, you don't want to get near them.

HOPE AND GLORY   1987

Dir: John Boorman. *Scr*: John Boorman. *Cast*: Ian Bannen (Grandfather George), Sebastian Rice-Edwards (Bill Rowan)

An old man tells his grandson how his children got their names.

> GEORGE
>
> You want to know why they're called Faith, Hope, Grace and Charity?
>
> BILL
>
> Why?
>
> GEORGE
>
> Your Grandmother. She named them after the virtues I lack. That's marriage for you.

BITTER MOON   1992

Dir: Roman Polanski. *Scr*: Roman Polanski, Gérard Brach, John Brownjohn, Jeff Gross. Based on a novel by Pascal Bruckner. *Cast*: Peter Coyote (Oscar)

Oscar, who is now in a wheelchair, reminisces about his turbulent relationship with his wife.

> OSCAR
>
> She came to see me when I got out of intensive care. She said, there's bad news and there's good news. You're paralysed from the waist down — permanently. Okay, I said, let's have the good news. That was the good news, she said. The bad news is that from now on, I'm taking care of you.

PULP FICTION   1994

Dir: Quentin Tarantino. *Scr*: Quentin Tarantino, Roger Avary. *Cast*: Samuel L. Jackson (Jules Winnfield), Quentin Tarantino (Jimmie Dimmick)

Two hit-men drink coffee with Jimmie in his kitchen.

> JULES
>
> Mmmm... Goddamn, Jimmie! This is some serious gourmet shit. Usually, me and Vince would be happy with some freeze-dried Taster's Choice right, but he springs this serious gourmet shit on us. What flavour is this?
>
> JIMMIE
>
> Knock it off, Julie.
>
> JULES
>
> What?
>
> JIMMIE
>
> I don't need you to tell me how fucking good my coffee is, okay? I'm the one who buys it. I

know how good it is. When Bonnie goes shopping she buys shit. I buy the gourmet expensive stuff because when I drink it I want to taste it. But you know what's on my mind right now? It ain't the coffee in my kitchen, it's the dead nigger in my garage.

> JULES
> Oh, Jimmie, don't even worry about that —

> JIMMIE
> No, no, no — let me ask you a question. When you came pulling in here, did you notice a sign out in front of my house that said 'Dead Nigger Storage'?

> JULES
> Jimmie, you know I ain't seen no. . .

Jimmie is getting angry now.

> JIMMIE
> Did you notice a sign out in front of my house that said 'Dead Nigger Storage'?

> JULES
> No. I didn't.

> JIMMIE
> You know why you didn't see that sign?

> JULES
> Why?

> JIMMIE
> 'Cause it ain't there. 'Cause storing dead niggers ain't my fucking business, that's why!

Tarantino wrote the roles of Winston 'The Wolf', Honey Bunny, Pumpkin, and Jules specifically for Harvey Keitel, Amanda Plummer, Tim Roth, and Samuel L. Jackson. The word 'fuck' is used two hundred sixty-five times – once every thirty-five seconds.

HEAT   1995

Dir: Michael Mann. *Scr*: Michael Mann. *Cast*: Al Pacino (Lieutenant Vincent Hanna), Robert De Niro (Neil McCauley)

Vincent, a detective, and Neil, a bank robber, realize they have met their match in each other.

> VINCENT
>
> You know, we're sitting here, you and I, like
> a couple of regular fellas. You do what you do,
> and I do what I gotta do. And now that we've
> been face-to-face, if I'm there and I gotta put
> you away, I won't like it. But I tell you, if
> it's between you and some poor bastard whose
> wife you're gonna turn into a widow, brother,
> you are going down.
>
> NEIL
>
> There is a flip side to that coin. What if you
> do got me boxed in and I gotta put you down?
> 'Cause no matter what, you will not get in my
> way. We've been face-to face, yeah. But I will
> not hesitate. Not for a second.

Michael Mann originally wrote and directed the story as *L.A. Takedown* (1989), a television pilot which was never commissioned. *Heat* itself, not so much a remake as a revision, was the first film in which Pacino and De Niro acted together (in *The Godfather: Part II* they never actually appeared on screen at the same time).

THE ICE STORM 1997

Dir: Ang Lee. *Scr*: James Schamus. Based on a novel by Rick Moody. *Cast*: Kevin Kline (Ben Hood)

Ben hopes to persuade his fellow dinner guests how solid his marriage is.

>   BEN
>   The only big fight we've had in years is about
>   whether to go back into couples therapy.

ROUNDERS 1998

Dir: John Dahl. *Scr*: David Levien, Brian Koppelman. *Cast*: Edward Norton (Lester 'Worm' Murphy), Famke Janssen (Petra)

Worm and Petra worry that their friend is in a dead-end relationship.

>   WORM
>   She's really got him by the balls.

>   PETRA
>   That's not so bad, is it?

>   WORM
>   It depends on the grip!

TOPSY-TURVY 1999

Dir: Mike Leigh. *Scr*: Mike Leigh. *Cast*: Jim Broadbent (W. S. Gilbert), Allan Corduner (Sir Arthur Sullivan)

Librettist Gilbert and composer Sullivan argue over suitable material for their next production, *The Mikado*.

>   GILBERT
>   Every theatrical performance is a contrivance by
>   its very nature.

> **SULLIVAN**
>
> Yes, but this piece consists entirely of an artificial and implausible situation.

> **GILBERT**
>
> If you wish to write a grand opera about a prostitute dying of consumption in a garret, I suggest you contact Mr Ibsen in Oslo. I am sure he will be able to furnish you with something suitably dull.

Gilbert's reference is to Verdi's opera *La Traviata*. His dismissal of Ibsen as 'dull' is somewhat unfair as his play *A Doll's House* was considered deeply risqué and was actually banned in many countries.

AUTHOR, AUTHOR

> I've seen horrors. Horrors that you've seen. But you have no right to call me a murderer. You have a right to kill me. You have a right to do that. But you have no right to judge me...
>
> We train young men to drop fire on people, but their commanders won't allow them to write 'fuck' on their airplanes because it's obscene...
>
> Have you ever considered any real freedoms? Freedoms from the opinions of others. Even the opinions of yourself. Did they say why, Willard? Why they wanted to terminate my command?

When Colonel Kurtz (Marlon Brando), half-obscured by lamplight in *Apocalypse Now* (1979), delivers these lines in his final scenes, whose words are we hearing? Are they by:

- Joseph Conrad, whose short novel *Heart of Darkness* (1899) about a renegade ivory trader in the African Congo inspired the film's story;
- Screenwriter John Milius, who transplanted the narrative to Vietnam in a script originally called 'The Psychedelic Soldier';
- Anthropologist James Frazer, whose study *The Golden Bough* (1890) appears as a prop in Kurtz's compound and is a source for many of the cultural themes in the story;
- T. S. Eliot, whose poem 'The Hollow Men' (1925) is quoted by Kurtz ('The horror, the horror') and which begins itself with an epigraph from Conrad's *Heart of Darkness*;
- Vietnam War reporter Michael Herr, whose book *Dispatches* (1977) was a key reference (Herr also wrote the voice-over narration for the film);
- Francis Ford Coppola, who directed the film and rewrote scenes constantly during the shoot;
- Marlon Brando, who disliked the draft he was sent and improvised much of his dialogue.

There can, of course, be no real answer – just as it is impossible to determine creative authorship for a jazz recording whose chord sequence is traditional, but whose performance is the result of every player's talents.

What Coppola understood above all is that in the hands of a truly visionary director, 'writing' is a process that transcends the actual words of the shooting script. Every stage he supervises is transformative, from the initial collaboration with (co)writers to discussions with production designers about *mise-en-scène* and the casting of actors who may want to improvise their own dialogue. Film editing of imagery as well as dialogue can radically reshape the way the story unfolds.

Although when credits roll it seems clear who is responsible for the screenplay, the actual truth is often murkier. Phil Alden Robinson (*Field of Dreams*, 1989) warns: 'No one can trust a writing credit. Nobody knows who really wrote the film.' Remarkably few projects are taken from inception to delivery by a sole author; directors, producers and actors (depending on their power) may all contribute to changes in the story, although it is rare for any of them to demand acknowledgement since their job is understood to involve a degree of influence. The process of attribution is trickier when a writer is brought in to make substantial changes to earlier drafts – and trickier still when others are added to the mix.

The opening titles for *The Wizard of Oz* (1939) list the following:

Screenplay: Noel Langley, Florence Ryerson,
    Edgar Allan Woolf
Adaptation: Noel Langley
Based on the book by: L. Frank Baum

The Internet Movie Database lists a further thirteen uncredited contributing writers, including the poet Ogden Nash and the Oscar-winning Herman J. Mankiewicz; at one point Langley, Nash and Mankiewicz were all working on the film at the same time without knowing the others had been hired. The other two formally credited authors, Ryerson and Woolf, were brought on board much later to bring the other drafts closer to L. Frank Baum's original novel.

Today, the Writers Guild of America has clear guidelines for settling disputes, which affect not only credits but residual payments (royalties) and eligibility for awards. Between 1993 and 1997, they supervised 415 arbitrations – roughly a third of all films submitted.

REMEMBER THE TITANS   2000

Dir: Boaz Yakin. *Scr*: Gregory Allen Howard. *Cast*: Denzel Washington (Herman Boone)

An American football coach takes his racially mixed team on a training run to a Civil War battlefield.

> HERMAN
>
> Anybody know what this place is? This is
> Gettysburg. This is where they fought the battle
> of Gettysburg. Fifty thousand men died right
> here on this field, fightin' the same fight
> that we're still fightin' amongst ourselves
> today. This green field right here, painted red,
> bubblin' with the blood of young boys. Smoke
> and hot lead pourin' right through their bodies.
> Listen to their souls, men. I killed my brother
> with malice in my heart. Hatred destroyed my
> family. You listen, you take a lesson from the
> dead. If we don't come together right now on
> this hallowed ground, we too will be destroyed
> just like they were. I don't care if you like
> each other right now, but you will respect each
> other. And maybe — I don't know, maybe we'll
> learn to play this game like men.

CHICAGO   2002

Dir: Rob Marshall. *Scr*: Bill Condon. Based on a musical by Bob Fosse, Fred Ebb and a play by Maurine Dallas Watkins. *Cast*: Catherine Zeta-Jones (Velma Kelly)

A woman awaiting trial for murder explains how she found her husband's body.

> VELMA
>
> My sister Veronica and I had this double act,
> and my husband Charlie travelled around with

us. Now for the last number in our act, we did
these twenty acrobatic tricks in a row. One,
two, three, four, five, splits, spread-eagles,
backflips, flip-flops, one right after the other.
So this one night before the show, we're down at
the Hotel Cicero. The three of us boozin', having
a few laughs. And we ran out of ice, so I go out
to get some. I come back... open the door...
and there's Veronica and Charlie, doing number
seventeen: the Spread-eagle. Well, I was in such
a state of shock I completely blacked out, I
can't remember a thing. It wasn't until later
when I was washing the blood off my hands I even
knew they were dead.

Renée Zellweger had no singing or dancing training prior to this film; Catherine Zeta-Jones cut her hair into a bob so her face would always be visible, proving that she never used stand-ins for the complicated choreography.

BEFORE SUNSET   2004

Dir: Richard Linklater. *Scr*: Richard Linklater, Julie Delpy, Ethan Hawke, Kim Krizan. *Cast*: Ethan Hawke (Jesse)

Jesse tells an old lover how he feels about his marriage.

         JESSE
I feel like I'm running a small nursery with
someone I used to date.

CRASH   2004

Dir: Paul Haggis. *Scr*: Paul Haggis, Robert Moresco. *Cast*: Don Cheadle (Detective Graham Waters), Jennifer Esposito (Ria)

Graham, an African-American, and Ria, a Latino woman, make love. The telephone rings. Frustrated, Graham answers the phone.

GRAHAM

Mom, I can't talk to you right now, okay? I'm
having sex with a white woman.

He hangs up. Ria gets out of bed.

GRAHAM

OK, where were we?

RIA

I was white, and you were about to jerk off in the
shower.

GRAHAM

Oh, shit. Come on. I would have said you were
Mexican, but I don't think it would have pissed
her off as much.

RIA

Why do you keep everybody a certain distance,
huh? What, you start to feel something and panic?

GRAHAM

Come on, Ria. You're just pissed 'cause I
answered the phone.

RIA

That's just where I begin to get pissed. I mean,
really, what kind of man speaks to his mother
that way, huh?

GRAHAM

Oh, this is about my mother. What do you know
about my mother?

RIA

If I was your father, I'd kick your fucking ass.

GRAHAM

OK, I was raised badly. Why don't you take your
clothes off, get back into bed, and teach me a
lesson?

RIA

You want a lesson? I'll give you a lesson. How
'bout a geography lesson? My father's from Puerto
Rico. My mother's from El Salvador. Neither one
of those is Mexico.

GRAHAM

Ah. Well then I guess the big mystery is, who
gathered all those remarkably different cultures
together and taught them all how to park their
cars on their lawns?

ETERNAL SUNSHINE OF THE SPOTLESS MIND   2004

Dir: Michel Gondry. *Scr*: Michel Gondry, Charlie Kaufman, Pierre Bismuth.
Cast: Jim Carrey (Joel Barish)

Joel tells his girlfriend he fears the spark has disappeared from their
relationship.

JOEL

Are we like couples you see in restaurants? Are
we the dining dead?

The film's title is taken from the poem by Alexander Pope about
two devoted lovers, *Eloisa to Abelard*:
    'How happy is the blameless vestal's lot!
    The world forgetting, by the world forgot.
    Eternal sunshine of the spotless mind!
    Each pray'r accepted, and each wish resign'd.'

MR & MRS SMITH   2005

Dir: Doug Liman. *Scr*: Simon Kinberg. *Cast*: Brad Pitt (John Smith)

A married couple – both contract killers – discover they have both been hired to murder the other.

> JOHN
>
> We have an unusual problem here, Jane. You obviously want me dead, and I'm less and less concerned for your well-being.

IN BRUGES   2008

Dir: Martin McDonagh. *Scr*: Martin McDonagh. *Cast*: Brendan Gleeson (Ken), Colin Farrell (Ray)

Two hit-men waiting for an assignment in Bruges find the excitements of the city are quickly exhausted.

> KEN
>
> We shall strike a balance between culture and fun.

> RAY
>
> Somehow, Ken, I believe that the balance shall tip in the favour of culture, like a big fat fucking retarded fucking black girl on a see-saw.

REVOLUTIONARY ROAD   2008

Dir: Sam Mendes. *Scr*: Justin Haythe. Based on a novel by Richard Yates. *Cast*: Kate Winslet (April Wheeler)

Frank and April dream of rekindling their passion for life until Frank confesses he has been unfaithful.

> APRIL
>
> No one forgets the truth, Frank. They just get better at lying.

THE KING'S SPEECH

2010

Dir: Tom Hooper. *Scr*: David Seidler. *Cast*: Geoffrey Rush (Lionel Logue), Colin Firth (King George VI)

A speech therapist tries to cure the reluctant king of his stammer.

>   LOGUE
> Would I lie to a prince of the realm to win
> twelve pennies?
>
>   GEORGE VI
> I have no idea what an Australian might do for
> that sort of money.

The film contains seventeen uses of the word 'fuck' and was originally given a 15 certificate. The producers wanted a less restrictive rating; after some negotiation the expletives remained but the certificate was relaxed to 12A with the bizarre warning 'contains strong language in a speech therapy context'.

ROOM

2015

Dir: Lenny Abrahamson. *Scr*: Emma Donoghue, based on her own novel. *Cast*: Brie Larson (Ma), Jacob Tremblay (Jack)

Held captive for seven years, a mother convinces her young son that one day they will escape.

>   MA
> You're gonna love it.
>
>   JACK
> What?
>
>   MA
> The world.

LOVE

THE PETRIFIED FOREST   1936

Dir: Archie Mayo. *Scr*: Charles Kenyon, Delmer Daves. Based on a play by Robert E. Sherwood. *Cast*: Leslie Howard (Alan Squier)

A world-weary writer finds that love brings him alive.

> ALAN
> Any woman's worth everything that any man has to
> give: anguish, ecstasy, faith, jealousy, love,
> hatred, life or death. Don't you see that's the
> whole excuse for our existence? It's what makes
> the whole thing possible and tolerable.

THE WIZARD OF OZ   1939

Dir: Victor Fleming. *Scr*: Noel Langley, Florence Ryerson, Edgar Allan Woolf. Based on a novel by L. Frank Baum. *Cast*: Judy Garland (Dorothy Gale), Jack Haley (Tin Man)

Dorothy says goodbye to her companions as she returns home to Kansas.

> DOROTHY
> Goodbye, Tin Man. Oh, don't cry! You'll rust so
> dreadfully. Here's your oil can.

> TIN MAN
> Now I know I've got a heart, 'cause it's
> breaking.

CASABLANCA   1942

Dir: Michael Curtiz. *Scr*: Julius J. Epstein, Philip G. Epstein, Howard Koch. Based on a play by Murray Burnett, Joan Alison. *Cast*: Humphrey Bogart (Rick Blaine), Ingrid Bergman (Ilsa Lund), Claude Rains (Captain Louis Renault)

Rick tries to persuade Ilsa she must flee Casablanca with her husband.

RICK

Last night we said a great many things. You said
I was to do the thinking for both of us. Well,
I've done a lot of it since then, and it all adds
up to one thing: you're getting on that plane
with Victor where you belong.

ILSA

But, Richard, no, I... I...

RICK

Now, you've got to listen to me! You have any idea
what you'd have to look forward to if you stayed
here? Nine chances out of ten, we'd both wind up
in a concentration camp. Isn't that true, Louie?

CAPTAIN RENAULT

I'm afraid Major Strasser would insist.

ILSA

You're saying this only to make me go.

RICK

I'm saying it because it's true. Inside of us,
we both know you belong with Victor. You're part
of his work, the thing that keeps him going. If
that plane leaves the ground and you're not with
him, you'll regret it. Maybe not today. Maybe not
tomorrow, but soon and for the rest of your life.

ILSA

But what about us?

RICK

We'll always have Paris. We didn't have... we'd
lost it until you came to Casablanca. We got it
back last night.

> ILSA
>
> When I said I would never leave you.

> RICK
>
> And you never will. But I've got a job to do,
> too. Where I'm going, you can't follow. What I've
> got to do, you can't be any part of. Ilsa, I'm
> no good at being noble, but it doesn't take much
> to see that the problems of three little people
> don't amount to a hill of beans in this crazy
> world. Someday you'll understand that.

Ilsa is crying now.

> RICK
>
> Now, now . . .

He lifts her face and holds her gaze.

> RICK
>
> Here's looking at you, kid.

The Naked Gun (1988) contains a *hommage* to the classic line: 'It's a topsy-turvy world, and maybe the problems of two people don't amount to a hill of beans. But this is our hill. And these are our beans!'

A MATTER OF LIFE AND DEATH (aka *Stairway to Heaven*) 1946

Dir: Michael Powell, Emeric Pressburger. *Scr*: Michael Powell, Emeric Pressburger.
Cast: Kim Hunter (June), David Niven (Squadron Leader Peter Carter)

A radio operator receives a message from a stricken bomber pilot.

> JUNE
>
> Are you receiving me? Repeat, are you receiving
> me? Request your position. Come in, Lancaster.

PETER

You seem like a nice girl. I can't give you my
position, instruments gone, crew gone too — all
except Bob here, my sparks, he's dead. The rest
all bailed out on my orders, time 03.35. Did you
get that?

JUNE

Crew bailed out 03.35.

PETER

Station Warrenden, bomber group A, G George, send
them a signal. Got that?

JUNE

Station Warrenden, bomber group A apple, G George.

PETER

They'll be sorry about Bob — we all liked him.

JUNE

Hello, G George, hello, G George, are you all
right? Are you going to try to land? Do you want
a fix?

PETER

Name's not G George, it's P Peter — Peter D.
Carter. D's for David, Squadron Leader Peter
Carter. No, I'm not going to land — undercarriage
is gone, inner port's on fire. I'm bailing out
presently. I'm bailing out.

JUNE

Received your message, we can hear you. Are you
wounded? Repeat, are you wounded? Are you bailing
out?

PETER

What's your name?

JUNE

June.

PETER

Yes, June, I'm bailing out. I'm bailing out but
there's a catch — I've got no parachute.

JUNE

Hello, hello, Peter — do not understand. Hello,
Peter, can you hear me?

PETER

Hello, June, don't be afraid. It's quite simple,
we've had it and I'd rather jump than fry. After
the first thousand feet what's the difference?
I shan't know anything anyway. I say, I hope I
haven't frightened you.

JUNE

No, I'm not frightened.

PETER

Good girl.

JUNE

Your sparks, you said he was dead — hasn't he got
a chute?

PETER

Cut to ribbons — cannon shell.

Pause.

PETER

June? Are you pretty?

She sounds surprised.

> JUNE

Not bad, I...

> PETER

Can you hear me as well as I can hear you?

> JUNE

Yes.

> PETER

You've got a good voice. You've got guts too. It's funny, I've known dozens of girls — I've been in love with some of them, but it's an American girl whom I've never seen and never shall see who'll hear my last words — it's funny, it's rather sweet. June, if you're around when they pick me up, turn your head away —

> JUNE

Perhaps we can do something, Peter, let me report it.

> PETER

No, no one can help, only you. Let me do this in my own way. I want to be alone with you, June. Where were you born?

> JUNE

Boston.

> PETER

Mass.?

> JUNE

Yes.

PETER

That's a place to be born, history was made there.
Are you in love with anybody? No, no, don't answer
that.

JUNE

I could love a man like you, Peter.

PETER

I love you, June — you're life, and I'm leaving
you. Where do you live? On the station?

JUNE

No, in a big country house about five miles
from here — Lee Wood House.

PETER

Old house?

JUNE

Yes, very old.

PETER

Good, I'll be a ghost and come and see you.
You're not frightened of ghosts, are you? It
would be awful if you were.

JUNE

I'm not frightened.

PETER

What time will you be home?

JUNE

Well, I'm on duty until six. I have breakfast
in the mess and then I have to cycle half an

hour. I often go along the sands . . . this
is such nonsense.

                    PETER
No it's not, it's the best sense I've ever
heard. I was lucky to get you, June. Can't
be helped about the parachute — I'll have my
wings soon anyway, big white ones. I hope they
haven't gone all modern — I'd hate to have a
prop instead of wings. What do you think the
next world's like? I've got my own ideas—

                    JUNE

She interrupts him.

                    JUNE
Oh, Peter—

                    PETER
I think it starts where this one leaves off, or
where this one could leave off if we'd listened
to Plato and Aristotle and Jesus. With all our
little earthly problems solved, but with greater
ones worth the solving. I'll know soon enough
anyway. I'm signing off now, June, goodbye.
Goodbye, June.

Silence.

                    JUNE
Hello, G for George, hello, G George, Hello, G
George, hello—

For the scene where Peter's body is washed up on the beach, cameraman Jack Cardiff breathed on the lens to create condensation.

IN A LONELY PLACE   1950

Dir: Nicholas Ray. *Scr*: Andrew Solt, Edmund H. North. Based on a novel by
Dorothy B. Hughes. *Cast*: Humphrey Bogart (Dixon Steele)

```
                    STEELE
    I was born when she kissed me. I died when she
    left me. I lived a few weeks while she loved me.
```

SABRINA   1954

Dir: Billy Wilder. *Scr*: Billy Wilder, Ernest Lehman, Samuel A. Taylor. Based on
a play by Samuel A. Taylor. *Cast*: Marcel Dalio (Baron St Fontanel)

```
                BARON ST FONTANEL
    A woman happily in love, she burns the soufflé.
    A woman unhappily in love, she forgets to turn on
    the oven.
```

BE FUNNY OR THEY'LL KILL YOU

Billy Wilder (1906–2002) is one of only seven men to have
won Oscars for best picture as well as director and screenplay
but at heart he remained, as he had begun, a writer.

Born an Austrian Jew, he moved to Berlin in the late 1920s
to work as a journalist before teaming up with Curt and Robert
Siodmak to write the silent film *Menschen am Sonntag* (*People
on Sunday*, 1930). Fleeing Germany as Hitler rose to power,
he arrived in America in 1933 unable to speak a word of
English and his work always reflected an Old World sensibility
energized by New World opportunities. Vincent Canby of the
New York Times described him as 'the brightest, wittiest, most
perceptive, most resourceful' talent of his generation and noted
approvingly that his creations were like 'sugar laced with acid'.

His private life displayed the same balance of romanticism and cynicism. When Wilder was pursuing the actress Audrey Young, he confessed: 'I'd worship the ground you walk on if you lived in a better neighbourhood'; blessed with an equally robust sense of humour, she married him.

Throughout his career he remained devoted to the craft of writing, although he freely admitted: 'It's such an exhausting thing, you know, facing that empty page in the morning.' His usual solution to the problem was to work with a partner, and his long-standing collaborations with Charles Brackett and subsequently I. A. L. Diamond gave us such classics as *Ninotchka* (1939), *The Lost Weekend* (1945), *Sunset Boulevard* (1950), *Some Like It Hot* (1959) and *The Apartment* (1960). Despite his wit and urbane manner, his reputation as a co-writer was fearsome; Harry Kurnitz once remarked: 'Billy Wilder at work is actually two people – Mr Hyde and Mr Hyde.' Wilder might well have pleaded guilty, since he once admitted: 'A director must be a policeman, a midwife, a psychoanalyst, a sycophant and a bastard.'

Perhaps surprisingly, his greatest tenderness was reserved for his public:

- An audience is never wrong. An individual member of it may be an imbecile, but a thousand imbeciles together in the dark – that is critical genius.

- Don't be too clever for an audience. Make it obvious. Make the subtleties obvious also.

- In certain pictures I do hope they will leave the cinema a little enriched, but I don't make them pay a buck and a half and then ram a lecture down their throats.

His greatest reverence was for the irreverent:

- In a serious picture you don't hear them being bored, but in a comedy you can hear them not laughing.

- If you're going to tell people the truth, be funny or they'll kill you.

His comment on his craft remains his finest epitaph:

- The best director is the one you don't see.

THE NIGHT OF THE HUNTER   1955

Dir: Charles Laughton, Robert Mitchum (uncredited). *Scr*: James Agee. Based on a novel by Davis Grubb. *Cast*: Robert Mitchum (Reverend Harry Powell)

A murderous preacher explains the tattoos on his knuckles.

> REVEREND POWELL
> Ah, little lad, you're staring at my fingers.
> Would you like me to tell you the little story
> of right hand, left hand? The story of good
> and evil? H-A-T-E! It was with this left hand
> that old brother Cain struck the blow that
> laid his brother low. L-O-V-E! You see these
> fingers, dear hearts? These fingers has veins
> that run straight to the soul of man. The right
> hand, friends, the hand of love. Now watch, and
> I'll show you the story of life. Those fingers,
> dear hearts, is always a-warring and a-tugging,
> one agin t'other. Now watch 'em! Old brother
> left hand, left hand he's a-fighting, and it
> looks like love's a goner. But wait a minute!
> Hot dog, love's a-winning! Yes, sirree! It's
> love that's won, and old left hand hate is
> down for the count!

Mitchum, despite other memorable roles in *Out of the Past* (1947), *Cape Fear* (1962) and *Farewell My Lovely* (1975), suffered from none of the self-importance of his actor colleagues. When asked by an interviewer what he looked for in a script, he replied crisply: 'Days off.'

Although the film is now considered a *noir* classic and influenced directors as diverse as David Lynch, Martin Scorsese, Terrence Malick and the Coen brothers, it was not well received on its release. Charles Laughton was so disappointed that he never directed a film again.

ALFIE   1966

Dir: Lewis Gilbert. *Scr*: Bill Naughton, based on his play. *Cast*: Michael Caine (Alfie Elkins)

Jack-the-lad Alfie is not afraid to lie to get what he wants.

> **ALFIE**
> I've never told her that I love her — except at those times when you've got to say something for appearance's sake.

IF...   1968

Dir: Lindsay Anderson. *Scr*: David Sherwin, John Howlett. *Cast*: Malcolm McDowell (Mick Travis)

Rebellious schoolboy Mick still has a romantic streak.

> **MICK**
> There's only one thing you can do with a girl like this. Walk naked into the sea together as the sun sets. Make love once . . . Then die.

The film features the first instance of a full-frontal female nude passed by the British Board of Film Classification.

LOVE AND DEATH   1975

Dir: Woody Allen. *Scr*: Woody Allen. *Cast*: Diane Keaton (Sonja)

Neurotic intellectual Sonja discusses the nature of love with her
equally intense cousin.

> ### SONJA
> To love is to suffer. To avoid suffering one
> must not love. But then one suffers from not
> loving. Therefore, to love is to suffer; not
> to love is to suffer; to suffer is to suffer.
> To be happy is to love. To be happy, then, is
> to suffer, but suffering makes one unhappy.
> Therefore, to be unhappy, one must love or
> love to suffer or suffer from too much
> happiness. I hope you're getting this down.

FELLINI'S CASANOVA / *Il Casanova di Federico Fellini*   1976

Dir: Federico Fellini. *Scr*: Federico Fellini, Bernardino Zapponi. Based on
the autobiography of Giacomo Casanova. *Cast*: Donald Sutherland (Giacomo
Casanova)

> ### CASANOVA
> A man who never speaks ill of women does not love
> them. For, to understand them and to love them
> one must suffer at their hands. Then and only
> then can you find happiness at the lips of your
> beloved.

The film's distributors originally hoped to cast Robert Redford in
the lead role but Fellini refused. The director defended his choice
of Donald Sutherland thus: 'A sperm-filled waxwork with the eyes
of a masturbator; as far removed as you could imagine from an
adventurer and seducer like Casanova, but nonetheless a serious,
studied, professional actor.'

SUPERMAN 1978

Dir: Richard Donner. *Scr*: Mario Puzo, David Newman, Leslie Newman, Robert Benton. Based on characters created by Jerry Siegel, Joe Shuster. *Cast*: Margot Kidder (Lois Lane)

Lois Lane holds an imaginary conversation with Superman as he flies with her above Metropolis.

> LOIS
>
> Can you read my mind? Do you know what it is
> that you do to me? I don't know who you are.
> Just a friend from another star. Here I am like
> a kid out of school. Holding hands with a god.
> I'm a fool. Will you look at me? Quivering.
> Like a little girl shivering. You can see
> right through me. Can you read my mind? Can you
> picture the things I'm thinking of? Wondering
> why you are all the wonderful things you are.
> You can fly! You belong in the sky. You and
> I could belong to each other. If you need a
> friend, I'm the one to fly to. If you need to
> be loved, here I am. Read my mind.

Steven Spielberg was a contender to direct the film but on hearing his salary demands the producers preferred to hedge their bets until they saw how his 'fish movie' (*Jaws*, 1975) performed. The shoot was so complex that at one point there were seven units working on different parts of the story; the credits sequence alone cost more than the budget of an average production at that time. Various approaches were explored to show Superman in flight: a dummy launched from a catapult, a model aircraft carrying a painting of the character and traditional animation. In the end the traditional technique of wire suspension with projected background plates proved most convincing.

NOSFERATU THE VAMPYRE
Nosferatu: Phantom der Nacht   **1979**

Dir: Werner Herzog. *Scr*: Werner Herzog. Based on a novel by Bram Stoker. *Cast*:
Klaus Kinski (Count Dracula)

COUNT DRACULA
The absence of love is the most abject pain.

In one scene where thousands of grey rats were needed, only the
white variety was available: the director ordered them to be painted.

GREGORY'S GIRL   **1981**

Dir: Bill Forsyth. *Scr*: Bill Forsyth. *Cast*: John Gordon Sinclair (Gregory
Underwood), William Greenlees (Steve)

Gregory confides to a classmate that he has fallen for the girl who
replaced him on the school football team.

GREGORY
Have you ever been in love? I'm in love.

STEVE
Since when?

GREGORY
This morning. I feel restless and dizzy. I bet I
won't get any sleep tonight.

STEVE
Sounds like indigestion.

HANNAH AND HER SISTERS   **1986**
Dir: Woody Allen. *Scr*: Woody Allen. *Cast*: Woody Allen (Mickey Sachs)

Mickey used to be married to Hannah but has now wed her
sister Lee.

MICKEY

You know, I was talking to your father before,
and I was telling him that it's ironic — I used
to always have Thanksgiving with Hannah, and I
never thought that I could love anybody else.
And here it is years later and I'm married to
you and completely in love with you. The heart
is a very, very resilient little muscle, it
really is.

Woody Allen said he was inspired to write the film after rereading Tolstoy's *Anna Karenina*. It took over $40 million [$93.5 million] at the box office in America alone and a lobby group was formed to propose that the screenplay be eligible for a Pulitzer prize.

IT'S ALL THERE ON THE PAGE

Emma Thompson has won Oscars both as an actor (*Howards End*, 1992) and writer (*Sense and Sensibility*, 1995). In her memoir of the making of the Jane Austen novel she recalls how the producer clarified the distinction between her twin roles on the project: 'Lindsay goes round the table and introduces everyone – making it clear that I am present in the capacity of writer rather than actress, therefore no one has to be too nice to me.' Most actors - on the record, at least – accord the creator of their characters suitable deference:

- You don't improvise with a Cameron Crowe script.
  Orlando Bloom

- I only sound intelligent when there's a good script writer around.
  Christian Bale

- I see myself as an actor first because writing is what you do when you are ready and acting is what you do when someone else is ready.
  Steve Martin

- When I'm the one who sits down and looks at the blank page and writes it out all the way, then I'll call it my script.
  Edward Norton

- You can have a million-dollar, twenty-million-dollar budget or sixty-million-dollar budget and if you don't have a good script, it doesn't mean a thing.
  Tippi Hedren

- With indies, all they have is their script and it's very important to them. The characters are better drawn, the stories more precise and the experience greater than with studio films where sometimes they fill in the script as they're shooting.
  Mark Ruffalo

- Well, first of all, you read the script a million times. Because what the script gives you are given circumstances. Given circumstances are all the facts of your character... And then, using my imagination, and then after all that, I have to tackle the scene.
  Viola Davis

- Every time you say yes to a film there's a certain percentage of your 'yes' that has to do with the director, a certain percentage to do with the story, a certain percentage with the character, the location, etc... I feel I do my best work when it's all there on the page, and I feel that the character is very vivid as I read the script and I'm not having to create stuff and trying to cobble

together something. If I have to do that, then I don't entirely trust what I'm doing.
Guy Pearce

- A script for an actor is like a bible. You carry it with you, you read it over and over, you go to your passages.
Cameron Diaz

- All of the good movies are based on how that story was told. And you cannot do it with a bad script, that's for sure, no matter who.
Javier Bardem

- There's a certain arrogance to an actor who will look at a script and feel like, because the words are simple, maybe they can paraphrase it and make it better.
Mary Steenburgen

Not all actors, however, are convinced that a script is a foolproof guide:

- Good actors never use the script unless it's amazing writing. All the good actors I've worked with, they all say whatever they want to say.
Jessica Alba

- Normally you read a screenplay – and I read a lot of them – and the characters don't feel like people. They feel like plot devices or cliches or stereotypes.
Joseph Gordon-Levitt

- I wasn't comfortable in the beginning. But the longer I'm in the business, you see a lot of times these screenplays have been rewritten five times and you're not really offending an author. It's a studio that keeps banging out money having a writer rewrite portions. I've learned that you actually do have some freedom and

you're not necessarily stepping on somebody's toes if you come in and say, 'Hey, this thing isn't working for me but I'm still interested in making this film.'
Edward Burns

Laura Linney is open about her intelligent engagement with material she feels is flawed:

- My experience is that's rare that you have a script that is what they call 'film-ready'. These days, many scripts are written to be financed, not to be acted . . . and so the agenda behind the writing is to explain, as opposed to give cues and hints to an actor to act. You don't have to say things all the time; you can act them. Otherwise, you have a character who doesn't connect to anything because they talk too much.

MOONSTRUCK   1987

Dir: Norman Jewison. *Scr*: John Patrick Shanley. *Cast*: Nicolas Cage (Ronny Cammareri)

Ronny tries to persuade Loretta to abandon her fears and follow his passion.

> RONNY
>
> Love don't make things nice, it ruins everything! It breaks your heart, it makes things a mess. We, we aren't here to make things perfect. Snowflakes are perfect, stars are perfect. Not us! Not us! We're here to ruin ourselves and — and to break our hearts and love the wrong people and, and die! I mean that the storybooks are bullshit. Now I want you to come upstairs with me and get in my bed.

WHEN HARRY MET SALLY... 1989

Dir: Rob Reiner. *Scr*: Nora Ephron. *Cast*: Billy Crystal (Harry Burns)

HARRY

I love that you get cold when it's seventy-one
degrees out; I love that it takes you an hour
and a half to order a sandwich; I love that you
get a little crinkle above your nose when you're
looking at me like I'm nuts; I love that after
I spend a day with you I can still smell your
perfume on my clothes, and I love that you are
the last person I want to talk to before I go to
sleep at night. And it's not because I'm lonely,
and it's not because it's New Year's Eve. I came
here tonight because when you realize you want
to spend the rest of your life with somebody, you
want the rest of your life to start as soon as
possible.

PRETTY WOMAN 1990

Dir: Garry Marshall. *Scr*: J. F. Lawton. *Cast*: Julia Roberts (Vivian Ward)

Vivian, an escort, is weary of always being 'the other woman'.

VIVIAN

When I was a little girl my mama used to lock me
in the attic when I was bad, which was pretty
often. And I would pretend I was a princess
trapped in a tower by a wicked queen. And then
suddenly this knight on a white horse with these
colours flying would come charging up and draw
his sword. And I would wave. And he would climb
up the tower and rescue me. But never in all the
time . . . that I had this dream did the knight say

to me, 'Come on, baby, I'll put you up in a great condo.'

When Vivian meets her client Edward at the start of the film they go to see Verdi's *La Traviata*. The opera is about a courtesan who abandons her calling because she falls in love.

THE ENGLISH PATIENT   1996

Dir: Anthony Minghella. *Scr*: Anthony Minghella. Based on a novel by Michael Ondaatje. *Cast*: Ralph Fiennes (Count László de Almásy), Kristin Scott Thomas (Katharine Clifton)

In pre-war Cairo, an adulterous couple share a rare stolen moment together.

> ALMÁSY
> When were you most happy?

> KATHARINE
> Now.

> ALMÁSY
> And when were you least happy?

> KATHARINE
> Now.

BEAUTIFUL GIRLS   1996

Dir: Ted Demme. *Scr*: Scott Rosenberg. *Cast*: Rosie O'Donnell (Gina Barrisano)

Gina is tired of her male friends' obsession with youthful beauty.

> GINA
> No matter how perfect the nipple, how supple the
> thigh, unless there's some other shit going on in
> the relationship besides physical it's going get

old, okay? And you guys, as a gender, have got to
get a grip otherwise the future of the human race
is in jeopardy.

THE DEVIL'S ADVOCATE   1997

Dir: Taylor Hackford. *Scr*: Jonathan Lemkin, Tony Gilroy. Based on a novel
by Andrew Neiderman. *Cast*: Keanu Reeves (Kevin Lomax), Al Pacino (John
Milton)

Kevin questions Milton, who is actually the Devil disguised as a
New York lawyer.

> KEVIN
>
> What about love?

> MILTON
>
> Overrated. Biochemically no different than eating
> large quantities of chocolate.

Lawyer John Milton was named after the seventeenth-century
author of *Paradise Lost*. The poem contains the line 'Better to reign
in Hell than serve in Heaven'.

YOU'VE GOT MAIL   1998

Dir: Nora Ephron. *Scr*: Nora Ephron, Delia Ephron. Based on a play by Miklós
László. *Cast*: Meg Ryan (Kathleen Kelly)

Kathleen writes a heartfelt email to a man she has never even met.

> KATHLEEN
>
> I like to start my notes to you as if we're
> already in the middle of a conversation. I
> pretend that we're the oldest and dearest friends
> — as opposed to what we actually are, people who
> don't know each other's names and met in an 'Over
> 30' chatroom where we both claimed we'd never
> been before. What will NY152 say today, I wonder.

```
I turn on my computer, I wait impatiently as it
boots up. I go on line, and my breath catches in
my chest until I hear three little words: You've
got mail. I hear nothing, not even a sound on
the streets of New York, just the beat of my own
heart. I have mail. From you.
```

Nora Ephron adapted her script from *The Shop Around the Corner*, a play by Miklós László in which the two protagonists fall in love while corresponding by post.

A BEAUTIFUL MIND   2001

Dir: Ron Howard. *Scr*: Akiva Goldsman. Based on a book by Sylvia Nasar. *Cast*: Russell Crowe (John Nash), Jennifer Connelly (Alicia Nash)

A brilliant mathematician finds himself emotionally awkward with his lover.

```
              NASH
    Alicia, does our relationship warrant long-term
    commitment? I need some kind of proof, some kind
    of verifiable, empirical data.

              ALICIA
    I'm sorry, just give me a moment to redefine my
    girlish notions of romance.
```

THE RULES OF ATTRACTION   2002

Dir: Roger Avary. *Scr*: Roger Avary. Based on a novel by Bret Easton Ellis. *Cast*: James van der Beek (Sean Bateman)

Lauren discovers her partner Sean has slept with her roommate.

```
              SEAN
    I only had sex with her because I'm in love with
    you.
```

Dir: Tim Burton. *Scr*: John August. Based on a novel by Daniel Wallace. *Cast*: Billy Crudup (Will Bloom)

Will suspects his mother may have idealized her relationships in the past.

>   WILL
> I know better than to argue romance with a French
> woman.

STARRING

Sean O'Fearna is regularly ranked among the twentieth century's greatest directors. His collaboration with rising star Marion Morrison on *Stagecoach* won the Best Picture Oscar in 1940; a screen legend for over thirty years, Morrison eventually won in the acting category for *True Grit* (1969). Thomas Mapother IV has been nominated for three Academy Awards and was Hollywood's highest-earning star in 2012, while Allan Stewart Konigsberg has won four from his twenty-three nominations but only attended the ceremony once. Who would have foreseen Paul Georg Julius Hernreid Ritter von Wassel-Waldingau would flee Casablanca with Ingrid Bergman, leaving Humphrey Bogart alone and heartbroken? And who can forget Bernard Schwartz as a cross-dressing saxophonist consoling Norma Jeane Mortenson as she complains she always gets 'the fuzzy end of the lollipop'?

Shrewd agents, perhaps. O'Fearna was the birth name of John Ford, Marion Morrison became John Wayne, Mapother is Tom Cruise and Mr Konigsberg is Woody Allen. Herr Wassel-Waldingau is better known as Paul Henreid, Schwartz as Tony Curtis, and Miss Mortenson ended her career worshipped but alone as Marilyn Monroe.

Many talented artists from Europe who fuelled Hollywood's boom through the 1930s were persuaded by immigration officials, studio bosses and plain common sense to give their real names a more user-friendly ring. Some, in a career where identity was increasingly synonymous with brand, just wanted to stand apart. Still others, saddled with a lack of poetry in their birth certificate, just wanted a zippier start.

For some it was easy enough: Ethel Zimmerman shed her youthful Zim to become Ethel Merman, while Frederick Austerlitz dropped Rick and Litz to take off as Fred Astaire. Others found a trim perfectly sufficient: Clint(on) Eastwood, Jr., James (Baum)garner, Walter Matuschanskayasky (Matthau), while the homophonous Dominic Felix Amici (Don Ameche) and Leo Jacoby (Lee J. Cobb) found stardust in spelling. Catherine Jones borrowed a Zeta- before marrying Michael Delaney Dowd, Jr (Michael Douglas, son of Issur Danielovitch – better known as Kirk Douglas).

Mel Columcille Gerard Gibson tactfully buried his middle names, Eldred Gregory Peck abandoned his first and Jennifer Anastassakis (Aniston) seems to have grown bored of hers halfway through. In some cases, professions dictated a certain style: Hulk Hogan may be forgiven for doubting Terry Jene Bollea would look imposing splashed across billboards, and Virginia McMath put a spring in her step to become Ginger Rogers. The rest hardly need to justify themselves:

- Anne Bancroft: Anna-Maria Louisa Italiano
- Ben Kingsley: Krishna Banji
- Brigitte Bardot: Camille Javal
- Bruce Willis: Walter Willison
- Claudette Colbert: Lily Chauchoin
- Cyd Charisse: Tula Ellice Finklea

- Demi Moore: Demetria Gene Guynes
- Diana Dors: Diana Fluck
- Doris Day: Doris von Kappelhoff
- Edward G. Robinson: Emmanuel Goldenberg
- James Dean: Seth Ward
- Joaquin Phoenix: Joaquin Rafael Bottom
- Judy Garland: Frances Gumm
- Lauren Bacall: Betty Joan Perske
- Michael Caine: Maurice Micklewhite
- Red Buttons: Aaron Chwatt
- Rita Hayworth: Margarita Cansino
- Whoopi Goldberg: Caryn Johnson

For readers who feel cheated by these false identities, the Internet Movie Database lists 139 entries under plain John Smith, although one had actually been persuaded by his agent that a straightforward name was more promising than his former one: Robert Errol Van Orden. The various John Smiths have been responsible for the following credits:

- Actor: *Crazy*
- Actor: *Emergency!*
- Actor: *At Death's Door*
- Producer: *England's Worst Ever Football Team*
- Director: *Bound and Thrashed*
- Transportation Department: *Up in the Air*
- Production Manager: *The Labyrinth of Love*
- Miscellaneous Crew: *Tortoise in Love*
- Composer: *Stuff*

- Self: *The Porn King, the Strippers and The Bent Coppers*
- Self: *The Harlem Globetrotters Popcorn Machine*
- Self: *Super High Me*
- Thanks: *Recalculating*

LOVE ACTUALLY 2003

Dir: Richard Curtis. *Scr*: Richard Curtis. *Cast*: Hugh Grant (David, the Prime Minister)

            PRIME MINISTER
Whenever I get gloomy with the state of the
world, I think about the arrivals gate at
Heathrow Airport. General opinion's starting to
make out that we live in a world of hatred and
greed, but I don't see that. It seems to me that
love is everywhere. Often, it's not particularly
dignified or newsworthy, but it's always there -
fathers and sons, mothers and daughters, husbands
and wives, boyfriends, girlfriends, old friends.
When the planes hit the Twin Towers, as far as
I know, none of the phone calls from the people
on board were messages of hate or revenge - they
were all messages of love. If you look for it,
I've got a sneaking suspicion... love actually
is all around.

When casting the part of Sarah, writer/director Richard Curtis auditioned many British actors, but kept saying, 'I want someone like Laura Linney...' The casting director eventually snapped and said, 'Oh, for fuck's sake, get Laura Linney then.' Linney auditioned and got the part.

ANCHORMAN: THE LEGEND OF RON BURGUNDY 2004

Dir: Adam McKay. *Scr*: Will Ferrell, Adam McKay. *Cast*: Paul Rudd (Brian Fantana), Will Ferrell (Ron Burgundy)

Two chauvinistic journalists discuss their hapless love lives.

> BRIAN
>
> I think I was in love once.

> RON
>
> Really? What was her name?

> BRIAN
>
> I don't remember.

> RON
>
> That's not a good start, but keep going.

> BRIAN
>
> She was Brazilian or Chinese or something weird. I met her in the bathroom of a Kmart and we made out for hours. Then we parted ways, never to see each other again.

> RON
>
> I'm pretty sure that's not love.

> BRIAN
>
> Damn it.

CLOSER   2004

Dir: Mike Nichols. *Scr*: Patrick Marber, based on his play. *Cast*: Clive Owen (Larry Gray), Natalie Portman (Alice Ayres)

Larry, who has just broken up with his lover, visits a strip club where he runs into Alice, an old acquaintance.

                    LARRY

All the girls in this hell hole . . . the pneumat-
ic robots, the coked-up babydolls . . . and you're
no different. You all use stage names to con
yourselves you're someone else so you don't feel
ashamed when you show your cunts and assholes to
complete fucking strangers! I'm trying to have a
conversation here!

                    ALICE

You're out of cash, buddy.

                    LARRY

I paid for this room!

                    ALICE

This is extra.

                    LARRY

We met last year.

                    ALICE

Wrong girl.

                    LARRY

Talk to me!

                    ALICE

I am.

                    LARRY

Talk to me in real life. I didn't know you'd be
here. I know who you are. I love you. I love
everything about you. The hurt.

He laughs - then begins to cry.

LARRY

She won't even see me. You feel the same. I know
you feel the same.

ALICE

You can't cry in here.

LARRY

Hold me. Let me hold you.

ALICE

We're not allowed to touch.

LARRY

Well, come home with me. It's safe. Let me look
after you.

ALICE

I don't need looking after.

LARRY

Everybody needs looking after.

ALICE

I'm not your revenge fuck.

LARRY

I'll pay you.

ALICE

I don't need your money.

LARRY

You have my money.

ALICE

Thank you.

LARRY

'Thank you.' 'Thank you.' Is that some kind of
rule?

ALICE

Just being polite.

LARRY

Get a lot of grown men crying their guts out, do
you?

ALICE

Occupational hazard.

THE SECRET LIFE OF WORDS   2005

Dir: Isabel Coixet. *Scr*: Isabel Coixet. *Cast*: Tim Robbins (Josef), Sarah Polley
(Hanna)

Josef tries to persuade Hanna to break free from her fearful, repetitive
life.

JOSEF

I thought, um, you and I, maybe we could go
away somewhere. Together. One of these days.
Today. Right now. Come with me.

HANNA

No, I don't think that's going to be possible.

JOSEF

Why not?

HANNA

Because I think that if we go away to someplace
together, I'm afraid that one day, maybe not
today, maybe... maybe not tomorrow either, but
one day suddenly, I may begin to cry and cry so

very much that nothing or nobody can stop me
and the tears will fill the room, and I won't
be able to breathe and I will pull you down
with me and we'll both drown.

                    JOSEF
I'll learn how to swim, Hanna. I swear, I'll
learn how to swim.

RED   2010

Dir: Robert Schwentke. *Scr*: Jon Hoeber, Erich Hoeber. Based on a graphic novel
by Warren Ellis, Cully Hamner. *Cast*: Helen Mirren (Victoria), Mary-Louise
Parker (Sarah Ross)

Secret agent Victoria – Retired, Extremely Dangerous – reveals her
past to her hostage.

                    VICTORIA
I was in love with an agent once.

                    SARAH
What happened?

                    VICTORIA
Well, I was with MI6 and the relationship
wasn't sanctioned. So when it came to light,
my loyalty was questioned and I was ordered to
kill him. It was a test.

                    SARAH
What did you do?

                    VICTORIA
I put three bullets in his chest.

In Bulgaria, the film was distributed under the title *BSP: Besni
Strashni Pensii* – which means 'Furious Frightful Pensioners'.

Dir: Joe Wright. *Scr*: David Farr, Seth Lochhead. Based on a story by Seth Lochhead. *Cast*: Saoirse Ronan (Hanna Heller), Álvaro Cervantes (Feliciano)

A young woman raised in seclusion by her father encounters other people for the first time.

>   HANNA
> Are we going to kiss now?

>   FELICIANO
> Would you like to?

>   HANNA
> Kissing requires a total of thirty-four facial
> muscles and a hundred and twelve postural
> muscles. The most important muscle involved
> is the orbicularis oris muscle, because it is
> used to pucker the lips.

LIBIDO

NINOTCHKA   1939

Dir: Ernst Lubitsch. *Scr*: Charles Brackett, Billy Wilder, Walter Reisch. Based on a story by Melchior Lengyel. *Cast*: Melvyn Douglas (Count Leon d'Algout)

>   LEON
>
>   It's midnight. One half of Paris is making love
>   to the other half.

GONE WITH THE WIND   1939

Dir: Victor Fleming. *Scr*: Sidney Howard. Based on a novel by Margaret Mitchell. *Cast*: Vivien Leigh (Scarlett O'Hara), Clark Gable (Rhett Butler)

>   SCARLETT
>   Rhett, don't. I shall faint.
>
>   RHETT
>   I want you to faint. This is what you were
>   meant for. None of the fools you've ever known
>   have kissed you like this, have they?

Gary Cooper turned down the part of Rhett Butler, saying not only '*Gone with the Wind* is going to be the biggest flop in Hollywood history,' but also 'I'm just glad it'll be Clark Gable who's falling on his face and not Gary Cooper.' Measured on its US box office receipts and adjusted for inflation, the film remains the most profitable release in the history of cinema.

BALL OF FIRE   1941

Dir: Howard Hawks. *Scr*: Charles Brackett, Billy Wilder, Thomas Monroe. *Cast*: Gary Cooper (Bertram Potts)

A mild-mannered lexicographer hopes to learn contemporary slang from a nightclub performer.

>   POTTS
> I shall regret the absence of your keen mind.
> Unfortunately, it is inseparable from an
> extremely disturbing body.

THE MAJOR AND THE MINOR   1942

Dir: Billy Wilder. *Scr*: Charles Brackett, Billy Wilder. Based on a story by Fanny Kilbourne and a play by Edward Childs Carpenter. *Cast*: Robert Benchley (Mr Albert Osborne)

>   OSBORNE
> Why don't you get out of that wet coat and into
> a dry martini?

'WHEN WOMEN GO WRONG, MEN GO RIGHT AFTER THEM'

Mae West (1893–1980) began her career as a child actor before turning to vaudeville; in 1926 she wrote, directed and starred in the Broadway play *Sex*. Arrested on charges of obscenity, she served ten days in jail on Welfare Island where she delighted in telling reporters she had worn silk underwear throughout her stay. The controversy ensured her – aged thirty-eight – a contract with Paramount. During her first film, *Night After Night* (1932), West insisted on rewriting many of her scenes, prompting her co-star George Raft to declare: 'she stole everything but the cameras'.

Although a supporter of women's liberation, she never declared herself a feminist and remained as famous for her sexual innuendo in real life as on screen. Memorable quips include:

- When women go wrong, men go right after them.

- When caught between two evils I generally pick the one I've never tried before.

- When I'm good, I'm very good. But when I'm bad, I'm better.

- Good girls go to heaven. Bad girls go everywhere else.

- I used to be Snow White, but I drifted.

- Ten men waiting for me at the door? Send one of them home, I'm tired.

- A hard man is good to find.

- I believe in censorship. After all, I made a fortune out of it.

- I only like two kinds of men: domestic and foreign.

- To err is human, but it feels divine.

- Is that a gun in your pocket or are you just glad to see me?

- Marriage is a great institution, but I'm not ready for an institution yet.

- Those who are easily shocked should be shocked more often.

- I'm the lady who works at Paramount all day…and Fox all night.

- I always save one boyfriend for a rainy day… and another in case it doesn't rain.

- Sex is an emotion in motion… Love is what you make it and who you make it with.

MILDRED PIERCE 1945

Dir: Michael Curtiz. *Scr*: Ranald MacDougall. Based on a novel by James M. Cain. *Cast*: Zachary Scott (Monte Beragon)

            MONTE
   In the spring a young man's fancy lightly turns
   to what he's been thinking about all winter.

THE BIG SLEEP 1946

Dir: Howard Hawks. *Scr*: William Faulkner, Leigh Brackett, Jules Furthman. Based on a novel by Raymond Chandler. *Cast*: Humphrey Bogart (Philip Marlowe)

            MARLOWE
   She tried to sit in my lap while I was standing up.

Hawks claims that when producer Jack Warner gave him $50,000 [$660,000] to buy the rights to *The Big Sleep* he paid Chandler $5,000 [$66,000] and kept the rest for himself. Bogart and Bacall argued for years about whose idea it had been for Marlowe to adopt his flustered disguise, conveniently forgetting that Chandler's novel already contained the line: 'I had my horn-rimmed glasses on. I put my voice high and let a bird twitter in it.'

GILDA 1946

Dir: Charles Vidor. *Scr*: Marion Parsonnet, E. A. Ellington. *Cast*: Rita Hayworth (Gilda Mundson Farrell), Glenn Ford (Johnny Farrell)

Two lovers meet again years after their acrimonious split.

            GILDA
   You do hate me, don't you, Johnny?

            JOHNNY
   I don't think you have any idea of how much.

                    GILDA
    Hate is a very exciting emotion. Haven't you
    noticed? Very exciting. I hate you too, Johnny.
    I hate you so much I think I'm going to die from
    it. Darling...

They kiss passionately.

                    GILDA
    I think I'm going to die from it.

THE SEVEN YEAR ITCH   1955

Dir: Billy Wilder. *Scr*: Billy Wilder, George Axelrod. Based on a play by George
Axelrod. *Cast*: Oskar Homolka (Dr Brubaker), Tom Ewell (Richard Sherman)

Sherman confesses to his analyst that he is restless in his marriage.

                    DR BRUBAKER
    When something itches, my dear sir, the natural
    tendency is to scratch.

                    SHERMAN
    Last night I scratched.

PILLOW TALK   1959

Dir: Michael Gordon. *Scr*: Stanley Shapiro, Maurice Richlin. *Cast*: Doris Day
(Jan Morrow)

Jan, happily single, resents having to share a telephone line with
Brad Allen, a relentless womanizer.

                    JAN
    Mr Allen, this may come as a shock to you, but
    there are some men who don't end every sentence
    with a proposition.

PEEPING TOM 1960

Dir: Michael Powell. *Scr*: Leo Marks. *Cast*: Bartlett Mullins (Mr Peters), Karlheinz Böhm (Mark Lewis)

Lewis, a psychopathic photographer, is interviewed for a job shooting glamour pictures.

>   MR PETERS
>   Got a question for you. Which magazines sell the
>   most copies?
>
>   MARK
>   Those with girls on the front covers and no front
>   covers on the girls.

Writer Leo Marks was a noted cryptographer during the Second World War. The thriller explored many of Freud's theories in a sophisticated but shocking manner; censors savaged the released version and the public was outraged by its subject matter. The furore destroyed Powell's hitherto glittering career, although the film is now hailed as a masterpiece. As Powell noted ruefully in his autobiography, 'I make a film that nobody wants to see and then, thirty years later, everybody has either seen it or wants to see it.' *Peeping Tom* remains banned in Finland to this day.

HUD 1963

Dir: Martin Ritt. *Scr*: Irving Ravetch, Harriet Frank Jr. Based on a novel by Larry McMurtry. *Cast*: Paul Newman (Hud Bannon)

Ruthless hedonist Hud takes a single-minded approach in matters of love.

>   HUD
>   The only question I ever ask any woman is 'What
>   time is your husband coming home?'

ONE FLEW OVER THE CUCKOO'S NEST   1975

Dir: Miloš Forman. *Scr*: Lawrence Hauben, Bo Goldman. Based on a novel by Ken Kesey. *Cast*: Jack Nicholson (Randle 'Mac' McMurphy)

McMurphy has been undergoing electroconvulsive therapy against his will.

> MCMURPHY
>
> They was giving me ten thousand watts a day, you know, and I'm hot to trot. The next woman takes me on's gonna light up like a pinball machine and pay off in silver dollars!

SCARFACE   1983

Dir: Brian De Palma. *Scr*: Oliver Stone. Based on a 1932 film of the same name, and on a novel by Armitage Trail. *Cast*: Al Pacino (Tony Montana)

Tony dances with Elvira but grows frustrated as she resists his advances.

> TONY
>
> Hey baby, what is your problem? Huh, you got a problem? You're good-looking, you got a beautiful body, beautiful legs, beautiful face, all these guys in love with you. Only you got a look in your eye like you haven't been fucked in a year.

PERSONAL SERVICES   1987

Dir: Terry Jones. *Scr*: David Leland. *Cast*: Julie Walters (Christine Painter)

After a raid on her brothel, Christine Painter is interviewed by police.

> CHRISTINE
>
> I'm responsible, not the men. You can't expect

the men to be responsible. When the balls are
full, the brain is empty.

A FISH CALLED WANDA   1988

Dir: Charles Crichton, John Cleese (uncredited). *Scr*: John Cleese, Charles
Crichton. *Cast*: John Cleese (Archie Leach)

Repressed English lawyer Archie finds himself so in love with Wanda
that he throws caution to the wind.

```
                ARCHIE
Wanda, do you have any idea what it's like being
English? Being so correct all the time, being
so stifled by this dread of, of doing the wrong
thing, of saying to someone 'Are you married?'
and hearing 'My wife left me this morning,' or
saying, uh, 'Do you have children?' and being
told they all burned to death on Wednesday. You
see, Wanda, we're all terrified of embarrassment.
That's why we're so . . . dead. Most of my friends
are dead, you know — we have these piles of
corpses to dinner. But you're alive, God bless
you, and I want to be, I'm so fed up with all
this. I want to make love with you, Wanda. I'm a
good lover — at least I used to be, back in the
early fourteenth century. Can we go to bed?
```

Cleese named his character Archibald Leach, the real name of screen
idol Cary Grant. When an interviewer once offered that 'Everybody
would like to be Cary Grant', Grant reputedly replied: 'So would
I.' He also decried the many rumours about his reputation, saying:
'Hell, if I'd jumped on all the dames I'm supposed to have jumped
on, I'd have had no time to go fishing.'

Dir: Rob Reiner. *Scr*: Nora Ephron. *Cast*: Billy Crystal (Harry Burns), Meg Ryan (Sally Albright)

Meeting by chance, old acquaintances Harry and Sally seem unsure how things stand between them.

>   HARRY
> You realize, of course, that we could never be
> friends.
>
>   SALLY
> Why not?
>
>   HARRY
> What I'm saying is, and this is not a come-on in
> any way, shape or form, is that men and women
> can't be friends because the sex part always gets
> in the way.
>
>   SALLY
> That's not true. I have a number of men friends
> and there is no sex involved.
>
>   HARRY
> No, you don't.
>
>   SALLY
> Yes, I do.
>
>   HARRY
> No, you don't.
>
>   SALLY
> Yes, I do.
>
>   HARRY
> You only think you do.

SALLY

You say I'm having sex with these men without my
knowledge?

HARRY

No, what I'm saying is they all want to have sex
with you.

SALLY

They do not.

HARRY

Do too.

SALLY

How do you know?

HARRY

Because no man can be friends with a woman
that he finds attractive. He always wants to
have sex with her.

SALLY

So, you're saying that a man can be friends
with a woman he finds unattractive?

HARRY

No. You pretty much want to nail them too.

SALLY

What if they don't want to have sex with you?

HARRY

Doesn't matter, because the sex thing is
already out there so the friendship is ultimately
doomed and that's the end of the story.

SALLY

Well, I guess we're not going to be friends then.

> **HARRY**
>
> I guess not.
>
> **SALLY**
>
> That's too bad. You were the only person
> that I knew in New York.

According to screenwriter Nora Ephron, the infamous 'I'll have what she's having' line was actually suggested by Billy Crystal.

PRETTY WOMAN   1990

Dir: Garry Marshall. *Scr*: J. F. Lawton. *Cast*: Julia Roberts (Vivian Ward), Richard Gere (Edward Lewis)

A high-class call girl negotiates her nightly fee with an attractive client.

> **VIVIAN**
>
> I would have stayed for two thousand.
>
> **EDWARD**
>
> I would have paid four.

The modern Cinderella story struck a chord with many women – but not all. As Laney Boggs says in *She's All That* (1999): 'I feel just like Julia Roberts in *Pretty Woman*. You know, except for the whole hooker thing.'

The studio didn't initially want to cast Julia Roberts as Vivian; along the way they considered Meg Ryan, Kim Basinger, Kathleen Turner, Debra Winger, Geena Davis, Carrie Fisher, Bo Derek, Kelly McGillis, Melanie Griffith, Sharon Stone, Michelle Pfeiffer, Madonna, Jamie Lee Curtis, Emma Thompson, Rosanna Arquette, Heather Locklear, Jennifer Jason Leigh, Joan Cusack, Phoebe Cates, Elisabeth Shue, Tatum O'Neal, Bridget Fonda, Lori Loughlin, Diane Lane and Justine Bateman.

Dir: David Lynch. *Scr*: David Lynch. Based on a novel by Barry Gifford. *Cast*: Nicolas Cage (Sailor Ripley)

Romantic Southern outlaw Sailor Ripley has a way with words.

```
                    SAILOR
     Man, I had a boner with a capital 'O'.
```

A FONT FOR SCHMUCKS

Producer Jack Warner once dismissively referred to the staff contracted to work at his studio: 'Actors? Schmucks. Screenwriters? Schmucks with Underwoods.' (The latter was a famous brand of manual typewriter.) Warner reputedly demanded his team deliver a minimum number of pages a week and used to stand outside the writers' building ready to burst in if he did not hear the reassuring clack of machinery and the familiar carriage return bell.

It was during Warner's heyday in the 1930s that the screenplay format took its enduring shape and its conventions remain today. Fifty years after the widespread acceptance of the electric typewriter (and thirty years after the personal computer became commonplace), the typeface used a century ago is still used by the vast majority of film writers.

The original font emulating the manuscript look for printing was designed by Howard Kettler in 1955. Originally named 'Messenger' it was finally christened 'Courier', as Kettler explained: 'A letter can be [from] an ordinary messenger, or it can be [from a] courier, which radiates dignity, prestige, and stability.' His creation endured as the standard typeface for the US State Department until 2004, doubtless lending the font an air of respectability to modern readers.

One of its advantages for the film industry is that it is monospaced – that is, each letter takes up the same width on the page, which regularizes formatting and word counts. The result gives fifty-five average length lines per page, approximating handily to a rule of thumb that each sheet represents a minute of screen time.

A further commonplace is that a one-sentence scene with traditional spacing and numbering takes up an eighth of a page, and thus represents around seven seconds of action. Sometimes writers resent the notion that their work can be mathematically analysed and cheekily compress complicated scenes to frustrate assistant directors.

An action-packed war episode might read as follows:

```
38. DAY EXTERIOR — PEARL HARBOR — QUAYSIDE —
(1/8 page)

CIVILIANS race for cover and hundreds of
NAVY GUNNERS open fire as the cloudless sky
is filled with JAPANESE AIRCRAFT releasing
TORPEDOES and BOMBS on the entire US FLEET.
```

WAYNE'S WORLD   1992

Dir: Penelope Spheeris. *Scr*: Mike Myers, Bonnie Turner, Terry Turner. *Cast*: Mike Myers (Wayne Campbell), Dana Carvey (Garth Algar)

Two teenagers recording a home video introduce a tribute to the model Claudia Schiffer.

> WAYNE
> Schwing!

> GARTH
> Schwing!

                    WAYNE
Tent pole! She's a babe!

                    GARTH
She's magically babelicious.

                    WAYNE
She tested very high on the strokability scale.

BASIC INSTINCT   1992
Dir: Paul Verhoeven. *Scr*: Joe Eszterhas. *Cast*: George Dzundza (Gus)

Gus worries his detective partner is allowing an attractive suspect to distract him.

                    GUS
Well, she got that magna cum laude pussy on her
that done fried up your brain.

Joe Eszterhas claimed to have written the uncommissioned script in thirteen days; a bidding war between studios raised the price of the screenplay to an unprecedented $3 million [$5.5 million]. Eszterhas and director Paul Verhoeven fell out several times during production over the edgy material, but the American public had no such reservations; the film took $350 million [$640 million] at the box office.

SCENT OF A WOMAN   1992
Dir: Martin Brest. *Scr*: Bo Goldman. Based on the film *Profumo di donna* by Ruggero Maccari, Dino Risi, and on a novel by Giovanni Arpino. *Cast*: Al Pacino (Lieutenant Colonel Frank Slade)

A retired US Army Ranger refuses to let his blindness compromise his passion for life.

                    FRANK
Ooh, but I still smell her . . . Women! What

could you say? Who made 'em? God must have been
a fuckin' genius. The hair — they say the hair
is everything, you know. Have you ever buried
your nose in a mountain of curls, just wanted
to go to sleep forever? Or lips — and when they
touched yours were like that first swallow of
wine after you just crossed the desert. Tits.
Hoo-hah! Big ones, little ones, nipples starin'
right out at ya, like secret searchlights. Mmm.
Legs. I don't care if they're Greek columns
or secondhand Steinways. What's between 'em
— passport to heaven. I need a drink. Yes, Mr
Simms, there's only two syllables in this whole
wide world worth hearin': pussy. Hah! Are you
listenin' to me, son? I'm givin' ya pearls here.

NAKED GUN 33⅓ : THE FINAL INSULT   1994

Dir: Peter Segal. *Scr*: Pat Proft, David Zucker, Robert LoCash. Based on a
TV series by Jim Abrahams, David Zucker, Jerry Zucker. *Cast*: Leslie Nielsen
(Lieutenant Frank Drebin)

Hapless detective Frank Drebin resists an invitation to a ménage à
trois.

>   FRANK
> I like my sex the way I play basketball — one on
> one, with as little dribbling as possible.

BOOGIE NIGHTS   1997

Dir: Paul Thomas Anderson. *Scr*: Paul Thomas Anderson. *Cast*: Burt Reynolds
(Jack Horner)

A Los Angeles porn film producer discovers – quite literally – a huge
new male talent.

> **JACK**
> I got a feeling that behind those jeans is
> something wonderful just waiting to get out.

The film opens with an unbroken shot lasting almost three minutes. Although Orson Welles' *A Touch of Evil* (1958) pioneered this technique on a single exterior set, Paul Thomas Anderson's camera move sweeps from a real Los Angeles cityscape through traffic shots and crowds before entering a nightclub where it introduces us to almost every key character in the subsequent story on the packed dance floor.

COLORS   1988
Dir: Dennis Hopper. *Scr*: Michael Schiffer. *Cast*: Sean Penn (Danny McGavin)

An over-confident young cop offers his wisdom about women.

> **DANNY**
> You don't wanna get laid, man. It leads to
> kissing and pretty soon you gotta talk to 'em.

The producers hired genuine L.A. gang members as guardians as well as actors but two of them were shot during filming.

ANALYZE THIS   1999
Dir: Harold Ramis. *Scr*: Kenneth Lonergan, Peter Tolan, Harold Ramis. *Cast*: Billy Crystal (Dr Ben Sobel), Robert De Niro (Paul Vitti)

A Mafia boss forces a psychoanalyst to take him on as a client.

> **DR SOBEL**
> What happened with your wife last night?
>
> **PAUL**
> I wasn't with my wife, I was with my girlfriend.
>
> **DR SOBEL**
> Are you having marriage problems?

```
                    PAUL
No.


                  DR SOBEL
Then why do you have a girlfriend?

                    PAUL
What, are you gonna start moralizing on me?

                  DR SOBEL
No, I'm not — I'm just trying to understand.
Why do you have a girlfriend?

                    PAUL
I do things with her I can't do with my wife.

                  DR SOBEL
Why can't you do them with your wife?

                    PAUL
Hey, that's the mouth she kisses my kids
goodnight with! What are you, crazy?
```

HIGH FIDELITY   2000

Dir: Stephen Frears. *Scr*: D. V. DeVincentis, Steve Pink, John Cusack, Scott Rosenberg. Based on a novel by Nick Hornby. *Cast*: John Cusack (Rob Gordon)

Rob cannot shake the thought that his ex-girlfriend is now with a new partner.

```
                    ROB
You are as abandoned and noisy as any character
in a porn film, Laura. You are Ian's plaything,
responding to his touch with shrieks of orgasmic
delight. No woman in the history of the world is
having better sex than the sex you are having
with Ian . . . in my head.
```

ABOUT SCHMIDT 2002

Dir: Alexander Payne. *Scr*: Alexander Payne, Jim Taylor. Based on a novel by Louis Begley. *Cast*: Kathy Bates (Roberta Hertzel)

Roberta, mother of the bride-to-be, reassures the groom's father about their children's future.

> ROBERTA
> You already know how famously they get along
> as friends, but did you know that their sex life
> is positively white-hot? The main reason both of
> my marriages failed was sexual. I'm an extremely
> sexual person, I can't help it, it's just how
> I'm wired, you know, even when I was a little
> girl. I had my first orgasm when I was six
> in ballet class. Anyway, the point is that I
> have always been very easily aroused and very
> orgasmic; Jeannie and I have a lot in common
> that way. Clifford and Larry, they were nice
> guys, but they just could not keep up with
> me. Anyway, I don't want to betray Jeannie's
> confidence, but let me just assure you that
> whatever problems those two kids may run into
> along the way, they will always be able to
> count on what happens between the sheets to
> keep them together. More soup?

BORAT: CULTURAL LEARNINGS OF AMERICA FOR MAKE BENEFIT GLORIOUS NATION OF KAZAKHSTAN 2006

Dir: Larry Charles. *Scr*: Sacha Baron Cohen, Anthony Hines, Peter Baynham, Dan Mazer. *Cast*: Sacha Baron Cohen (Borat)

Borat has travelled to the US from Kazakhstan seeking the freedom – and pleasures – of the West.

> **BORAT**
>
> A man yesterday tell me, if I buy a car I must
> buy one with pussy magnet.

The Kazakh government described *Borat* as 'a concoction of bad taste and ill manners which is incompatible with the ethics and civilized behavior of Kazakhstan's people' and ran a four-page advertisement in the *New York Times* correcting the misperceptions Sacha Baron Cohen had spread. Much of the film was staged as 'reality' and the police were called to the set on ninety-two occasions.

A DANGEROUS METHOD   2011

Dir: David Cronenberg. *Scr*: Christopher Hampton. Based on a play by Christopher Hampton and a book by John Kerr. *Cast*: Vincent Cassel (Otto Gross)

A psychoanalyst proposes that society has an unhealthy attitude towards sex.

> **GROSS**
>
> It seems to me the measure of the true perversity
> of the human race is that one of its very few
> reliably pleasurable activities should be the
> subject of so much hysteria and repression.

PADDINGTON 2   2017

Dir: Paul King. *Scr*: Paul King, Simon Farnaby. Based on the novels by Michael Bond. *Cast*: Stewart Gilchrist (Chakrabatics Instructor)

> **CHAKRABATICS INSTRUCTOR**
> Open your minds, and your legs will follow.

BRUISERS

THE PALM BEACH STORY   1942

Dir: Preston Sturges. *Scr*: Preston Sturges. *Cast*: Rudy Vallée (John D. Hackensacker III)

      HACKENSACKER

That's one of the tragedies of this life — that the men who are most in need of a beating up are always enormous.

OUT OF THE PAST   1947

Dir: Jacques Tourneur. *Scr*: Daniel Mainwaring. *Cast*: Kirk Douglas (Whit Sterling)

A gangster threatens a private investigator he intends to frame.

      WHIT

You're gonna take the rap and play along. You're gonna make every exact move I tell you. If you don't, I'll kill you. And I'll promise you one thing: it won't be quick. I'll break you first. You won't be able to answer a telephone or open a door without thinking, 'This is it'. And when it comes, it still won't be quick. And it won't be pretty. You can take your choice.

KIND HEARTS AND CORONETS   1949

Dir: Robert Hamer. *Scr*: Robert Hamer, John Dighton. Based on a novel by Roy Horniman. *Cast*: Dennis Price (Louis Mazzini)

Murderer Louis Mazzini is scrupulous in his professional etiquette.

      LOUIS

It is so difficult to make a neat job of killing people with whom one is not on friendly terms.

WHITE HEAT   1949

Dir: Raoul Walsh. *Scr*: Ivan Goff, Ben Roberts. Based on a story by Virginia Kellogg. *Cast*: James Cagney (Arthur 'Cody' Jarrett)

Cody Jarrett celebrates his escape from jail shortly before he is killed in a blaze in a chemical plant.

> CODY
> Made it, Ma! Top of the world!

Jack Dawson (Leonardo DiCaprio) reprises Cagney's line – and triumphant pose – as he yells from the ship's bow in *Titanic* (1997): 'I'm the king of the world!'

CHEESE

In 2004, British bakery Warburtons celebrated a new line of Cheddar-flavoured crumpets by inviting its customers to nominate the cheesiest movie lines of all time. Here are their top ten:

I'm the king of the world!
Titanic (1997)

Nobody puts Baby in the corner.
Dirty Dancing (1987)

Is it still raining? I hadn't noticed.
Four Weddings and a Funeral (1994)

SAM WHEAT: I love you.
MOLLY JENSEN: Ditto.
Ghost (1990)

You can be my wingman any time.
Top Gun (1986)

I'm just a girl standing in front of a boy
asking him to love her.
Notting Hill (1999)

Today we celebrate our Independence Day!
Independence Day (1996)

They may take our lives, but they will not take
our freedom!
Braveheart (1995)

You had me at hello.
Jerry Maguire (1996)

BLIND WOMAN: You're a godsend, a saviour.
POSTMAN: No, I'm a postman.
The Postman (1997)

There are plenty of other classics which might have given these
winners a run for their money:

One thing's sure. Inspector Clay is dead.
Murdered. And somebody's responsible.
Plan 9 From Outer Space (1959)

It makes you kill yourself. Just when you
thought there couldn't be any more evil that
can be invented.
The Happening (1966)

You know, hot dogs get a bad rap. They got a cool
shape, they got protein.
The Happening (1966)

If Pazuzu comes for you, I will spit a leopard.
Exorcist II: The Heretic (1977)

Okay, cocksucker. Fuck with me and we'll see
who shits on the sidewalk.
Death Race 2000 (1975)

You have a great body. May I use it?
Saturn 3 (1980)

Flash! I love you, but we only have 14 hours
to save the earth!
Flash Gordon (1980)

I eat Green Berets for breakfast. And right now,
I'm very hungry!
Commando (1985)

The dingo took my baby!
A Cry in the Dark (1988)

EDWARD: So what happens after he climbs up and
rescues her?
VIVIAN: She rescues him right back.
Pretty Woman (1990)

Kenner, just in case we get killed, I wanted to
tell you. You have the biggest dick I've ever
seen on a man.
Showdown in Little Tokyo (1991)

CRISTAL: You have great tits. They're really
beautiful.
NOMI: Thank you.
CRISTAL: I like nice tits. I always have, how
about you?
NOMI: I like having nice tits.
Showgirls (1995)

Swoon, I'll catch you.
The English Patient (1996)

You complete me.
Jerry Maguire (1996)

You're why cavemen chiselled on walls.
As Good As It Gets (1997)

I hate to disappoint you, but rubber lips are immune to your charms.
Batman & Robin (1997)

I said, put the bunny back in the box.
Con Air (1997)

It's like looking in a mirror. Only not.
Face/Off (1997)

Did you just have a brain fart?
G.I. Jane (1997)

KITANA: Mother! You're alive!
SINDEL: Too bad. You will die!
Mortal Kombat 2: Annihilation (1997)

A bird may love a fish, Signore, but where will they live?
Ever After: A Cinderella Story (1998)

He's got space dementia.
Armageddon (1998)

Dancing's just a conversation between two people. Talk to me.
Hope Floats (1998)

You better hold on tight, spider-monkey.
Twilight (1998)

While you were still learning how to spell
your name, I was being trained to conquer
galaxies.
Battlefield Earth: A Saga of the Year 3000 (2000)

God was showing off when he made you.
Keeping the Faith (2000)

This is Walker. We need to get those planes
fuelled and loaded right now!... I think
World War Two has just hit us.
Pearl Harbor (2001)

Well, you might be a cunning linguist, but I
am a master debater.
Austin Powers in *Goldmember* (2002)

I'm really wired. What do you say I take you
home and eat your pussy?
Shark Attack 3: Megalodon (2002)

I don't like sand. It's coarse and rough and
irritating, and it gets everywhere.
Star Wars: Episode II – Attack of the Clones (2002)

You know what happens when a toad gets struck
by lightning? The same thing that happens to
everything else.
X-Men (2002)

It's turkey time. Gobble gobble.
Gigli (2003)

Are you a Mexican or a Mexi-can't?
Once Upon a Time in Mexico (2003)

Are you sure you saw what you think you thought
you saw?
Hellbreeder (2004)

I've always been standing in your doorway.
Spider-Man 2 (2004)

BRENDA: I know Tai Kwon Do!
MADEA: And I know 'Whoop Your Ass'!
Diary of a Mad Black Woman (2005)

Hold me, like you did by the lake on Naboo.
Star Wars: Episode III – Revenge of the Sith (2005)

Forgive my lips. They find joy in the most
unusual places.
A Good Year (2006)

It's a pressure valve. It won't open unless
there's tremendous pressure.
Poseidon (2006)

Spartans! Ready your breakfast and eat hearty.
For tonight, we dine in hell!
300 (2006)

Not the bees!
The Wicker Man (2006)

THE ASPHALT JUNGLE   1950

Dir: John Huston. *Scr*: Ben Maddow, John Huston. Based on a novel by W. R. Burnett. *Cast*: Louis Calhern (Alonzo D. Emmerich)

Crooked lawyer Emmerich finds it easy to forgive himself.

> EMMERICH
> Crime is only a left-handed form of human
> endeavour.

ACE IN THE HOLE   1951

Dir: Billy Wilder. *Scr*: Billy Wilder, Lesser Samuels, Walter Newman. *Cast*: Jan Sterling (Lorraine Minosa)

Lorraine is puzzled by the motives of an unscrupulous journalist.

> LORRAINE
> I met a lot of hard-boiled eggs in my life, but
> you — you're twenty minutes.

THE WILD ONE   1953

Dir: László Benedek. *Scr*: John Paxton. Based on a story by Frank Rooney. *Cast*: Peggy Maley (Mildred), Marlon Brando (Johnny Strabler)

A young woman questions a Hell's Angel who has ridden into town.

> MILDRED
> Hey Johnny, what are you rebelling against?

> JOHNNY
> Whadda you got?

Triumph, manufacturers of the motorcycle Brando rides, were not happy to be associated with the film until they realized it had substantially boosted sales.

POINT BLANK   1967

Dir: John Boorman. *Scr*: Alexander Jacobs, David Newhouse, Rafe Newhouse. Based on a novel by Donald E. Westlake (as Richard Stark). *Cast*: Carroll O'Connor (Brewster)

Crime boss Brewster plans to eliminate one of his partners.

> BREWSTER
>
> Fairfax is dead. He just doesn't know it yet.

TRUE GRIT   1969

Dir: Henry Hathaway. *Scr*: Marguerite Roberts. Based on a novel by Charles Portis. *Cast*: John Wayne (Reuben J. 'Rooster' Cogburn), Jeremy Slate (Emmett Quincy)

US Marshal Rooster Cogburn suspects Ned Pepper is harbouring the man he is pursuing.

> ROOSTER
>
> When's the last time you saw Ned Pepper?

> EMMETT
>
> I don't remember any Ned Pepper.

> ROOSTER
>
> Short feisty fella, nervous and quick, got a messed-up lower lip.

> EMMETT
>
> That don't bring nobody to mind. A funny lip?

> ROOSTER
>
> Wasn't always like that, I shot him in it.

> EMMETT
>
> In the lower lip? What was you aiming at?

ROOSTER
His upper lip.

Between 1926 and 1976 John Wayne starred in over 170 films; this was the only one that won him an Oscar.

GET CARTER   1971

Dir: Mike Hodges. *Scr*: Mike Hodges. Based on a novel by Ted Lewis. *Cast*: Bryan Mosley (Cliff Brumby), Michael Caine (Jack Carter)

Small-time crook Jack Carter hears Cliff Brumby has been trying to get rid of him.

BRUMBY
Listen, I don't like it when some tough nut
comes pushing his way in and out of my house
in the middle of the night! Bloody well tell me
who sent you.

CARTER
You're a big man, but you're in bad shape. With
me it's a full-time job. Now behave yourself.

THE GODFATHER   1972

Dir: Francis Ford Coppola. *Scr*: Francis Ford Coppola, Mario Puzo. Based on a novel by Mario Puzo. *Cast*: Al Pacino (Michael Corleone), Diane Keaton (Kay Adams)

MICHAEL
Well, when Johnny was first starting out, he was
signed to a personal services contract with this
big-band leader. And as his career got better
and better, he wanted to get out of it. But the
band leader wouldn't let him. Now, Johnny is

my father's godson. So my father went to see
this band leader and offered him $10,000 to let
Johnny go, but the band leader said no. So the
next day, my father went back, only this time
with Luca Brasi. Within an hour, he had a signed
release for a certified check of $1,000.

                    KAY
How did he do that?

                    MICHAEL
My father made him an offer he couldn't refuse.

                    KAY
What was that?

                    MICHAEL
Luca Brasi held a gun to his head, and my
father assured him that either his brains or
his signature would be on the contract.

'DON'T QUIT. MAKE THEM FIRE YOU'

It's easy to look back on *The Godfather* and believe it sprang
fully formed from the talents of Mario Puzo, Francis Ford
Coppola and their stellar cast. Who else could have delivered
the screen-searing power of Don Corleone but Marlon
Brando? Try these names for size, Paramount's original
suggestions: Ernest Borgnine, Edward G. Robinson, Orson
Welles, Danny Thomas, Richard Conte, Anthony Quinn and
George C. Scott. Even Coppola himself first wanted Laurence
Olivier for the role.

The studio hated Coppola's second choice of Brando
and offered him the minimum fee permitted by the Screen

Actors Guild; one of the producers later said the star received $50,000 [$300,000] plus a percentage of the profits, which he sold back to the studio to pay for an expensive divorce. The film went on to make $135 million [$810 million] in its US theatrical release alone.

During pre-production the film received numerous threats from the Mafia, who controlled the 'teamsters' – drivers and labourers for the film industry. One of the producers eventually met with Joseph Colombo, boss of one of New York's Five Families organizations, and agreed that if the mobsters permitted the production to go ahead undisturbed the script would not include the terms 'Mafia' or 'Cosa Nostra'.

The early days of the project were so dogged by arguments and setbacks that Coppola returned from a location scout to find a telegram from his agent, urging him: 'Don't quit. Make them fire you.' His persistence paid off, although he said afterwards: 'Every film creates its own identity and it's possible to rivet the audience without the obvious tools. I was more surprised than anyone that this picture seemed to work the way it did.'

The Godfather won Oscars for Best Picture, Best Screenplay and Best Actor. Even the ceremony itself had its memorable clashes: three other cast members (James Caan as Sonny, Robert Duvall as Tom Hagen and Al Pacino as Michael Corleone) were all nominated for Best Supporting Actor but Pacino boycotted the awards as he calculated his 'secondary' role had more screen time than Brando's; Brando refused to collect his own Oscar, sending instead rights activist Sacheen Littlefeather to deliver a speech about the film industry's mistreatment of Native American Indians.

CHATO'S LAND   1972

Dir: Michael Winner. *Scr*: Gerald Wilson. *Cast*: Jack Palance (Captain Quincey Whitmore)

Whitmore's men grow restless as he leads them deeper into hostile territory.

> **CAPTAIN WHITMORE**
> For a thirsty man in a dry land, you gotta lotta talk.

BRING ME THE HEAD OF ALFREDO GARCIA   1974

Dir: Sam Peckinpah. *Scr*: Sam Peckinpah, Gordon T. Dawson. *Cast*: Warren Oates (Bennie)

Bennie hopes to claim the bounty on a wanted man who is already dead.

> **BENNIE**
> There ain't nothing sacred about a hole in the ground — or the man that's in it.

Although Peckinpah was reportedly desperate, drunk and depressed while directing the film, many consider it his finest work. Banned in many countries on its release and panned by the *Wall Street Journal* as being 'grotesque, sadistic, irrational, obscene and incompetent', the film was hailed by Roger Ebert as 'some kind of bizarre masterpiece'.

BLAZING SADDLES   1974

Dir: Mel Brooks. *Scr*: Mel Brooks, Norman Steinberg, Andrew Bergman, Richard Pryor, Alan Uger. *Cast*: Slim Pickens (Taggart), Harvey Korman (Hedley Lamarr)

Hedley Lamarr recruits a gang of thugs to evict the townsfolk of Rock Ridge.

What do you want me to do, sir?

HEDLEY
I want you to round up every vicious criminal and
gunslinger in the West. Take this down.

*Taggart looks for a pen and paper while Hedley
talks.*

HEDLEY
I want rustlers, cut-throats, murderers, bounty
hunters, desperadoes, mugs, pugs, thugs,
nitwits, halfwits, dimwits, vipers, snipers,
conmen, Indian agents, Mexican bandits, muggers,
buggerers, bushwhackers, hornswogglers, horse
thieves, bull dykes, train robbers, bank robbers,
ass-kickers, shit-kickers and Methodists!

Taggart finally finds a pen and paper.

TAGGART
Could you repeat that, sir?

CHINATOWN   1974

Dir: Roman Polanski. *Scr*: Robert Towne. *Cast*: Faye Dunaway (Evelyn Mulwray),
Jack Nicholson (Jake Gittes)

Private investigator Jake Gittes is under no illusion about the
integrity of his profession.

EVELYN
Hollis seems to think you're an innocent man.

JAKE
Well, I've been accused of a lot of things
before, Mrs Mulwray, but never that.

Jack Nicholson is a devoted LA Lakers fan and was persistently late for filming because he was following their games on TV in his trailer. After one heated argument, director Polanski smashed the television set with a mop.

NIGHT MOVES   1975

Dir: Arthur Penn. *Scr*: Alan Sharp. *Cast*: Gene Hackman (Harry Moseby), James Woods (Quentin)

Private investigator Harry Moseby quizzes a reluctant suspect.

>   HARRY
> What happened to your face?
>
>   QUENTIN
> I won second prize in a fight.

As a struggling actor Hackman had jobs as a doorman, furniture mover, soda jerk and pharmacy assistant. During his rise to fame he turned down the lead role in *Jaws*, *Close Encounters of the Third Kind*, *Raiders of the Lost Ark* and *One Flew Over the Cuckoo's Nest*. He later said: 'I was trained to be an actor, not a star. I was trained to play roles, not to deal with fame and agents and lawyers and the press.'

JAWS   1975

Dir: Steven Spielberg. *Scr*: Carl Gottlieb, Peter Benchley. Based on a novel by Peter Benchley. *Cast*: Robert Shaw (Quint)

Quint, a local fisherman, interrupts a town meeting about a man-eating shark terrorizing their beach.

>   QUINT
> Y'all know me. Know how I earn a livin'. I'll
> catch this bird for you, but it ain't gonna be
> easy. Bad fish. Not like going down the pond

chasin' bluegills and tommycods. This shark,
swallow you whole. Little shakin', little
tenderizin', an' down you go. And we gotta do it
quick, that'll bring back your tourists, put all
your businesses on a payin' basis. But it's not
gonna be pleasant. I value my neck a lot more
than three thousand bucks, chief. I'll find him
for three, but I'll catch him, and kill him, for
ten. But you've gotta make up your minds. If you
want to stay alive, then ante up. If you want to
play it cheap, be on welfare the whole winter. I
don't want no volunteers, I don't want no mates,
there's just too many captains on this island.
$10,000 for me by myself. For that you get the
head, the tail, the whole damn thing.

TAXI DRIVER   1976

Dir: Martin Scorsese. *Scr*: Paul Schrader. *Cast*: Robert De Niro (Travis Bickle)

A disturbed Vietnam vet takes a job as a New York taxi driver.

        TRAVIS
All the animals come out at night — whores,
skunk pussies, buggers, queens, fairies, dopers,
junkies. Sick, venal. Someday a real rain'll come
and wash all this scum off the streets. I go all
over. I take people to the Bronx, Brooklyn, I
take 'em to Harlem. I don't care. Don't make no
difference to me. It does to some. Some won't
even take spooks. Don't make no difference to me.

Bizarrely, one of the studios who read the script suggested Neil
Diamond for the lead role. The famous scene where Travis Bickle
talks to himself was ad-libbed by Robert De Niro. The screenplay
just read: 'Travis looks in the mirror.'

SHAFT   1971

Dir: Gordon Parks. *Scr*: Ernest Tidyman, John D. F. Black. Based on a novel by
Ernest Tidyman. *Cast*: Richard Roundtree (John Shaft)

Private investigator John Shaft warns a suspect not to interrupt him.

> **SHAFT**
> Don't let your mouth get your ass in trouble.

SCARFACE   1983

Dir: Brian De Palma. *Scr*: Oliver Stone. Based on a 1932 film of the same name,
and on a novel by Armitage Trail. *Cast*: Al Pacino (Tony Montana)

Drug lord Tony Montana is determined to safeguard his empire
on his own terms.

> **TONY**
> All I have in this world is my balls and my word,
> and I don't break them for no one.

When Saddam Hussein set up a front company to launder money
from various illegal enterprises, he named it Montana Management
after the main character in the film.

'STICKS NIX HICK PIX'

One of the most famous media headlines ever printed, this
terse 1935 splash in *Variety* announces that films about country
life do not play well with rural audiences – proof, perhaps, that
the Hollywood dream of fleeing a small-town existence for the
bright lights of the big city had already taken root. Further
epigrammatic utterances include:

- Cruise Boozer Brews Snooze (1988: audiences are
  finding Tom Cruise's *Cocktail* less than thrilling)

- A Wing-Ding for the King (2004: *The Lord of the Rings: The Return of the King* proves a success at the box office)
- Bay's Bots Rock Box (2007: director Michael Bay's *Transformers* is a hit in cinemas).

Variety was first published in 1905 as a trade magazine for the entertainment industry and soon formulated its own shorthand for familiar aspects of the business. Its 'Slanguage Dictionary' includes the following terms to deal with movies and their production:

- Ankle – a classic (and enduring) *Variety* term meaning to quit or be dismissed from a job, without necessarily specifying which; instead, it suggests walking; 'Alan Smithee has ankled his post as production prexy at U.'
- Aud – audience; 'Liza Minnelli has always had a special rapport with her aud.'
- Biopic – a *Variety* coinage meaning biographical film; '*Coal Miner's Daughter*, about Loretta Lynn, is one of the most successful biopics ever produced.'
- Boff (also boffo, boffola) – outstanding (usually refers to box office performance); '*My Best Friend's Wedding* has been boffo at the B.O.' (See also socko, whammo)
- Chopsocky – a martial arts film; 'Chopsocky star Chuck Norris will make a guest appearance on *Seinfeld* this season.'
- Click – a hit; 'Disney click *The Lion King* is slated to air on ABC this season.'
- Crix – critics; 'While the director's last film was a flop with auds, the crix were in his corner.'
- Gotham – New York City; 'Film production in Gotham has been on the rise for the past several years.'

- Horse opera – Western film; 'John Carradine appeared in numerous horse operas throughout his career.'

- Hotsy – strong performance at the box office; '*The Devil's Advocate* made a hotsy bow last weekend.'

- Huddle – (v.) to have a meeting; (n.) a meeting; 'The exec was in a huddle and was not available for comment.'

- Legs – stamina at the box office; 'The film opened big but rival distribs are dubious about its legs.'

- Lense – to film a motion picture; 'The project will lense in Rome and New York.'

- Meller – melodrama; 'The company is in pre-production on a meller about a blind woman held hostage on a New York City subway.'

- Moppet – child, especially child actor; 'Elizabeth Taylor is one of the few moppets who made the transition to adult star.'

- Mouse (also Mouse House) – the Walt Disney Co. or any division thereof, a reference to the company's most famous animated character, Mickey Mouse; 'The Mouse's music division is reuniting with talent manager Alan Smithee on a joint-venture label.'

- (The) o.o. – the once-over; to examine something; 'Sylvester Stallone gave the script the o.o. before passing on it.'

- Pen – (v.) to write; 'Alan Smithee has been inked to pen the biopic about Abraham Lincoln.'

- Percenter (also tenpercenter) – agent; 'Mike Ovitz was a percenter before becoming a talent manager.'

- Pour – cocktail party; 'Universal held a pour for the press in New York to promote its upcoming release.'

- Praiser – publicist; 'A praiser for the star had no comment on the deal.'

- Preem – (n.) an opening-night or première performance; (v.) to show a completed film for the first time; 'Several of the pic's stars were on hand for the preem' or 'The pic will preem Dec. 18.'

- Prexy (also prez) – president; 'The studio has no plans to fill the prexy post in the wake of the exec's resignation.'

- Shingle – a small business, often set up by an actor or established player at a larger company; 'Tom Green has launched production shingle Tom Green Films.'

- Solon – an authority; someone in the know; from the ancient Greek wise man, Solon; 'Solons say the deal is likely to go down by the end of the week.'

- Sprocket opera – film festival; 'The actor plans to attend the annual Sundance sprocket opera next year.'

- Tentpole – Movie expected by a studio to be its biggest grossing blockbuster of the season, usually summer. Often the pic is the start of, or an instalment in, a franchise; '*Armageddon* was a successful tentpole in 1998.'

- Topline – to star; to be billed above the title of a show or film; 'Julia Roberts will topline the director's next pic.'

- Turnaround – no longer active; a project put into 'turnaround' has been abandoned by one studio and may be shopped to another.

- Unspool – to screen a film; 'More than thirty films are set to unspool at the upcoming festival.'

- Wrap – to finish production; 'The picture will wrap in the next two weeks.'

BARFLY

Dir: Barbet Schroeder. *Scr*: Charles Bukowski. *Cast*: Mickey Rourke (Henry Chinaski)

1987

A dissolute bohemian defends his lifestyle.

> HENRY
>
> Some people never go crazy. What truly horrible lives they must lead.

More famous for his novels than his screenplays, Bukowski was hailed by *Time Magazine* as a 'laureate of American lowlife'. His stories and films are shocking and touching in equal measure, but rarely lack his characteristic dark humour. The script contains several other bitter gems:

- It's hatred. It's the only thing that lasts.
- So you hired a dick to find an asshole?
- I'd hate to be you if I were me.
- Don't be sorry, just put on some new underwear.

THE UNTOUCHABLES

Dir: Brian De Palma. *Scr*: David Mamet. Based on a book by Oscar Fraley, Eliot Ness. *Cast*: Sean Connery (Jim Malone), Kevin Costner (Eliot Ness)

1987

Veteran Chicago patrolman Malone warns Federal agent Ness he will have to abandon his scruples if he hopes to bring Al Capone to justice.

> MALONE
>
> You said you wanted to get Capone. Do you really wanna get him? You see what I'm saying is, what are you prepared to do?

> NESS
>
> Anything within the law.

MALONE

And then what are you prepared to do? If you open
the can on these worms you must be prepared to
go all the way. Because they're not gonna give up
the fight, until one of you is dead.

NESS

I want to get Capone! I don't know how to do it.

MALONE

You wanna know how to get Capone? They pull a
knife, you pull a gun. He sends one of yours to
the hospital, you send one of his to the morgue.
That's the Chicago way. And that's how you get
Capone. Now, do you want to do that? Are you
ready to do that? I'm offering you a deal. Do you
want this deal?

NESS

I have sworn to capture this man with all legal
powers at my disposal and I will do so.

MALONE

Well, the Lord hates a coward.

He reaches out a hand. Ness shakes it.

MALONE

Do you know what a blood oath is, Mr Ness?

NESS

Yes.

MALONE

Good, 'cause you just took one.

MISSISSIPPI BURNING   1988

Dir: Alan Parker. *Scr*: Chris Gerolmo. *Cast*: Willem Dafoe (Alan Ward), Gene Hackman (Rupert Anderson)

FBI agent Anderson warns his younger colleague Ward not to underestimate the determination of the Ku Klux Klan.

> WARD
>
> Some things are worth dying for.

> ANDERSON
>
> Down here, things are different. Here, they believe some things are worth killing for.

THEY LIVE   1988

Dir: John Carpenter. *Scr*: John Carpenter. Based on a short story by Ray Nelson. *Cast*: Roddy Piper (Nada)

Nada seeks out aliens who have colonized the planet disguised as humans.

> NADA
>
> I've come here to chew bubblegum and kick ass . . . and I'm all out of bubblegum.

LICENCE TO KILL   1989

Dir: John Glen. *Scr*: Michael G. Wilson, Richard Maibaum. Based on characters created by Ian Fleming. *Cast*: Timothy Dalton (James Bond), Robert Davi (Franz Sanchez)

James Bond confronts drugs lord Sanchez.

> BOND
>
> In my business you prepare for the unexpected.

> SANCHEZ
>
> And what business is that?

```
                  BOND
   I help people with problems.

                  SANCHEZ
   Problem solver?

                  BOND
   More of a problem eliminator.
```

Putting a dampener on 007's swashbuckling style, the US credits for the film feature a tobacco warning from the United States Surgeon-General. The writers had originally intended the story to be set in the heroin-producing Golden Triangle, with sequences including a motorcycle chase along the Great Wall of China and a fight scene in the museum of the Terracotta Warriors, but the Chinese authorities vetoed the script.

The film was the first to use a title not directly taken from one of Ian Fleming's James Bond novels, although the phrase 'licence to kill' occurs frequently with reference to 007's powers. *Octopussy* (1983), *The Living Daylights* (1987) and *Quantum of Solace* (2008) all took their names from short stories featuring Bond. Remaining unadapted titles include 'Property of a Lady', '007 In New York', 'Risico' and 'The Hildebrand Rarity'.

GOODFELLAS   1990

Dir: Martin Scorsese. *Scr*: Nicholas Pileggi, Martin Scorsese. Based on a book by Nicholas Pileggi. *Cast*: Ray Liotta (Henry Hill)

A mobster recalls the moment of his arrest.

```
                  HENRY
   For a second I thought I was dead, but when I
   heard all the noise I knew they were cops. Only
   cops talk that way. If they had been wiseguys,
   I wouldn't have heard a thing. I would've been
   dead.
```

PULP FICTION   1994

Dir: Quentin Tarantino. *Scr*: Quentin Tarantino, Roger Avary. *Cast*: Bruce Willis (Butch Coolidge), Ving Rhames (Marsellus Wallace)

Butch has just liberated Marsellus from being sodomized by two hillbillies, who now lie prostrate on the floor.

> ### BUTCH
> You okay?

> ### MARSELLUS
> Naw man. I'm pretty fuckin' far from okay.

> ### BUTCH
> What now?

> ### MARSELLUS
> What now? Let me tell you what now. I'm a call a coupla hard, pipe-hittin' niggers who'll go to work on the homies here with a pair of pliers and a blow torch.

He turns to the rapists.

> ### MARSELLUS
> You hear me talkin', hillbilly boy? I ain't through with you by a damn sight. I'm a get medieval on your ass.

Quentin Tarantino (with Roger Avary) wrote many of the roles with specific actors in mind: Harvey Keitel as The Wolf, Amanda Plummer and Tim Roth as Honey Bunny and Pumpkin, and Samuel L. Jackson as Jules. Daniel Day-Lewis reportedly agreed to play Vincent but Tarantino overlooked him in favour of John Travolta; the film returned Travolta to major star status after several years of unremarkable roles. Tarantino, who plays Jimmie, had originally intended to take the part of drug dealer Lance but decided he would prefer to give his full attention as director in the scene where Mia

(Uma Thurman) overdoses; the shot where Vincent tries to revive Mia with a shot of adrenaline was filmed in reverse to avoid harming the actress with the needle. The film, with its abundant references to earlier *noir* classics, was described by some critics as a masterpiece of post-modernism. Tarantino explained that his idea was simply 'to take the oldest chestnuts that you've ever seen when it comes to crime stories… and then purposely having them run awry.'

GROSSE POINTE BLANK   1997

Dir: George Armitage. *Scr*: Tom Jankiewicz, D. V. DeVincentis, Steve Pink, John Cusack. *Cast*: Minnie Driver (Debi Newberry), John Cusack (Martin Q. Blank)

A professional hit-man attends his high school reunion but finds it hard to explain what he has been doing since he graduated.

> DEBI
>
> You're a psychopath.

> MARTIN
>
> No, no. Psychopaths kill for no reason. I kill for money. It's a job.

Martin later elucidates: 'I killed the president of Paraguay with a fork. How have you been?'

FIGHT CLUB   1999

Dir: David Fincher. *Scr*: Jim Uhls. Based on a novel by Chuck Palahniuk. *Cast*: Brad Pitt (Tyler Durden)

Tyler Durden founds an anarchic self-help group where members fight one another to vent their anger against a conformist, consumerist world.

> TYLER
>
> Welcome to Fight Club. The first rule of Fight Club is: you do not talk about Fight Club. The

```
second rule of Fight Club is: you do not talk
about Fight Club. The third rule of Fight Club:
someone yells stop, goes limp, taps out, the
fight is over. The fourth rule: only two guys to
a fight. The fifth rule: one fight at a time,
fellas. The sixth rule: no shirts, no shoes. The
seventh rule: fights will go on as long as they
have to. And the eighth and final rule: if this
is your first night at Fight Club, you have to
fight.
```

When Tyler first sleeps with Marla, she was supposed to shock him with the line: 'I want to have your abortion.' The studio objected, so director David Fincher agreed to change it provided the executives made no further comment. They agreed, so Fincher had Marla say: 'I haven't been fucked like that since grade school [primary school].' Author Chuck Palahniuk said he thought the film better than his novel.

THE CONTENDER   2000

Dir: Rod Lurie. *Scr*: Rod Lurie. *Cast*: Gary Oldman (Shelly Runyon)

Republican Congressman Shelly Runyon challenges Democrat President Evans over the appointment of a new vice president.

> SHELLY
> We're both sticking to our guns. The difference
> is, mine are loaded.

HEIST   2001

Dir: David Mamet. *Scr*: David Mamet. *Cast*: Danny DeVito (Mickey Bergman), Gene Hackman (Joe Moore)

Two gold thieves have fallen out over how to divide the spoils.

MICKEY
Don't you want to hear my last words?

JOE
I just did.

BEND OVER

David Mamet (b. 1947) rose to fame as a playwright, winning a Pulitzer Prize for Drama with *Glengarry Glen Ross* in 1984. Hollywood studios soon wooed him, hoping his terse, intelligent dialogue and tight plotting would translate into Oscar successes for their movies. The producers he worked with were soon to discover that his uncompromising working methods and dislike of leaving his home town Chicago made for a distinctly un-Californian partnership. His thoughts on the film industry are as lively as his screenplays:

- Working as a screenwriter, I always thought that 'Film is a collaborative business' only constituted half of the actual phrase. From a screenwriter's point of view the correct rendering should be 'Film is a collaborative business: bend over'.

- Life in the movie business is like the beginning of a new love affair: it's full of surprises, and you're constantly getting fucked.

- Thank God Hollywood people don't have souls so they don't have to suffer through their lives.

- Hollywood is like cocaine. You cannot understand its attraction until you are doing it. And when you are doing it, you are insane.

Nevertheless his Oscar nominations for *The Verdict* (1982) and

Wag the Dog (1997) and his success with *The Postman Always Rings Twice* (1981) and *The Untouchables* (1987) have kept him in fierce demand. Many of his statements in interviews have become mantras for screenwriters:

- We respond to a drama to that extent to which it corresponds to our dream life.

- Every scene should be able to answer three questions: 'Who wants what from whom? What happens if they don't get it? Why now?'

- People may or may not say what they mean, but they always say something designed to get what they want.

He often uses the fees he earns from uncredited rewriting on troubled projects to fund his own directorial efforts. These include *House of Games* (1987), *State and Main* (2000) and *Heist* (2001). The latter film contains much of his famous 'Mamet-speak', as well as some outstanding dark humour:

```
PINKY: My motherfucker is so cool, when he
goes to bed, sheep count him.
BERGMAN: Everybody needs money. That's why
they call it money.
BERGMAN: Do you want to tell me what made you
a criminal?

JOE MOORE: What made you a criminal?
BERGMAN: Nothing made me a criminal. I am
a criminal.


JOE MOORE: She could talk her way out of
a sunburn.
```

BOBBY BLANE: There's nothing wrong with
prayer. We knew this firefighter, this trooper,
who always carried a bible next to his heart.
We used to mock him, but that bible stopped a
bullet.
JIMMY: No shit.
BOBBY BLANE: Hand of God, that bible stopped
a bullet, would of ruined that fucker's heart.
And had he had another bible in front of his
face, that man would be alive today.

D.A. FRECCIA: You're a pretty smart fellow.
JOE MOORE: Ah, not that smart.
D.A. FRECCIA: If you're not that smart, how'd
you figure it out?

JOE MOORE: I tried to imagine a fellow smarter
than myself. Then I tried to think, 'what
would he do?'

IN BRUGES   2008

Dir: Martin McDonagh. *Scr*: Martin McDonagh. *Cast*: Ciarán Hinds (Priest),
Colin Farrell (Ray)

Ray goes to make a surprising confession.

> PRIEST
Why did you murder someone, Raymond?

> RAY
For money, father.

> PRIEST
For money? You murdered someone for money?

                    RAY

Yes, father. Not out of anger. Not out of
nothing. For money.

                  PRIEST

Who did you murder for money, Raymond?

                    RAY

You, father.

                  PRIEST

I'm sorry?

                    RAY

I said you, father. What are you, deaf?

He raises a pistol.

                    RAY

Harry Waters says hello.

BABY DRIVER   2017

Dir: Edgar Wright. *Scr*: Edgar Wright. *Cast*: Richard Marcos Taylor (Armie),
Jamie Foxx Weisz (Bats)

                  ARMIE

We've met before, right?

                   BATS

I dunno. You still alive, right?

                  ARMIE

Uh-huh.

                   BATS

Then I guess we ain't never met.

VAMPS

HELL'S ANGELS   1930

Dir: Howard Hughes. *Scr*: Howard Estabrook, Marshall Neilan, James Moncure March, Harry Behn. *Cast*: Jean Harlow (Helen)

Helen exchanges her fur wrap for a dressing gown.

>   HELEN
> Would you be shocked if I put on something more
> comfortable?

THE CABIN IN THE COTTON   1932

Dir: Michael Curtiz. *Scr*: Paul Green. Based on a novel by Harry Harrison Kroll. *Cast*: Bette Davis (Madge Norwood)

After asking Marvin out on a date, Madge finds herself bashful.

>   MADGE
> I'd like to kiss you, but I just washed my hair.

Davis claimed in an interview after she retired that this was her all-time favourite movie line. Her reputation as a competitive actress caused Vincent Sherman to say of her and Miriam Hopkins, who co-starred in *Old Acquaintance* (1930): 'I didn't direct them, I refereed.'

'EXCESSIVE OR LUSTFUL KISSING'

The Cinematograph Act of 1909 was introduced largely to protect the public from the hazards of highly flammable nitrate prints but the authorities quickly realized that the content of a motion picture could also be incendiary.

Although we tend to look back on the earliest surviving films as charming echoes of a bygone era, we should remember that some of the pioneers – Eisenstein, Griffith and Chaplin – were trying to tell stories as sophisticated as those of their literary peers. Crude technologies may have hampered them, but they dealt with controversial subjects such as racism, revolution and sexual desire. As early as 1906 some American cities passed local laws regulating content, but most forms of censorship proved unwieldy and unenforceable. Meanwhile, directors grew bolder and stars more smouldering.

At the same time, audiences were growing at an astonishing rate; by 1930 two thirds of Americans were going to the movies at least once a week. Governments remained slow to react to this new influence on their citizens and were forced to invoke outdated laws regulating obscenity, blasphemy and libel as guidelines; religious groups were far quicker to show outrage at themes they considered unsuitable for their congregations.

Incensed by the further danger of talking pictures, Daniel Lord, a leading American Catholic, wrote: 'Silent smut had been bad. Vocal smut cried to the censors for vengeance.' Some states tried to enact legislation but with little effect, so Lord and his Jesuit brother-in-arms Martin Quigley took their crusade directly to Hollywood.

Producers, aware that the vast majority of their customers were under twenty-five, feared that unless they joined forces to regulate their own output the business would destroy itself. They agreed to Lord and Quigley's proposals and on 19 February 1930 *Variety* published the Motion Picture Production Code. Will Hays, a Presbyterian Republican and President of the Motion Picture Producers and Distributors of America, was chosen to be its head of enforcement.

The Hays Code, as it became known, was widely ridiculed for its moralizing tone and was initially impossible to implement. Under the section 'The Don'ts and Be Carefuls', it stipulated:

Those things which are included in the following list shall not appear in pictures produced by the members of this

Association, irrespective of the manner in which they are treated:

- Pointed profanity – by either title or lip – this includes the words God, Lord, Jesus, Christ (unless they be used reverently in connection with proper religious ceremonies), hell, damn, Gawd, and every other profane and vulgar expression however it may be spelled;
- Any licentious or suggestive nudity, in fact or in silhouette;
- Any inference of sex perversion (homosexuality);
- White slavery;
- Miscegenation (sex relationships between the white and black races);
- Children's sex organs;
- Ridicule of the clergy.

It further advised that:

- Special care be exercised in the manner in which the following subjects are treated:
- Theft, robbery, safe-cracking, and dynamiting of trains, mines, buildings, etc. (having in mind the effect which a too-detailed description of these may have upon the moron);
- Brutality and possible gruesomeness;
- First-night scenes (one-night stands);
- Man and woman in bed together;
- Deliberate seduction of girls;
- The institution of marriage;
- Excessive or lustful kissing, particularly when one character or the other is a 'heavy'.

DUCK SOUP   1933

Dir: Leo McCarey. *Scr*: Bert Kalmar, Harry Ruby. *Cast*: Groucho Marx (Rufus T. Firefly)

Rufus encourages his brothers to defend Mrs Teasdale.

> **RUFUS T. FIREFLY**
> Remember, you're fighting for this woman's honour, which is probably more than she ever did.

I'M NO ANGEL   1933

Dir: Wesley Ruggles. *Scr*: Mae West. *Cast*: Cary Grant (Jack Clayton), Mae West (Tira)

Jack has fallen in love with Tira, a circus lion-tamer.

> **JACK**
> You were wonderful tonight.

> **TIRA**
> Yeah, I'm always wonderful at night.

> **JACK**
> Tonight you were especially good.

> **TIRA**
> Well, when I'm good, I'm very good. But when I'm bad, I'm better.

TO HAVE AND HAVE NOT   1944

Dir: Howard Hawks. *Scr*: Jules Furthman, William Faulkner. Based on a novel by Ernest Hemingway. *Cast*: Lauren Bacall (Marie 'Slim' Browning)

Slim Browning and Harry 'Steve' Morgan settle their differences with a kiss.

You know you don't have to act with me, Steve.
You don't have to say anything, and you don't
have to do anything. Not a thing. Oh, maybe just
whistle. You know how to whistle, don't you,
Steve? You just put your lips together and...
blow.

All great lines invite parody. In *Dead Men Don't Wear Plaid* (1982), the heroine purrs: 'If you need me, just call. You know how to dial, don't you? You just put your finger in the hole and make tiny little circles.'

THE BIG SLEEP   1946

Dir: Howard Hawks. *Scr*: William Faulkner, Leigh Brackett, Jules Furthman. Based on a novel by Raymond Chandler. *Cast*: Lauren Bacall (Vivian Rutledge), Humphrey Bogart (Philip Marlowe)

VIVIAN
Speaking of horses, I like to play them myself.
But I like to see them work out a little first,
see if they're front-runners or come from behind,
find out what their whole card is, what makes
them run.

MARLOWE
Find out mine?

VIVIAN
I think so.

MARLOWE
Go ahead.

VIVIAN
I'd say you don't like to be rated. You like to

get out in front, open up a little lead, take a
little breather in the backstretch, and then come
home free.

> MARLOWE

You don't like to be rated yourself.

> VIVIAN

I haven't met anyone yet that can do it. Any
suggestions?

> MARLOWE

Well, I can't tell till I've seen you over a
distance of ground. You've got a touch of class,
but I don't know how far you can go.

> VIVIAN

A lot depends on who's in the saddle.

NOTORIOUS   1946

Dir: Alfred Hitchcock. *Scr*: Ben Hecht. *Cast*: Cary Grant (T. R. Devlin), Ingrid
Bergman (Alicia Huberman)

Alicia, fond of both drink and men, falls for the man who has
recruited her as a spy.

> DEVLIN

Don't you need a coat?

> ALICIA

You'll do.

Director Hitchcock claimed the FBI had him under surveillance
during the shoot as the film dealt with uranium, a component of
nuclear weapons. The famous sequence where Cary Grant and Ingrid
Bergman kiss, only to separate and then resume, was designed to
circumvent the Hays Code ruling that a screen embrace should last
no more than three seconds.

WHITE HEAT   1949

Dir: Raoul Walsh. *Scr*: Ivan Goff, Ben Roberts. Based on a story by Virginia Kellogg. *Cast*: Virginia Mayo (Verna Jarrett), James Cagney (Arthur 'Cody' Jarrett)

Verna tries to persuade her gangster husband to buy her a present.

>   VERNA
>   I'd look good in a mink coat, honey.
>
>   CODY
>   You'd look good in a shower curtain.

In the days before 'squibs' – tiny explosive charges detonated by special effects teams – gunfights were recreated using trained marksmen to fire actual low-velocity bullets. Cagney, a fearless performer of many of his own stunts, was nearly hit on several occasions. Despite his huge box office success he remained remarkably modest, saying: 'I hate the word superstar… You don't hear them speak of Shakespeare as a superpoet. You don't hear them call Michelangelo a superpainter. They only apply the word to this mundane market.'

ALL ABOUT EVE   1950

Dir: Joseph L. Mankiewicz. *Scr*: Joseph L. Mankiewicz. Based on a story by Mary Orr. *Cast*: Bette Davis (Margo Channing)

Margo Channing, a famous actress, has lost none of her pride as she grows older.

>   MARGO
>   I'll admit I may have seen better days, but I'm
>   still not to be had for the price of a cocktail,
>   like a salted peanut.

The film shares the record for most the Oscar nominations – fourteen – with *Titanic* (1997) and *La La Land* (2016).

An icon evolves.

If you've got it…

… flaunt it.

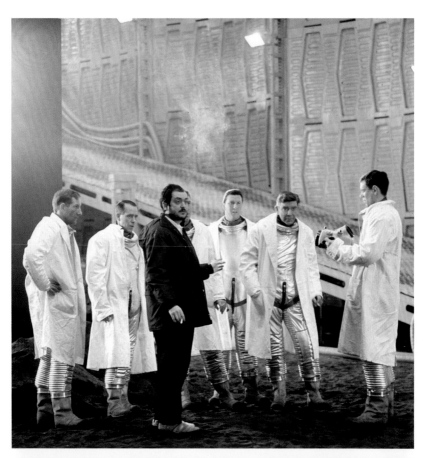

Kubrick demanded – and delivered – perfection…

… while Coppola captured madness by confronting it.

Sometimes the landscape is a character in itself…

… and sometimes the face is the canvas.

Spielberg rarely got his best shots from a director's chair.

AN AMERICAN IN PARIS   1951

Dir: Vincente Minnelli. *Scr*: Alan Jay Lerner. *Cast*: Gene Kelly (Jerry Mulligan),
Nina Foch (Milo Roberts)

> JERRY
>
> That's quite a dress you almost have on.
>
> MILO
>
> Thanks.
>
> JERRY
>
> What holds it up?
>
> MILO
>
> Modesty.

GENTLEMEN PREFER BLONDES   1953

Dir: Howard Hawks. *Scr*: Charles Lederer. Based on the musical by Joseph
Fields and a novel and play by Anita Loos. *Cast*: Marilyn Monroe (Lorelei Lee)

The wealthy Mr Esmond fears Lorelei's love for his son is more
mercenary than romantic.

> LORELEI
>
> Don't you know that a man being rich is like
> a girl being pretty? You wouldn't marry a girl
> just because she's pretty, but my goodness,
> doesn't it help?

GOLDFINGER   1964

Dir: Guy Hamilton. *Scr*: Richard Maibaum, Paul Dehn. Based on a novel by Ian
Fleming. *Cast*: Honor Blackman (Pussy Galore), Sean Connery (James Bond)

Criminal mastermind Auric Goldfinger has asked one of his
associates to take care of his prisoner James Bond.

PUSSY

My name is Pussy Galore.

BOND

I must be dreaming.

KEEPING THE BRITISH END UP

James Bond, commander in the Royal Naval Reserve but employed by the Secret Intelligence Service under the code name 007, first appeared in *Casino Royale* in 1952. Its opening sentence read: 'The scent and smoke and sweat of a casino are nauseating at three in the morning.'

Fleming – who had been involved in intelligence work during the Second World War – intended to portray the life of a secret agent in its full seamy, cynical reality. Of his creation he once said: 'Exotic things would happen to and around him but he would be a neutral figure – an anonymous blunt instrument wielded by a Government Department... Apart from the fact that he wears the same clothes that I wear, he and I really have little in common. I do rather envy him his blondes and his efficiency, but I can't say I much like the chap.'

Bond's sexual innuendo, more a hallmark of the films than of the original novels, echoes Fleming's own chauvinism: 'Men want a woman whom they can turn on and off like a light switch.' Ten years after 007's literary début, his creator admitted: 'The target of my books lay somewhere between the solar plexus and the upper thigh.'

Screenwriters, directors and actors for fifty years have responded to the challenge of portraying this enigmatic figure, yet audiences remain determined to champion a man whose humour remains as dry as his martinis:

BOND: It's just the right size — for me, that is.
From Russia With Love (1963)

BOND: Something big's come up.
Goldfinger (1964)

BOND: I'm afraid you've caught me with more
than my hands up.
Diamonds Are Forever (1971)

PLENTY O'TOOLE: Hi, I'm Plenty.
BOND: But of course you are.
PLENTY O'TOOLE: Plenty O'Toole.
BOND: Named after your father perhaps?
Diamonds Are Forever (1971)

BOND: Miss Anders! I didn't recognize you with
your clothes on.
The Man with the Golden Gun (1974)

BOND: Just keeping the British end up.
The Spy Who Loved Me (1977)

BOND: When one is in Egypt, one should delve
deeply into its treasures.
The Spy Who Loved Me (1977)

MINISTER OF DEFENCE: My God, what's Bond doing?
Q: I think he's attempting re-entry, sir.
Moonraker (1979)

FATIMA BLUSH: Oh, how reckless of me. I made
you all wet.
BOND: Yes, but my martini is still dry. My name
is James.
Never Say Never Again (1983)

BOND: You appear tense... That's too bad. Going down, one should always be relaxed.
Never Say Never Again (1983)

BOND: Well, my dear, I take it you spend quite a lot of time in the saddle.
JENNY FLEX: Yes, I love an early-morning ride.
BOND: Well, I'm an early riser myself.
A View to a Kill (1985)

XENIA ONATOPP: You don't need the gun, Commander.
BOND: Well, that depends on your definition of safe sex.
GoldenEye (1995)

MISS MONEYPENNY: You know, this sort of behaviour could qualify as sexual harassment.
BOND: Really. What's the penalty for that?
MISS MONEYPENNY: Someday, you'll have to make good on your innuendos.
GoldenEye (1995)

BOND: I always enjoyed learning a new tongue.
MISS MONEYPENNY: You always were a cunning linguist, James.
Tomorrow Never Dies (1997)

BOND: I was wrong about you.
CHRISTMAS JONES: Yeah, how so?
BOND: I thought Christmas only comes once a year.
The World Is Not Enough (1999)

DARLING   1965

Dir: John Schlesinger. *Scr*: Frederic Raphael. *Cast*: Dirk Bogarde (Robert Gold)

Robert has fallen in love with headstrong model Diana but is frustrated that she continues to have affairs.

> ROBERT
>
> Your idea of fidelity is not having more than one man in bed at the same time.

THE GRADUATE   1967

Dir: Mike Nichols. *Scr*: Calder Willingham, Buck Henry. Based on a novel by Charles Webb. *Cast*: Anne Bancroft (Mrs Robinson), Dustin Hoffman (Benjamin Braddock)

An older woman tries to seduce her daughter's boyfriend.

> MRS ROBINSON
>
> Sit down, Benjamin.

> BENJAMIN
>
> If you don't mind my saying so — this conversation is getting a little strange. Now I'm sure that Mr Robinson will be here any minute and—

> MRS ROBINSON
>
> No.

> BENJAMIN
>
> What?

> MRS ROBINSON
>
> My husband will be back quite late.

She makes her meaning clearer:

> MRS ROBINSON
>
> He should be gone for several hours.

She moves towards him.

BENJAMIN

Oh my God.

MRS ROBINSON

Pardon?

BENJAMIN

Oh no, Mrs Robinson, oh no.

MRS ROBINSON

What's wrong?

BENJAMIN

Mrs Robinson, you didn't — I mean you didn't
expect—

MRS ROBINSON

What?

BENJAMIN

I mean — you didn't really think that I would do
something like that.

MRS ROBINSON

Like what?

BENJAMIN

What do you think?

MRS ROBINSON

Well, I don't know.

BENJAMIN

For God's sake, Mrs Robinson, here we are, you've
got me into your house. You give me a drink.
You put on music, now you start opening up your
personal life to me and tell me your husband
won't be home for hours.

                    MRS ROBINSON
    So?

                    BENJAMIN
    Mrs Robinson — you *are* trying to seduce me.

He hesitates. She holds his gaze.

                    BENJAMIN
    Aren't you?

Mel Brooks had already cast Dustin Hoffman in his upcoming film *The Producers* and only let Hoffman audition for *The Graduate* because he was convinced the actor would never be right for the role of Benjamin. Hoffman got the part, and was bemused to find himself starring opposite Anne Bancroft – Mel Brooks's wife.

MYRA BRECKINRIDGE   1970

Dir: Michael Sarne. *Scr*: Michael Sarne, David Giler. Based on a novel by Gore Vidal. *Cast*: Mae West (Leticia Van Allen), Cal Bartlett (Actor)

Leticia, a libidinous seventy-year-old, runs a casting agency 'for leading men'.

                    LETICIA
    How tall are you, son?

                    ACTOR
    Ma'am, I'm six feet seven inches.

                    LETICIA
    Never mind about the six feet. Let's talk about
    the seven inches.

Bette Davis despised the script and refused the role of Leticia. *Time* magazine reviewed the film as 'an insult to intelligence, an affront to sensibility and an abomination to the eye'.

BEYOND THE VALLEY OF THE DOLLS   1970

Dir: Russ Meyer. *Scr*: Russ Meyer, Roger Ebert. *Cast*: Edy Williams (Ashley St Ives)

Porn star Ashley St Ives takes a shine to the manager of a rock band.

> ASHLEY
>
> You're a groovy boy. I'd like to strap you on
> sometime.

Director Russ Meyer trained as a cameraman in the US Army and some of the footage he shot during the Second World War can be seen in *Patton* (1970). He hoped to pursue a career as a cinematographer in Hollywood but strict union rules debarred him from membership, so he turned his hand to directing and developed a cult following for his cheerfully sleazy pictures. Defending his reputation as a salacious storyteller, he said: 'Nothing is obscene providing it is done in bad taste.'

LOOKING FOR MR GOODBAR   1977

Dir: Richard Brooks. *Scr*: Richard Brooks. Based on a novel by Judith Rossner. *Cast*: Eddie Garrett (Bartender), Diane Keaton (Theresa Dunn)

A bartender shares his views on drinking with a customer.

> BARTENDER
>
> Confidentially, with me . . . one's too many and a
> million's not enough.
>
> THERESA
>
> I got the same problem with men.

ALL THAT JAZZ   1979

Dir: Bob Fosse. *Scr*: Robert Alan Aurthur, Bob Fosse. *Cast*: uncredited

Two showgirls commiserate after an open casting call.

> DANCER BACKSTAGE 1
>
> Fuck him! He never picks me!

DANCER BACKSTAGE 2

Honey, I did fuck him and he never picks me
either.

DRESSED TO KILL   1980

Dir: Brian De Palma. *Scr*: Brian De Palma. *Cast*: Nancy Allen (Liz Blake),
Michael Caine (Dr Robert Elliott)

Call girl Liz finds herself attracted to a psychiatrist who may hold
the answer to an unsolved murder.

        LIZ

Do you want to fuck me?

        DR ELLIOTT

Oh, yes.

        LIZ

Then why don't you?

        DR ELLIOTT

Because I'm a doctor and...

        LIZ

Fucked a lot of doctors.

        DR ELLIOTT

... and I'm married.

        LIZ

Fucked a lot of them, too.

BODY HEAT   1981

Dir: Lawrence Kasdan. *Scr*: Lawrence Kasdan. *Cast*: William Hurt (Ned Racine),
Kathleen Turner (Matty Walker)

        NED

Maybe you shouldn't dress like that.

> **MATTY**
> This is a blouse and a skirt. I don't know what
> you're talking about.

> **NED**
> You shouldn't wear that body.

William Hurt and Kathleen Turner wanted to make sure the crew didn't feel bashful when they filmed their love scenes, so to break the ice they introduced themselves to everyone on the set – naked.

GORKY PARK   1983

Dir: Michael Apted. *Scr*: Dennis Potter. Based on a novel by Martin Cruz Smith. *Cast*: Alexei Sayle (Golodkin)

A Moscow black marketeer is accused of providing prostitutes for visitors.

> **GOLODKIN**
> Girls like screwing foreigners, don't they? It's
> almost as good as travel.

NOSTALGIA / *Nostalghia*   1983

Dir: Andrei Tarkovsky. *Scr*: Tonino Guerra, Andrei Tarkovsky. *Cast*: Domiziana Giordano (Eugenia)

Eugenia is unsure why she feels attracted to her married colleague Andrei.

> **EUGENIA**
> You're the kind of man I'd sleep with rather than
> explain why I don't feel like it.

Tarkovsky's first film shot outside the Soviet Union had to be awarded a special prize at the Cannes Festival in 1983 because the Soviet authorities had forbidden him to accept the prestigious Palme D'Or.

WHO FRAMED ROGER RABBIT?   1988

Dir: Robert Zemeckis. *Scr*: Jeffrey Price, Peter S. Seaman. Based on a novel by Gary K. Wolf. *Cast*: Kathleen Turner (voice of Jessica Rabbit)

Despite her curvaceous figure, cartoon character Jessica Rabbit knows how to sound bashful.

```
                  JESSICA RABBIT
    I'm not bad. I'm just drawn that way.
```

Bob Hoskins (starring opposite Jessica Rabbit) had to act with cut-outs and dummies representing the cartoon characters; he found the whole experience so disorienting that he began to suffer hallucinations.

The film offers cameos for many of cinema's most memorable animated characters, including Mickey Mouse, Minnie Mouse, Pluto, Donald Duck, Goofy, the Three Little Pigs and the Big Bad Wolf, Snow White and all seven dwarfs, Pinocchio and Jiminy Cricket, Dumbo, Bambi, Chicken Little, Peter and the Wolf, Tinker Bell from *Peter Pan*, the penguins from *Mary Poppins*, Bugs Bunny, Daffy Duck, Porky Pig, Tweety, Sylvester, Yosemite Sam, Foghorn Leghorn, Road Runner, Wile E. Coyote, Speedy Gonzales, Betty Boop and Woody Woodpecker.

AS SOON AS I GET THE REWRITE

Awarding the 2003 Oscar for Best Adapted Screenplay, Steve Martin quipped: 'I handed in a script last year and the studio didn't change one word. The word they didn't change was on page eighty-seven.' Screenwriters may be the unsung heroes of their own jokes but they are under no illusion about the way their talents are viewed by the industry:

> Did you hear about the dumb but ambitious starlet? She slept with the screenwriter.

The screenwriter of a Frank Capra comedy was watching a TV interview with the great director. An awestruck female reporter was heaping praise on a passage from the writer's script, and Frank explained the scene's charm by saying: 'That's the Capra touch.' The reporter continued to praise scenes in many other Capra movies. In each case the director's comment was: 'That's the Capra touch.' The writer responsible for the script couldn't take it any more so he stuffed 120 blank sheets of paper in an envelope and sent the package to the director with the note: 'Put the Capra touch on this.'

Q. How many screenwriters does it take to screw in a light bulb?
A. Does it really need to be changed?

Q. How many development executives does it take to change a light bulb?
A. One – but does it have to be a light bulb?

Q. How many screenwriters does it take to change a light bulb?
A. Ten.
　1st draft: Hero changes light bulb.
　2nd draft: Villain changes light bulb.
　3rd draft: Hero stops villain from changing light bulb. Villain falls to death.
　4th draft: Cut the light bulb.
　5th draft: Reinstate light bulb. Fluorescent instead of tungsten.
　6th draft: Villain breaks bulb, uses it to kill hero's mentor.

7th draft: Fluorescent not working. Back to tungsten.

8th draft: Hero forces villain to eat light bulb.

9th draft: Hero laments loss of light bulb. Doesn't change it.

10th draft: Hero changes light bulb.

Q. How many agents does it take to screw in a light bulb?

A. Three – one to screw it in, and two to hold down the screenwriter.

A screenwriter dies and is given the choice of going to heaven or to hell, so she decides to visit each place first. As she enters the satanic realms she sees a thousand writers shackled to their typewriters in a fiery furnace being lashed by overseers.

Shocked, she leaves and sets out to inspect heaven. There, she discovers another thousand writers chained to the same typewriters and receiving the same whipping. Turning to an angel, she says in surprise: 'But this is just the same as hell!'

The angel replies: 'Sure, but here your script goes into production.'

Two development execs meet in the hallway. One says, 'Hey, what's cooking?' The second one, extremely excited, replies, 'I just bought this script. It's the most perfect piece of writing I've ever seen. Characters, story, everything about it is A1. Academy Award time.'

'That's fantastic,' says the first one, dripping with envy. 'So when do you go into production?'

'As soon as I get the rewrite.'

BULL DURHAM   1988

Dir: Ron Shelton. *Scr*: Ron Shelton. *Cast*: Susan Sarandon (Annie Savoy)

A baseball groupie confesses she likes to read poetry to her lovers.

> ANNIE
> A guy'll listen to anything if he thinks it's
> foreplay.

WORKING GIRL   1988

Dir: Mike Nichols. *Scr*: Kevin Wade. *Cast*: Melanie Griffith (Tess McGill)

Tess is determined to stay true to herself in a tough corporate world.

> TESS
> I have a head for business and a bod for sin. Is
> there anything wrong with that?

WILD AT HEART   1990

Dir: David Lynch. *Scr*: David Lynch. Based on a novel by Barry Gifford. *Cast*:
Laura Dern (Lula Pace Fortune)

Lula makes no attempt to hide her passion for her lover.

> LULA
> Uh oh. . . Baby, you'd better get me back to that
> hotel. You got me hotter than Georgia asphalt.

THE LAST SEDUCTION   1994

Dir: John Dahl. *Scr*: Steve Barancik. *Cast*: Linda Fiorentino (Bridget Gregory),
Peter Berg (Mike Swale)

When Linda first meets Mike she makes her wishes crystal clear.

> BRIDGET
> You're my designated fuck.

MIKE

Designated fuck? Do they make cards for that?
What if I want to be more than your designated
fuck?

BRIDGET

Then I'll designate someone else.

DANGEROUS BEAUTY   1998

Dir: Marshall Herskovitz. *Scr*: Jeannine Dominy. Based on a book by Margaret
Rosenthal. *Cast*: Catherine McCormack (Veronica Franco)

A courtesan in sixteenth-century Venice defends herself against the
hypocrisy of her interrogators.

VERONICA

I confess that as a young girl I loved a man who
would not marry me for want of a dowry. I confess
I had a mother who taught me a different way
of life, one I resisted at first but learned to
embrace. I confess I became a courtesan, traded
yearning for power, welcomed many rather than
be owned by one. I confess I embraced a whore's
freedom over a wife's obedience. I confess I
find more ecstasy in passion than in prayer. Such
passion *is* prayer. I confess I pray still to feel
the touch of my lover's lips, his hands upon me,
his arms enfolding me . . . Such surrender has been
mine. I confess I pray still to be filled and
inflamed. To melt into the dream of us, beyond
this troubled place, to where we are not even
ourselves. To know that always, this is mine. If
this had not been mine — if I had lived any other
way — a child to her husband's will, my soul

hardened from lack of touch and lack of love . . .
I confess such endless days and nights would be
a punishment far greater than you could ever
mete out. You, all of you, you who hunger so for
what I give, yet cannot bear to see that kind of
power in a woman. You call God's greatest gift —
ourselves, our yearning, our need to love — you
call it filth and sin and heresy. . . I repent
there was no other way open to me. I do not
repent my life.

Y TU MAMÁ TAMBIÉN   2001

Dir: Alfonso Cuarón. *Scr*: Alfonso Cuarón, Carlos Cuarón. *Cast*: Maribel Verdú
(Luisa Cortés), Diego Luna (Tenoch Iturbide)

Seducing two young men at the same time, Luisa encourages them
to approach her tenderly.

> LUISA
> You have to make the clitoris your best friend.

> TENOCH
> What kind of friend is always hiding?

The Mexican film was released in most countries with its original
title. Its literal translation (*And Your Mother Too*) fails to convey its
common usage as a retort to a wide range of insults.

WET HOT AMERICAN SUMMER   2001

Dir: David Wain. *Scr*: David Wain, Michael Showalter. *Cast*: Marguerite Moreau
(Katie)

Katie leaves her summer camp admirer in no doubt about his
prospects as her boyfriend.

KATIE

Listen, Coop. Last night was really great. You
were incredibly romantic and heroic, no doubt
about it. And that's great. But I've thought
about it, and my thing is this. Andy is really
hot. And don't get me wrong, you're cute too, but
Andy is like, cut. From marble. He's gorgeous.
He has this beautiful face and this incredible
body, and I genuinely don't care that he's kinda
lame. I don't even care that he cheats on me.
And I like you more than I like Andy, Coop, but
I'm sixteen. And maybe it'll be a different
story when I'm ready to get married, but right
now, I am entirely about sex. I just wanna get
laid. I just wanna take him and grab him and
fuck his brains out, ya know? So that's where my
priorities are right now. Sex. Specifically with
Andy and not with you.

MONSTERS

DRACULA   1931

Dir: Tod Browning. *Scr*: Garrett Fort. Based on a play by Hamilton Deane, John L. Balderston, adapted from the novel by Bram Stoker. *Cast*: Bela Lugosi (Count Dracula)

          DRACULA
   I am Dracula. I bid you welcome.

No cosmetic modifications were made to Bela Lugosi's teeth for the film; his Dracula has no fangs. Cinematographer Karl Freund intensified the monster's piercing gaze by highlighting each eye with an individual keylight. Sound was still a recent innovation in films and the studio feared audiences would be confused by 'invisible' orchestral accompaniment, so the only time we hear music is during the title sequence and when Dracula meets Mina outside a theatre.

ISLAND OF LOST SOULS   1932

Dir: Erle C. Kenton. *Scr*: Waldemar Young, Philip Wylie. Based on a novel by H. G. Wells. *Cast*: Charles Laughton (Dr Moreau), Bela Lugosi (Sayer of the Law)

A scientist obsessed by evolution struggles to control the half-human creatures he has bred from wild animals.

          DR MOREAU
   What is the law?

          SAYER OF THE LAW
   Not to eat meat, that is the law. Are we not men?

          BEASTS
   Are we not men!

          DR MOREAU
   What is the law?

SAYER OF THE LAW

Not to go on all fours, that is the law. Are we
not men?

BEASTS

Are we not men!

DR MOREAU

What is the law?

SAYER OF THE LAW

Not to spill blood, that is the law. Are we not
men?

BEASTS

Are we not men!

KING KONG   1933

Dir: Merian C. Cooper (uncredited), Ernest B. Schoedsack (uncredited). *Scr*:
James Ashmore Creelman, Ruth Rose, Merian C. Cooper. Based on a story by
Edgar Wallace. *Cast*: Unknown (Police Lieutenant), Robert Armstrong (Carl
Denham)

King Kong's captor Denham pays wistful tribute as the giant ape is
killed.

POLICE LIEUTENANT

Well, Denham, the airplanes got him.

DENHAM

Oh no, it wasn't the airplanes — it was beauty
killed the beast.

Merian Cooper and Ernest Schoedsack jointly directed the film but
were also its producers, only taking the screen credit as the latter.
Conveniently they had both been wrestlers and were able to act
out the fight between Kong and the Tyrannosaurus Rex to help the
animators.

ANGELS WITH DIRTY FACES   1938

Dir: Michael Curtiz. *Scr*: Rowland Brown, John Wexley, Warren Duff. *Cast*:
James Cagney (Rocky Sullivan)

Recently released from a reformatory, Rocky is keen to make an
impression on his old neighbourhood associates.

> ROCKY
>
> Morning, gentlemen. Nice day for a murder.

THE WIZARD OF OZ   1939

Dir: Victor Fleming. *Scr*: Noel Langley, Florence Ryerson, Edgar Allan Woolf.
Based on a novel by L. Frank Baum. *Cast*: Margaret Hamilton (Wicked Witch
of the West)

> WICKED WITCH
>
> Oh, you cursed brat! Look what you've done.
> I'm melting! Melting! Oh, what a world! What a
> world! Who would have thought a good little girl
> like you could destroy my beautiful wickedness?

BEAUTY AND THE BEAST / *La Belle et la Bête*   1946

Dir: Jean Cocteau. *Scr*: Jean Cocteau. Based on a story by Jeanne-Marie Leprince
de Beaumont. *Cast*: Jean Marais (The Beast)

> THE BEAST
>
> Belle, you must not look into my eyes. You
> need not fear. You will never see me except
> each evening at seven when you will dine, and
> I will come to the great hall. And never look
> into my eyes.

Many of the Wicked Witch's scenes were trimmed or deleted, as
Margaret Hamilton's performance was deemed too frightening for
audiences.

THE SEVENTH SEAL / *Det sjunde inseglet*   **1957**

Dir: Ingmar Bergman. *Scr*: Ingmar Bergman, based on his play. *Cast*: Max von
Sydow (Antonius Block), Maud Hansson (Witch)

A wandering knight seeks the help of a witch in his struggle for
faith.

> ANTONIUS
> Have you met the devil? I want to meet him too.

> WITCH
> Why do you want to do that?

> ANTONIUS
> I want to ask him about God. He must know. He, if
> anyone.

The iconic shot of figures dancing behind Death on a distant hilltop
was nearly abandoned because most of the actors had left for the
day. Bergman only managed to complete it with the help of passing
tourists.

PSYCHO   **1960**

Dir: Alfred Hitchcock. *Scr*: Joseph Stefano. Based on a novel by Robert Bloch.
Cast: Anthony Perkins (Norman Bates), Janet Leigh (Marion Crane)

A shy motel owner tries to reassure a guest that the argument she
has overheard is nothing to worry about.

> NORMAN
> It's not like my mother is a maniac or a raving
> thing. She just goes a little mad sometimes. We
> all go a little mad sometimes. Haven't you?

> MARION
> Yes. Sometimes just one time can be enough.

Hitchcock was so keen to keep the ending a secret that after he secured the rights to the novel he tried to buy up all unsold copies to stop word spreading. Rumours circulated that he shot the film in black-and-white because the blood in the shower scene would be too shocking in colour, but later he said he was just curious to see if he could make a success of a production shot like a low-budget B-movie.

A BODY IN THE COACH

A 2007 poll of critics in the *Daily Telegraph* hailed Alfred Hitchcock (1899–1980) as 'Unquestionably the greatest filmmaker to emerge from these islands, [he] did more than any director to shape modern cinema … His flair was for narrative, cruelly withholding crucial information (from his characters and from us) and engaging the emotions of the audience like no one else.' The American magazine *MovieMaker* was more succinct, declaring him 'The most influential filmmaker of all time'.

Recurring themes of suspicion, anxiety and a mistrust of authority clearly have their roots in his upbringing. Born in the East End of London, he was educated by strict Jesuits, and his own father once sent him – at the age of five – to the local police station with a note asking the officer to lock him in a cell for five minutes as a punishment for bad behaviour.

Before finding his first film employment as a designer of title cards, he wrote short stories which further reflected his macabre, voyeuristic interests and fondness for surprising narrative twists. 'Gas' (1919) tells of a woman who dreams she is being assaulted, only to discover she has been hallucinating under the influence of a dentist's anaesthetic. 'And There Was No Rainbow' (1920) offers us a young man in search of a brothel who mistakenly seeks out the house of his best friend's girl.

Hitchcock's body of film work is remarkably consistent in its preoccupations and style. He worked from meticulous storyboards and avoided unnecessary extra angles or takes in order to prevent his producers from changing his vision during subsequent editing. Unsurprisingly, his comments about his work and the industry itself are self-aware and slyly humorous:

- I am a type(cast) director. If I made *Cinderella*, the audience would immediately be looking for a body in the coach.

- One of television's great contributions is that it brought murder back into the home, where it belongs.

- Give them pleasure – the same pleasure they have when they wake up from a nightmare.

- Blondes make the best victims. They're like virgin snow that shows up the bloody footprints.

- Reality is something that none of us can stand, at any time.

- Man does not live by murder alone. He needs affection, approval, encouragement and, occasionally, a hearty meal.

- In the documentary the basic material has been created by God, whereas in the fiction film the director is a God; he must create life.

- I enjoy playing the audience like a piano.

- If it's a good movie, the sound could go off and the audience would still have a perfectly clear idea of what was going on.

- When an actor comes to me and wants to discuss his character, I say, 'It's in the script'. If he says, 'But what's my motivation?', I say, 'Your salary'.

- The length of a film should be directly related to the endurance of the human bladder.

- I deny I ever said that actors are cattle. What I said was, 'Actors should be treated like cattle'.

Hitchcock, however, was bested in a debate about his technique during the shoot of *Lifeboat* (1944) when he told the composer Hugo Friedhofer it would be inappropriate to have a musical score as the characters were adrift on the open sea. After all, where could the sound of an orchestra possibly come from? Undeterred, Friedhofer is reported to have replied: 'The same place the camera came from, Mr Hitchcock.'

CAPE FEAR   1962

Dir: J. Lee Thompson. *Scr*: James R. Webb. Based on a novel by John D. MacDonald. *Cast*: Robert Mitchum (Max Cady), Gregory Peck (Sam Bowden)

Lawyer Sam Bowden has shot Max Cady – the murderer and former client who has been terrorizing his family – and readies himself to fire again.

> CADY
>
> Go ahead. I just don't give a damn.
>
> BOWDEN
>
> No. No! That would be letting you off too easy, too fast. Your words – do you remember? Well, I do. No, we're gonna take good care of you. We're gonna nurse you back to health. And you're strong, Cady. You're gonna live a long life . . . in a cage! That's where you belong and that's where you're going. And this time for life! Bang your head against the walls. Count the years – the months – the hours . . . until the day you rot!

The film was remade in 1991 by Martin Scorsese and writer Wesley Strick with Robert De Niro as the terrifying Cady, Nick Nolte as Sam Bowden and Jessica Lange as his wife Leigh. Interestingly, the final lines of their screenplay are a voice-over from Danielle, the teenage daughter of the family Cady menaces (played by Juliette Lewis):

> DANIELLE: We never spoke about what happened, at least not to each other. Fear, I suppose, that to remember his name and what he did would mean letting him into our dreams. And me, I hardly dream about him any more. Still, things won't ever be the way they were before he came. But that's all right because if you hang onto the past you die a little every day. And for myself, I know I'd rather live. (*She whispers*) The end.

THE EXTERMINATING ANGEL / *El Ángel exterminador*   1962

Dir: Luis Buñuel. *Scr*: Luis Buñuel. *Cast*: Patricia Morán (Rita Ugalde)

> RITA
> I believe the common people, the lower class people, are less sensitive to pain. Haven't you ever seen a wounded bull? Not a trace of pain.

2001: A SPACE ODYSSEY   1968

Dir: Stanley Kubrick. *Scr*: Stanley Kubrick, Arthur C. Clarke. *Cast*: Keir Dullea (Dave Bowman), Douglas Rain (voice of HAL)

An astronaut is barred from re-entering his spacecraft by its central computer.

> DAVE
> Hello, HAL. Do you read me, HAL?

                    HAL

Affirmative, Dave. I read you.

                    DAVE

Open the pod bay doors, HAL.

                    HAL

I'm sorry, Dave. I'm afraid I can't do that.

                    DAVE

What's the problem?

                    HAL

I think you know what the problem is just as well
as I do.

                    DAVE

What are you talking about, HAL?

                    HAL

This mission is too important for me to allow you
to jeopardize it.

                    DAVE

I don't know what you're talking about, HAL.

                    HAL

I know that you and Frank were planning to
disconnect me, and I'm afraid that's something I
cannot allow to happen.

Dave feigns innocence.

                    DAVE

Where the hell did you get that idea, HAL?

                    HAL

Dave, although you took very thorough precautions
in the pod against my hearing you, I could see
your lips move.

All right, HAL. I'll go in through the emergency
airlock.

                    HAL

Without your space helmet, Dave? You're going to
find that rather difficult.

                    DAVE

HAL, I won't argue with you any more! Open the
doors!

                    HAL

Dave, this conversation can serve no purpose any
more. Goodbye.

Chicago Sun-Times critic Roger Ebert re-evaluated the film in 1997:
'*2001: A Space Odyssey* is in many respects a silent film . . . The genius
is not in how much Stanley Kubrick does in [it] but in how little.
He reduces each scene to its essence, and leaves it onscreen long
enough for us to contemplate it, to inhabit it in our imaginations.
Alone among science fiction movies, *2001* is not concerned with
thrilling us, but with inspiring our awe.'

'YOU AIN'T HEARD NOTHIN' YET!'

Although some directors, including D. W. Griffith, had
incorporated audio recording into their productions during the
1920s, it was largely for musical accompaniment and ambient
sound effects. The kind of synchronized dialogue we now take
for granted was first used in a full-length feature in *The Jazz
Singer* (1927) when Al Jolson, dubbed 'The World's Greatest
Entertainer', delivered his trademark line: 'Wait a minute, wait
a minute, you ain't heard nothin' yet!'

The recording technology was temperamental, expensive and bulky and its use added further complications to the process of capturing a scene. Cameras now had to run at precise speeds to match the tape machines but were so loud they had to be soundproofed – often in boxes big enough to enclose the operator and assistant as well. Before the stages themselves were soundproofed, much filming had to be done at night to avoid traffic noise. On one occasion, a canny but penniless bit-player hired for a single scene brought a box of crickets and released them on the set. Production was halted; five days – and five pay cheques later – the crew were still hunting them down.

Many stars were sceptical of the invention as they had grown used to being icons, not actors. They now had to focus on all aspects of performance and an unfortunate number discovered they had been hired for their looks rather than their speaking voice – or, indeed, their actual acting abilities. Many Europeans had their studio contracts cancelled when their accents proved unpalatable to audiences, and many household names, including Lillian Gish, Buster Keaton, John Gilbert, Gloria Swanson, Douglas Fairbanks and Mary Pickford, all realized their heyday was over.

Directors also resented the fact that actors now had unprecedented freedom since it was no longer possible to shout comments at them during takes. One hated this loss of control so much that he devised a low voltage electrical system through which he could issue signals to guide his cast's performance while the camera was rolling. Much as perfectionists such as Tarkovsky, Hitchcock and Kubrick might regret it, this invention never took off but the public embraced the advent of sound unhesitatingly and by 1929 all major studios had stopped making silent pictures.

CHITTY CHITTY BANG BANG 1968

Dir: Ken Hughes. *Scr*: Roald Dahl, Ken Hughes, Richard Maibaum. Based on a novel by Ian Fleming. *Cast*: Robert Helpmann (Childcatcher)

Vulgaria's most feared official smells something amiss in a puppet workshop.

> **CHILDCATCHER**
>
> I don't trust a man who makes toys in a land where children are forbidden.

BARBARELLA 1968

Dir: Roger Vadim. *Scr*: Terry Southern, Roger Vadim and five others. Based on stories in *Barbarella* comics by Jean-Claude Forest, Claude Brulé. *Cast*: Milo O'Shea (Durand-Durand)

Fugitive scientist Durand-Durand has invented a weapon with which he threatens Earth.

> **DURAND-DURAND**
>
> I'll do things to you that are beyond all known philosophies! Wait until I get my devices!

A CLOCKWORK ORANGE 1971

Dir: Stanley Kubrick. *Scr*: Stanley Kubrick. Based on a novel by Anthony Burgess. *Cast*: Malcolm McDowell (Alex)

A violent thug with a fondness for Beethoven picks up a couple of girls in a record shop.

> **ALEX**
>
> What you got back home, little sister, to play your fuzzy warbles on? I bet you got little save pitiful, portable picnic players. Come with uncle and hear all proper! Hear angel trumpets and devil trombones. You are invited.

Anthony Burgess originally sold the rights to his novel to Mick Jagger for $500 [$3,300] because he was short of cash; Jagger had wanted his fellow Rolling Stones to play the droogs, the story's thuggish anti-heroes. Ken Russell was initially slated to direct; both Tim Curry and Jeremy Irons were approached to play the lead role of Alex but turned it down. Kubrick later said of the final casting that if Malcolm McDowell had not been available he would not have made the film.

DELIVERANCE   1972

Dir: John Boorman. *Scr*: James Dickey, based on his novel. *Cast*: Bill McKinney (Mountain Man), Herbert Coward (Toothless Man)

Two violent hillbillies humiliate the hikers they find in their territory.

> MOUNTAIN MAN
> What do you want to do now?

> TOOTHLESS MAN
> He got a real pretty mouth, ain't he?

> MOUNTAIN MAN
> That's the truth.

He turns to their victim.

> TOOTHLESS MAN
> You gonna do some prayin' for me, boy. And you
> better pray good.

THE EXORCIST   1973

Dir: William Friedkin. *Scr*: William Peter Blatty, based on his novel. *Cast*: Mercedes McCambridge (Demon), Jason Miller (Father Damian Karras)

A demon possessing Regan, a young girl, turns his attention to the priest who hopes to exorcize her.

                    DEMON
What an excellent day for an exorcism.

                    FATHER KARRAS
You would like that?

                    DEMON
Intensely.

                    FATHER KARRAS
But wouldn't that drive you out of Regan?

                    DEMON
It would bring us together.

                    FATHER KARRAS
You and Regan?

                    DEMON
You and us.

Author William Peter Blatty could only afford to take time off to write the novel after winning $10,000 [$55,000] on *You Bet Your Life*, a game show hosted by Groucho Marx.

When the film was banned by several local authorities in Britain, enterprising travel companies set up special 'Exorcist Bus Trips' to unaffected cinemas.

DAWN OF THE DEAD   1978

Dir: George A. Romero. *Scr*: George A. Romero. *Cast*: Ken Foree (Peter)

One of the survivors of a zombie attack explains why the corpses have risen.

                    PETER
When there's no more room in hell, the dead will walk the Earth.

Dir: Ridley Scott. *Scr*: Dan O'Bannon, Ronald Shusett. *Cast*: Sigourney Weaver
(Ripley), Ian Holm (Ash), Yaphet Kotto (Parker), Veronica Cartwright (Lambert)

Crew members of the *Nostromo*, an interstellar cargo ship with an
alien predator on board, discover their colleague Ash is an android.

> RIPLEY
>
> Ash, can you hear me? Ash?

*Ash's head has been torn from his body. His voice
sounds electronic now.*

> ASH
>
> Yes, I can hear you.

> RIPLEY
>
> What was your special order?

> ASH
>
> You read it. I thought it was clear.

> RIPLEY
>
> What was it?

> ASH
>
> Bring back life form. Priority One. All other
> priorities rescinded.

> PARKER
>
> The damn company. What about our lives, you son of
> a bitch?

> ASH
>
> I repeat, all other priorities are rescinded.

> RIPLEY
>
> How do we kill it, Ash? There's gotta be a way of
> killing it. How? How do we do it?

                    ASH

You can't.

                    PARKER

That's bullshit.

                    ASH

You still don't understand what you're dealing
with, do you? A perfect organism. Its structural
perfection is matched only by its hostility.

                    LAMBERT

You admire it.

                    ASH

I admire its purity. A survivor... unclouded by
conscience, remorse, or delusions of morality.

                    PARKER

I've heard enough of this, and I'm asking you to
pull the plug.

Ripley moves to shut Ash down.

                    ASH

Last word.

                    RIPLEY

What?

                    ASH

I can't lie to you about your chances, but...
you have my sympathies.

The infamous scene where an alien bursts from Kane's (John Hurt's)
chest was filmed in one take with four cameras; the rest of the cast
were not warned that real blood and guts were being used, ensuring
their genuine horror .

THE SHINING 1980

Dir: Stanley Kubrick. *Scr*: Stanley Kubrick, Diane Johnson. Based on a novel by Stephen King. *Cast*: Shelley Duvall (Wendy Torrance), Jack Nicholson (Jack Torrance)

Jack, caretaker of a lonely hotel, has been driven insane by its supernatural inhabitants. Wendy, his wife, tries to escape him.

> WENDY
>
> Stay away from me.

> JACK
>
> Why?

> WENDY
>
> I just wanna go back to my room!

> JACK
>
> Why?

> WENDY
>
> Well, I'm very confused, and I just need time to think things over.

> JACK
>
> You've had your whole fucking life to think things over, what good's a few minutes more gonna do you now?

> WENDY
>
> Please! Don't hurt me!

> JACK
>
> I'm not gonna hurt you.

> WENDY
>
> Stay away from me!

JACK

Wendy? Darling? Light of my life, I'm not gonna
hurt you. You didn't let me finish my sentence.
I said, I'm not gonna hurt you. I'm just going
to bash your brains in. Gonna bash 'em right the
fuck in!

TIME BANDITS   1981

Dir: Terry Gilliam. *Scr*: Michael Palin, Terry Gilliam. *Cast*: David Warner (Evil
Genius)

A malevolent sorcerer seeks a cosmic map which will allow him to
travel through time.

EVIL GENIUS

When I have the map I will be free and the
world will be different, because I have
understanding... of digital watches. And soon
I shall have understanding of videocassette
recorders and car telephones. And when I have
understanding of them, I shall have understanding
of computers. And when I have understanding of
computers, I shall be the Supreme Being! God
isn't interested in technology. He knows nothing
of the potential of the microchip or the silicon
revolution. Look how He spends His time! Forty-
three species of parrots! Nipples for men! Slugs!
He created slugs. They can't hear! They can't
speak! They can't operate machinery! I mean,
are we not in the hands of a lunatic? If I were
creating a world, I wouldn't mess about with
butterflies and daffodils. I would have started
with lasers, eight o'clock, day one!

```
He presses a button, unleashing the beam. An
assistant screams.
```

                    EVIL GENIUS
```
    Sorry.
```

As a joke to help with the casting of other main characters, Gilliam had written in the script: 'The warrior (Agamemnon) takes off his helmet, revealing someone who looks exactly like Sean Connery, or an actor of equal but cheaper stature.' To the director's surprise, someone gave Connery a copy. He liked it, and signed up.

THE FLY   1986

Dir: David Cronenberg. *Scr*: David Cronenberg, Charles Edward Pogue. Based on a story by George Langelaan. *Cast*: Joy Boushel (Tawney), Jeff Goldblum (Seth Brundle), Geena Davis (Veronica Quaife)

Scientist Seth Brundle tries to persuade a stranger to help with his teleportation experiments but his colleague Veronica knows it is too dangerous.

                    TAWNY
```
    I'm afraid.
```

                    SETH
```
    Don't be afraid.
```

                    VERONICA
```
    No! Be afraid. Be very afraid.
```

When Jeff Goldblum's character delivers the line 'I'm an insect who dreamed he was a man and loved it, but now that dream is over and the insect is awake,' he is referring to Franz Kafka's *The Metamorphosis* (1915), in which the narrator discovers he has been transformed into a cockroach.

Cronenberg's original conception featured several other biological mutations including an ape/cat hybrid and a child born with butterfly wings, but they were omitted from his final cut. Although a film's end credits typically give the director top billing, Cronenberg broke with precedent and listed Chris Walas first for his groundbreaking work in creating the special effects make-up for the creature. Walas duly won the Academy Award.

MISERY   1990
Dir: Rob Reiner:. *Scr*: William Goldman. Based on a novel by Stephen King. *Cast*: Kathy Bates (Annie Wilkes)

A writer is wounded in a car accident and held helpless by his rescuer, a woman obsessed by his work.

          ANNIE
  There's nothing to worry about. You're going to
  be just fine — I'm your number one fan.

THE SILENCE OF THE LAMBS   1991
Dir: Jonathan Demme. *Scr*: Ted Tally. Based on a novel by Thomas Harris. *Cast*: Anthony Hopkins (Dr Hannibal Lecter)

A serial killer renowned for cannibalism taunts an FBI agent who seeks his help.

          LECTER
  A census taker once tried to test me. I ate his
  liver with some fava beans and a nice Chianti.

The pattern on the moth's body in the poster was changed to echo Salvador Dalí's *In Voluptas Mors*, which shapes seven naked women into the image of a skull. The Tobacco horn worm moths used in the film received five-star treatment, being flown first-class in special carriers and kept in a climate-controlled room before being costumed in special body shields bearing a skull and crossbones.

SCHINDLER'S LIST 1993

Dir: Steven Spielberg. *Scr*: Steven Zaillian. Based on a novel by Thomas Keneally.
Cast: Ralph Fiennes (Amon Goeth)

SS officer Amon Goeth rallies his troops before a raid to eliminate the Jewish ghetto in Krakow.

> GOETH
>
> Today is history. Today will be remembered.
> Years from now the young will ask with wonder
> about this day. Today is history and you are
> part of it. Six hundred years ago when elsewhere
> they were footing the blame for the Black
> Death, Casimir the Great — so called — told
> the Jews they could come to Krakow. They came.
> They trundled their belongings into the city.
> They settled. They took hold. They prospered
> in business, science, education, the arts.
> With nothing they came and with nothing they
> flourished. For six centuries there has been
> a Jewish Krakow. By this evening those six
> centuries will be a rumour. They never happened.
> Today is history.

SE7EN 1995

Dir: David Fincher. *Scr*: Andrew Kevin Walker. *Cast*: Kevin Spacey (John Doe)

A serial killer exacts revenge on the detective pursuing him.

> JOHN DOE
>
> I visited your home this morning after you'd
> left. I tried to play husband. I tried to taste
> the life of a simple man. It didn't work out, so
> I took a souvenir: her pretty head.

THE USUAL SUSPECTS   1995

Dir: Bryan Singer. *Scr*: Christopher McQuarrie. *Cast*: Kevin Spacey (Roger 'Verbal' Kint)

A crippled conman describes the elusive criminal mastermind responsible for the deaths of his colleagues.

> **VERBAL**
> Who is Keyser Söze? He is supposed to be Turkish.
> Some say his father was German. Nobody believed
> he was real. Nobody ever saw him or knew anybody
> that ever worked directly for him, but to hear
> Kobayashi tell it, anybody could have worked
> for Söze. You never knew. That was his power.
> The greatest trick the Devil ever pulled was
> convincing the world he didn't exist. And like
> that, poof. He's gone.

The quote about the devil is by French poet Charles Baudelaire, although the film-makers were unaware of its origin. Strangely, a similar remark appears in *End of Days* (1999), also starring Gabriel Byrne and Kevin Pollak.

'WHO IS KEYSER SÖZE?'

Although filled with compelling characters and memorable dialogue, *The Usual Suspects* is a rare example of a thriller whose construction feels almost purely intellectual. Through flashbacks, contradiction, ambiguity and visual sleight-of-hand it draws the audience into a world where facts are unreliable and the very concept of 'writing' is shown to be a kind of game.

Director Bryan Singer's inspiration was the line in *Casablanca* where Captain Renault tells his men to 'round up the usual suspects'; Singer's subsequent conception consisted simply of five criminals who meet in a police line-up. When he asked writer Christopher McQuarrie what could have drawn the men together, McQuarrie remembered a true story he had read about a man who murdered his family and disappeared for decades. As McQuarrie began writing in lunch breaks at the law firm where he worked he was distracted by a cluttered notice board and decided to use it as a motif for the story. From these fragments they created a journey that was to be as immersive for its cast as for its audience.

In the line-up and interrogation scenes, shot before the rest of the film, McQuarrie fed the cast questions off-camera and they improvised answers. From the start of the process, the 'criminals' seemed to be united against the authorities (the film-makers), refusing to take the shooting seriously and constantly trying to make each other laugh. When Singer upbraided them, they ignored him; in the end he was forced to use the takes where they cracked up, and the editor put the scenes together in a way that showed the men were – quite genuinely – forging relationships with one another.

McQuarrie gave the suspects names from staff members at the law firm and this method of purely random invention became a key part of his storytelling. By the end of the film we realize that 'Verbal' Kint's statement to the detectives has been entirely fabricated using haphazard details from the police station where he is interrogated to provide 'evidence' and corroborative detail for his confession.

Singer used a similar trick to ensure realism in the actors' performances: because the police investigation revolves around exactly who criminal mastermind Keyzer Söze is, the director refused to give any of his cast the answer. Kevin Spacey revealed later that Singer had managed to persuade all the main players that they themselves were the anti-hero. When the film was first screened for the cast Gabriel Byrne (as Dean Keaton) was so shocked to discover he was not the central figure that he fled to the parking lot where he yelled at Singer for an hour. Debate still rages in internet movie chat rooms, where fans who have watched the film dozens of times offer their conclusions: most claim Kint is Söze (his surname means 'verbal' in Turkish) while others suggest the lawyer Kobayashi is the only character with enough knowledge to mastermind the entire story. Other aficionados insist Kobayashi himself is a fiction – just a name Kint saw on a detective's coffee mug.

Five different actors were used to play Söze as their conflicting viewpoints are explored, and the whole film initially seems to be an impenetrable construction of interlocking fictions. On repeated viewing, however, it displays a masterful confidence in its deceptions and once the truth is revealed a multitude of details prove that a careful observer might have followed the plot without distraction. As if to prove how much he enjoyed baffling us along the way, writer McQuarrie has a cameo as a police officer at the end when he just turns to the camera and laughs.

THE DEVIL'S ADVOCATE   1997

Dir: Taylor Hackford. *Scr*: Jonathan Lemkin, Tony Gilroy. Based on a novel by Andrew Neiderman. *Cast*: Al Pacino (John Milton)

Satan – in the form of a New York lawyer – warns that God will not save the human race from its own greed and selfishness.

```
               MILTON
You sharpen the human appetite to the point
where it can split atoms with its desire. You
build egos the size of cathedrals. Fibre-
optically connect the world to every ego
impulse. Grease even the dullest dreams with
```

these dollar-green, gold-plated fantasies until
every human becomes an aspiring emperor, becomes
his own god. Where can you go from there? And
as we're scrambling from one deal to the next,
who's got his eye on the planet? As the air
thickens, the water sours. Even the bees' honey
takes on the metallic taste of radioactivity —
and it just keeps coming, faster and faster...
And then it hits home: you gotta pay your own
way, Eddie. It's a little late in the game to
buy out now. Your belly's too full, your dick
is sore, your eyes are bloodshot, and you're
screaming for someone to help. But guess what?
There's no one there.

DECONSTRUCTING HARRY   1997

Dir: Woody Allen. *Scr*: Woody Allen. *Cast*: Billy Crystal (The Devil)

The Devil offers his view on life.

>   THE DEVIL
> It's like Vegas. You're up, you're down, but in
> the end the house always wins.

AUSTIN POWERS: THE SPY WHO SHAGGED ME   1999

Dir: Jay Roach. *Scr*: Mike Myers, Michael McCullers. *Cast*: Mike Myers (Dr Evil)

Dr Evil explains to his son why he abandoned him.

>   DR EVIL
> You're semi-evil. You're quasi-evil. You're
> the margarine of evil. You're the Diet Coke of
> evil. Just one calorie, not evil enough.

AMERICAN PSYCHO

2000

Dir: Mary Harron. *Scr*: Mary Harron, Guinevere Turner. Based on a novel by
Bret Easton Ellis. *Cast*: Christian Bale (Patrick Bateman)

A jaded killer hires two prostitutes to amuse him.

> PATRICK

Do you like Phil Collins? I've been a big
Genesis fan ever since the release of their
1980 album, *Duke*. Before that, I really didn't
understand any of their work. Too artsy,
too intellectual. It was on *Duke* where Phil
Collins' presence became more apparent. I think
Invisible Touch was the group's undisputed
masterpiece. It's an epic meditation on
intangibility. At the same time, it deepens
and enriches the meaning of the preceding three
albums. Christy, take off your robe. Listen
to the brilliant ensemble playing of Banks,
Collins and Rutherford. You can practically
hear every nuance of every instrument. Sabrina,
remove your dress. In terms of lyrical
craftsmanship, the sheer songwriting, this
album hits a new peak of professionalism.
Sabrina, why don't you, uh, dance a little.
Take the lyrics to 'Land of Confusion'. In this
song, Phil Collins addresses the problems of
abusive political authority. 'In Too Deep' is
the most moving pop song of the 1980s, about
monogamy and commitment. The song is extremely
uplifting. Their lyrics are as positive and
affirmative as anything I've heard in rock.
Christy, get down on your knees so Sabrina can
see your asshole. Phil Collins' solo career

seems to be more commercial and therefore more
satisfying, in a narrower way. Especially songs
like 'In the Air Tonight' and 'Against All
Odds'. Sabrina, don't just stare at it, eat
it. But I also think Phil Collins works better
within the confines of the group than as a solo
artist, and I stress the word artist. This is
'Sussudio': a great, great song, a personal
favourite.

THE DEVIL'S REJECTS   2005

Dir: Rob Zombie. *Scr*: Rob Zombie. *Cast*: Bill Moseley (Otis B. Driftwood)

A murderous kidnapper confronts his victims.

> ### DRIFTWOOD
> I am the devil, and I am here to do the devil's
> work.

THE DEVIL WEARS PRADA   2006

Dir: David Frankel. *Scr*: Aline Brosh McKenna. Based on a novel by Lauren
Weisberger. *Cast*: Meryl Streep (Miranda Priestly)

The haughty editor of a fashion magazine upbraids her assistant.

> ### MIRANDA
> Details of your incompetence do not interest
> me. Tell Simone I'm not going to approve that
> girl that she sent me for the Brazilian layout.
> I asked for clean, athletic, smiling. She sent
> me dirty, tired and paunchy. And RSVP 'yes' to
> Michael Kors' party - I want the driver to drop
> me off at 9:30 and pick me up at 9:45 sharp. Call
> Natalie at Glorious Foods and tell her no for
> the fortieth time. No! I don't want dacquoise,

I want tortes filled with warm rhubarb compote.
Then call my ex-husband and remind him that the
parent—teacher conference is at Dalton tonight.
Then call my husband, ask him to meet me for
dinner at that place I went to with Massimo. Tell
Richard I saw the pictures that he sent for that
feature on the female paratroopers and they're
all so deeply unattractive. Is it impossible to
find a lovely, slender, female paratrooper? Am I
reaching for the stars here? Not really. Also, I
need to see all the things that Nigel has pulled
for Gwyneth's second cover try. I wonder if she's
lost any of that weight yet.

Miranda is widely held to be a portrait of Anna 'Nuclear' Wintour, editor of the New York edition of *Vogue*. Wintour allegedly told fashion designers who had been approached to play cameo roles that if they accepted, their collections would never again appear in her publication.

NO COUNTRY FOR OLD MEN   2007

Dir: Ethan Coen, Joel Coen. *Scr*: Ethan Coen, Joel Coen. Based on a novel by Cormac McCarthy. *Cast*: Javier Bardem (Anton Chigurh), Gene Jones (Proprietor)

Anton Chigurh, a hired killer, stops at a gas station but realizes the owner may be able to identify him.

                    CHIGURH
How much?

He points to a bag of nuts.

                    PROPRIETOR
Sixty-nine cents.

                    CHIGURH
This. And the gas.

PROPRIETOR

Y'all getting any rain up your way?

CHIGURH

What way would that be?

PROPRIETOR

I seen you was from Dallas.

CHIGURH

What business is it of yours where I'm from,
friendo?

PROPRIETOR

I didn't mean nothing by it.

CHIGURH

Didn't mean nothing.

PROPRIETOR

I was just passing the time. If you don't wanna
accept that, I don't know what else to do for
you. Will there be something else?

CHIGURH

I don't know. Will there?

PROPRIETOR

Is something wrong?

CHIGURH

With what?

PROPRIETOR

With anything?

CHIGURH

Is that what you're asking me? Is there something
wrong with anything?

The proprietor sounds afraid.

> PROPRIETOR
>
> Will there be anything else?

> CHIGURH
>
> You already asked me that.

> PROPRIETOR
>
> Well... I need to see about closing.

> CHIGURH
>
> See about closing.

> PROPRIETOR
>
> Yessir.

> CHIGURH
>
> What time do you close?

> PROPRIETOR
>
> Now. We close now.

> CHIGURH
>
> Now is not a time. What time do you close?

Directors Joel and Ethan Coen based Chigurh's bizarre hairdo on a 1979 photograph they found of a man visiting a brothel. When the normally suave Javier Bardem saw the results of the styling, he complained to the Coens: 'Now I won't get laid for the next two months.' The brothers just high-fived each other.

THE DARK KNIGHT 2008

Dir: Christopher Nolan. *Scr*: Jonathan Nolan, Christopher Nolan. *Cast*: Michael Caine (Alfred Pennyworth)

Alfred warns Bruce Wayne (aka Batman) not to query their adversary's motives.

>   ALFRED
> Some men just want to watch the world burn.

When Heath Ledger, playing the Joker, first appeared in a scene with Michael Caine, his performance was so frightening that Caine forgot his lines.

SHUTTER ISLAND   2010

Dir: Martin Scorsese. *Scr*: Laeta Kalogridis. Based on a novel by Dennis Lehane. *Cast*: Leonardo DiCaprio (Teddy Daniels), Mark Ruffalo (Chuck Aule)

Two US Marshals investigate a murder in a mental hospital on a remote island.

>   TEDDY
> You know, this place makes me wonder.

>   CHUCK
> Yeah, what's that, boss?

>   TEDDY
> Which would be worse — to live as a monster? Or to die as a good man?

WAR DOGS   2016

Dir: Todd Phillips. *Scr*: Stephen Chin, Todd Phillips. *Cast*: Bradley Cooper (Henry Girard)

>   HENRY
> I'm not a bad man, but in a certain situation I have to ask myself, 'What would a bad man do?'

POWER

CITIZEN KANE 1941

Dir: Orson Welles. *Scr*: Herman J. Mankiewicz, Orson Welles. *Cast*: Orson Welles (Charles Foster Kane)

Kane admits the newspaper he owns is an expensive folly.

> **KANE**
> You're right, I did lose a million dollars last
> year. I expect to lose a million dollars this
> year. I expect to lose a million dollars next
> year. You know, Mr Thatcher, at the rate of a
> million dollars a year, I'll have to close this
> place in... sixty years.

Citizen Kane topped *Sight and Sound* magazine's poll as best film for over fifty years from 1962 to 2012, but was so unpopular on its release that at the 1941 Oscars it was booed every time one of its nine nominations was announced.

YOUR ONLY COMPETITION IS IDIOTS

Herman J. Mankiewicz (1897–1953) was one of cinema's most talented writers, responsible for seventy-eight films including *Citizen Kane*, *It's a Wonderful World* and *The Pride of St Louis*. Shortly after moving to Los Angeles, he cabled his journalist friend Ben Hecht (*Scarface*, *Notorious*, *Wuthering Heights*): 'Will you accept $300 per week to work for Paramount? All expenses paid. $300 is peanuts. Millions are to be grabbed out here and your only competition is idiots. Don't let this get around.'

Writers have always had a conflicted relationship with film; for many, it feels like a choice between money and integrity. Many start out as acclaimed playwrights, novelists or journalists and resent the fact that in the world of screenplays their freedom diminishes in inverse proportion to the size of their pay cheque. As Harry Zimm says in *Get Shorty* (1995): 'I once asked this literary agent what kind of writing paid the best. He said, "Ransom notes".'

Mankiewicz probably didn't spend much time pondering this dilemma, since within a month of beginning his new career he was earning $400 [$5,700] a week. Hecht was similarly rewarded, with the additional advantage that he turned in his work with startling speed; he delivered *Scarface* (1932) in nine days.

At the time this new breed of writer was arriving on the West Coast the industry was still in upheaval following the advent of sound and it was the perfect opportunity to transform film from a medium of mute spectacle into a more sophisticated art form. Mankiewicz already had a reputation as the cleverest, funniest man in New York – Hecht famously described him as 'the Central Park West Voltaire' – and his style was perfectly suited to giving audiences the blend of fast-paced, intelligent and gritty humour we now associate with that era.

Perhaps the one aspect of cinema that didn't change once sound had become universally accepted was its hierarchy of talent. In the theatre, a successful playwright will have a higher billing than the director: the work is essentially his. But the legacy of silent films meant that audiences paid primarily to see the actors. They might remember the studio and the director's name, but the idea of going to the pictures on the basis of who had written the film remained largely irrelevant.

Mankiewicz was well aware he would never be as famous as the films he wrote, although he never lost his sense of humour about the way the industry operated:

'In a novel the hero can lay ten girls and marry a virgin for the finish. In a movie this is not allowed. The villain can lay anybody he wants, have as much fun as he wants cheating and stealing, getting rich and whipping the servants. But you have to shoot him in the end. When he falls with a bullet in his forehead, it is advisable that he clutch at the Gobelin tapestry on the wall and bring it down over his head like a symbolic shroud. Also, covered by such a tapestry, the actor does not have to hold his breath while being photographed as a dead man.'

Not surprisingly, his outspoken manner caused plenty of battles with his paymasters. Pauline Kael recounts of one lost screenplay:

'When a studio attempted to punish him for his customary misbehaviour by assigning him to a *Rin Tin Tin* picture, he rebelled by turning in a script that began with the craven dog frightened by a mouse and reached its climax with a house on fire and the dog taking a baby into the flames.'

Sometimes, it seemed, he longed for a quieter life, settling down with one of the leading ladies from his films. Even then, his tongue remained firmly in his cheek:

'Barbara Stanwyck is my favorite. My God, I could just sit and dream of being married to her, having a little cottage out in the hills, vines around the door. I'd come home from the office tired and weary, and I'd be met by Barbara, walking through the door holding an apple pie she had cooked herself. And wearing no drawers.'

MAJOR BARBARA   1941

Dir: Gabriel Pascal. *Scr*: George Bernard Shaw, based on his play. *Cast*: Robert Morley (Andrew Undershaft)

Undershaft is not afraid to tell his daughter what he feels about his money.

> **UNDERSHAFT**
> My religion? My dear, I'm a millionaire. That's
> my religion.

THE MAN WHO CAME TO DINNER   1942

Dir: William Keighley. *Scr*: Julius J. Epstein, Philip G. Epstein. Based on a play by George S. Kaufman, Moss Hart. *Cast*: Monty Woolley (Sheridan Whiteside)

Whiteside terrorizes everyone in the house where he stays as a guest.

> **WHITESIDE**
> Now will you all leave quietly, or must I ask
> Miss Cutler to pass among you with a baseball
> bat?

THE DAY THE EARTH STOOD STILL   1951

Dir: Robert Wise. *Scr*: Edmund H. North. Based on a story by Harry Bates. *Cast*: Michael Rennie (Klaatu)

Klaatu, a visitor from outer space, brings a message to all humanity.

> **KLAATU**
> Now, we do not pretend to have achieved
> perfection, but we do have a system, and it
> works. I came here to give you these facts.
> It is no concern of ours how you run your own
> planet, but if you threaten to extend your
> violence, this Earth of yours will be reduced
> to a burned-out cinder. Your choice is simple:

join us and live in peace, or pursue your
present course and face obliteration. We shall
be waiting for your answer. The decision rests
with you.

STRANGERS ON A TRAIN   1951

Dir: Alfred Hitchcock. *Scr*: Raymond Chandler, Czenzi Ormonde, Whitfield
Cook. Based on a novel by Patricia Highsmith. *Cast*: Patricia Hitchcock (Barbara
Morton)

Barbara seems at ease with the political world her family inhabits.

> BARBARA
>
> Oh, Daddy doesn't mind a little scandal. He's a
> senator.

Raymond Chandler, one of the screenwriters, did not enjoy his
collaboration with Hitchcock. As the director arrived for one story
meeting, Chandler yelled out of the window: 'Look at the fat bastard
trying to get out of his car!'

THE TEAHOUSE OF THE AUGUST MOON   1956

Dir: Daniel Mann. *Scr*: John Patrick, adapted from his play. Based on a book by
Vern J. Sneider. *Cast*: Paul Ford (Colonel Purdy), Glenn Ford (Captain Fisby)

After the war, American troops are sent to Okinawa to teach the
locals democracy.

> COLONEL PURDY
> You'll need an interpreter.

> CAPTAIN FISBY
> I can study the language.

> COLONEL PURDY
> No need. We won the war.

SWEET SMELL OF SUCCESS   1957

Dir: Alexander Mackendrick. *Scr*: Clifford Odets, Ernest Lehman. Based on a novella by Ernest Lehman. *Cast*: Unknown (Jimmy Weldon)

Musician Jimmy is furious that his expensive publicity agent is not advancing his career.

> JIMMY
> It's a dirty job, but I pay clean money for it.

12 ANGRY MEN   1957

Dir: Sidney Lumet. *Scr*: Reginald Rose. *Cast*: Lee J. Cobb (Juror #3), Henry Fonda (Juror #8)

Twelve jurors deliberate their verdict in a murder trial.

> JUROR #3
> You're talking about a matter of seconds. Nobody can be that accurate.

> JUROR #8
> Well, I think that testimony that can put a boy into the electric chair *should* be that accurate.

Henry Fonda, at that time a huge star, was asked by United Artists to make the film and he acted as producer as well as leading man; he personally chose Sidney Lumet to direct. The process was intense, as Lumet insisted on long rehearsals in which the cast remained in the jurors' room without respite to create the feeling of a group under relentless pressure.

The film lasts ninety-six minutes, of which ninety-three take place in the room where the jurors congregate; the set was a mere sixteen by twenty-four feet. As the story progresses, Lumet gradually increased the focal length of the camera's lenses and lowered the angle of the shots to intensify his portraits of the characters and emphasize the claustrophobia of their surroundings.

TOUCH OF EVIL   1958

Dir: Orson Welles. *Scr*: Orson Welles. Based on a novel by Whit Masterson. *Cast*: Charlton Heston (Miguel 'Mike' Vargas)

VARGAS

A policeman's job is only easy in a police state.

JUDGMENT AT NUREMBERG   1961

Dir: Stanley Kramer. *Scr*: Abby Mann. *Cast*: Spencer Tracy (Judge Dan Haywood)

An American judge passes sentence on a German counterpart accused of war crimes.

JUDGE HAYWOOD

Janning, to be sure, is a tragic figure.
We believe he loathed the evil he did. But
compassion for the present torture of his soul
must not beget forgetfulness of the torture and
death of millions by the government of which
he was a part. Janning's record and his fate
illuminate the most shattering truth that has
emerged from this trial. If he and the other
defendants were all depraved perverts — if
the leaders of the Third Reich were sadistic
monsters and maniacs — these events would have
no more moral significance than an earthquake
or other natural catastrophes. But this trial
has shown that under the stress of a national
crisis, men — even able and extraordinary men
— can delude themselves into the commission
of crimes and atrocities so vast and heinous
as to stagger the imagination. No one who has
sat through this trial can ever forget. The
sterilization of men because of their political

```
beliefs, the murder of children — how easily
that can happen. There are those in our country
today, too, who speak of the 'protection' of
the country. Of 'survival'. The answer to
that is: survival as what? A country isn't a
rock. And it isn't an extension of one's self.
It is what it stands for — when standing for
something is the most difficult. Before the
people of the world — let it now be noted in
our decision here that this is what we stand
for: justice, truth — and the value of a single
human being.
```

Many of the cast worked for less than their usual salary because they believed the subject matter was so important. Some of the court scenes feature actual footage from the concentration camps.

KNIFE IN THE WATER / *Nóż w wodzie*   1964

Dir: Roman Polanski. *Scr*: Jakub Goldberg, Roman Polanski, Jerzy Skolimowski. *Cast*: Leon Niemczyk (Andrzej)

Andrzej and a mysterious traveller become antagonistic on a sailing trip.

```
              ANDRZEJ
   If two men are on board, one is the skipper.
```

MY FAIR LADY   1964

Dir: George Cukor. *Scr*: Alan Jay Lerner. Based on a play by George Bernard Shaw. *Cast*: Wilfrid Hyde-White (Colonel Hugh Pickering), Stanley Holloway (Alfred P. Doolittle)

Pickering has offered to pay for Eliza Doolittle's elocution lessons, but Eliza's father demands a share of his generosity too.

PICKERING

Have you no morals, man?

DOOLITTLE

Nah, can't afford 'em. Neither could you, if you
were as poor as me.

A MAN FOR ALL SEASONS   1966

Dir: Fred Zinnemann. *Scr*: Robert Bolt, based on his play. *Cast*: Paul Scofield (Sir
Thomas More), Leo McKern (Thomas Cromwell)

Cromwell, a minister of Henry VIII, applies political pressure to Sir
Thomas More.

SIR THOMAS MORE

You threaten like a dockside bully.

CROMWELL

How should I threaten?

SIR THOMAS MORE

Like a minister of state. With justice.

CROMWELL

Oh, justice is what you're threatened with.

SIR THOMAS MORE

Then I am not threatened.

Writer Robert Bolt took the title for his play from this contemporaneous description of the statesman: 'More is a man of an angel's wit and singular learning; I know not his fellow. For where is the man of that gentleness, lowliness and affability? And, as time requireth, a man of marvellous mirth and pastimes, and sometime of as sad gravity: a man for all seasons.'

COOL HAND LUKE   1967

Dir: Stuart Rosenberg. *Scr*: Frank Pierson, Donn Pearce. Based on a novel by
Donn Pierce. *Cast*: Clifton James (Carr), Paul Newman (Luke Jackson)

Cool Hand Luke meets Carr, his prison warder.

              CARR
Them clothes got laundry numbers on them. You
remember your number and always wear the ones
that has your number. Any man forgets his number
spends a night in the box. These here spoons you
keep with you. Any man loses his spoon spends
a night in the box. There's no playing grab-ass
or fighting in the building. You got a grudge
against another man, you fight him Saturday
afternoon. Any man playing grab-ass or fighting
in the building spends a night in the box. First
bell's at five minutes of eight when you will
get in your bunk. Last bell is at eight. Any man
not in his bunk at eight spends the night in the
box. There is no smoking in the prone position
in bed. To smoke you must have both legs over
the side of your bunk. Any man caught smoking
in the prone position in bed. . . spends a night
in the box. You get two sheets. Every Saturday,
you put the clean sheet on the top. . . the top
sheet on the bottom. . . and the bottom sheet you
turn in to the laundry boy. Any man turns in the
wrong sheet spends a night in the box. No one'll
sit in the bunks with dirty pants on. Any man
with dirty pants on sitting on the bunks spends
a night in the box. Any man don't bring back
his empty pop bottle spends a night in the box.
Any man loud talking spends a night in the box.
You got questions, you come to me. I'm Carr, the
floor walker. I'm responsible for order in here.
Any man don't keep order spends a night in. . .

LUKE

. . . the box.

CARR

I hope you ain't going to be a hard case.

THE LION IN WINTER   1968

Dir: Anthony Harvey. *Scr*: James Goldman, based on his play. *Cast*: Katharine Hepburn (Eleanor of Aquitaine)

Eleanor of Aquitaine begs her sons to settle the succession to their father's throne without bloodshed.

ELEANOR

We are the origins of war. Not history's
forces, nor the times, nor justice, nor the
lack of it, nor causes, nor religions, nor
ideas, nor kinds of government nor any other
thing! We are the killers; we breed war. We
carry it, like syphilis, inside. Dead bodies
rot in field and stream because the living
ones are rotten. For the love of God, can't
we love each other just a little? That's how
peace begins. We have so much to love each
other for. We have such possibilities, my
children; we could change the world.

IF...   1968

Dir: Lindsay Anderson. *Scr*: David Sherwin, John Howlett. *Cast*: Malcolm McDowell (Mick Travis)

Mick rebels against his conservative, repressive schooling.

MICK

One man can change the world with a bullet
in the right place.

A WORD TO THE WISE

Producer Samuel Goldwyn famously said: 'Pictures are for entertainment – messages should be delivered by Western Union.' Even so, film-makers can rarely resist an opportunity to share a little wisdom. Some of the following lines are as pithy as aphorisms, others as impenetrable as a Zen koan, but if you take their advice, choose carefully...

Front seldom tell truth. To know occupants of house, always look in backyard.
Charlie Chan in London (1934)

Never do nothing you wouldn't want printed on the front page of the New York Times.
Born Yesterday (1950)

Don't ever hit your mother with a shovel. It leaves a dull impression on her mind.
Butch Cassidy and the Sundance Kid (1969)

A little nonsense now and then is relished by the wisest men.
Willy Wonka & the Chocolate Factory (1971)

Two wrongs don't make a right but three rights will make a left.
Caddyshack (1980)

Named must your fear be before banish it you can.
Star Wars V: The Empire Strikes Back (1980)

It's such a fine line between stupid and clever.
This Is Spinal Tap (1984)

There are three rules that I live by: never get less than twelve hours sleep; never play cards with a guy who has the same first name as a city; and never get involved with a woman with a tattoo of a dagger on her body.
Teen Wolf (1985)

I don't make things difficult. That's the way they get, all by themselves.
Lethal Weapon (1987)

A fool and his money are lucky enough to get together in the first place.
Wall Street (1987)

Truth hurts. Maybe not as much as jumping on a bicycle with the seat missing, but it hurts.
The Naked Gun 2½: The Smell of Fear (1991)

You know what the trouble about real life is? There's no danger music.
The Cable Guy (1996)

You are not a beautiful or unique snowflake. You're the same decaying organic matter as everything else.
Fight Club (1999)

The best way to get over a man is to get under a new one.
Good Advice (2001)

Worrying is like a rocking chair. It gives you something to do but it doesn't get you anywhere.
Van Wilder (2002)

Never trust a guy who fumbles for the check.
Anything Else (2003)

Never pat a burning dog.
A Good Year (2006)

The further you run from your sins, the more
exhausted you are when they catch up to you.
Inside Man (2006)

That which does not kill you only makes you...
stranger.
The Dark Knight (2008)

At the end of a war you need some soldiers
left, or else it looks like you've lost.
In the Loop (2009)

When you go fishing you can catch a lot of
fish, or you can catch a big fish. You ever
walk into a guy's den and see a picture of him
standing next to fourteen trout?
The Social Network (2010)

W.R.: MYSTERIES OF THE ORGANISM /
W.r.- Misterije Organizma **1971**

Dir: Dušan Makavejev. *Scr*: Dušan Makavejev. *Cast*: Zoran Radmilović (Zoran Radmilović)

A Communist party member vents his frustration with the system.

> RADMILOVIĆ
>
> Gentlemen, in our democracy everyone is entitled
> to a doughnut. Some get the doughnut, others get
> the hole in the doughnut.

AGUIRRE, WRATH OF GOD / *Aguirre, der Zorn Gottes* **1972**

Dir: Werner Herzog. *Scr*: Werner Herzog. *Cast*: Klaus Kinski (Don Lope de Aguirre)

Insane, ambitious conquistador Aguirre leads his men in search of El Dorado.

> AGUIRRE
>
> I, the wrath of God, will marry my own daughter
> and with her I will found the purest dynasty the
> earth has ever seen.

Despite being shot entirely in Peru, the crew for the production consisted of only eight people. Most of the film was shot on a 35mm camera Herzog stole from his film school.

CHINATOWN **1974**

Dir: Roman Polanski. *Scr*: Robert Towne. *Cast*: John Huston (Noah Cross)

A private investigator confronts Noah Cross, an unscrupulous property developer.

> NOAH
>
> Of course I'm respectable. I'm old. Politicians,

ugly buildings and whores all get respectable if
they last long enough.

THE GODFATHER: PART II   1974

Dir: Francis Ford Coppola. *Scr*: Francis Ford Coppola, Mario Puzo. Based on a
novel by Mario Puzo. *Cast*: Al Pacino (Michael Corleone)

                    MICHAEL
If anything in this life is certain, if history
has taught us anything, it is that you can kill
anyone.

MONTY PYTHON AND THE HOLY GRAIL   1975

Dir: Terry Gilliam, Terry Jones. *Scr*: Graham Chapman, John Cleese, Eric
Idle, Terry Gilliam, Terry Jones, Michael Palin. *Cast*: Graham Chapman (King
Arthur), Terry Jones (Woman), Michael Palin (Dennis)

                    KING ARTHUR
I am your king.

                    WOMAN
Well, I didn't vote for you.

                    KING ARTHUR
You don't vote for kings.

                    WOMAN
Well, how did you become king then?

                    KING ARTHUR
The Lady of the Lake, her arm clad in the
purest shimmering samite, held aloft Excalibur
from the bosom of the water, signifying by
divine providence that I, Arthur, was to carry
Excalibur. That is why I am your king.

DENNIS
```
Listen, strange women lying in ponds
distributing swords is no basis for a system
of government. Supreme executive power derives
from a mandate from the masses, not from some
farcical aquatic ceremony.
```

The film's tight budget did not allow for many lavish historic locations. Another of the story's highlights – Lancelot's running dash to Swamp Castle – was filmed on Hampstead Heath beside one of London's busiest road junctions.

NASHVILLE   1975

Dir: Robert Altman. *Scr*: Joan Tewkesbury. *Cast*: Thomas Hal Phillips (Hal Phillip Walker)

Party candidate Hal hopes to woo voters with an unpretentious speech.

HAL
```
Who do you think is running Congress? Farmers?
Engineers? Teachers? Businessmen? No, my friends.
Congress is run by lawyers. A lawyer is trained
for two things and two things only. To clarify
– that's one. And to confuse – that's the other.
He does whichever is to his client's advantage.
Did you ever ask a lawyer the time of day? He
told you how to make a watch, didn't he? Ever ask
a lawyer how to get to Mr Jones' house in the
country? You got lost, didn't you?
```

The film contains a huge cast of characters and the dialogue was almost entirely improvised by them from the story outline. All the actors playing musicians wrote and performed their own songs, and all the onscreen music was recorded live.

ALL THE PRESIDENT'S MEN   1976

Dir: Alan J. Pakula. *Scr*: William Goldman. Based on a book by Carl Bernstein and Bob Woodward. *Cast*: Jason Robards (Ben Bradlee)

The editor of the *Washington Post* berates two reporters who have been uncovering the story of the Watergate break-in.

> BRADLEE
>
> You know the results of the latest Gallup Poll? Half the country never even heard of the word Watergate. Nobody gives a shit. You guys are probably pretty tired, right? Well, you should be. Go on home, get a nice hot bath. Rest up. . . fifteen minutes. Then get your asses back in gear. We're under a lot of pressure, you know, and you put us there. Nothing's riding on this except the, uh, First Amendment to the Constitution, freedom of the press, and maybe the future of the country. Not that any of that matters, but if you guys fuck up again, I'm going to get mad. Goodnight.

MONTY PYTHON'S THE MEANING OF LIFE   1983

Dir: Terry Jones, Terry Gilliam. *Scr*: Graham Chapman, John Cleese, Terry Gilliam, Eric Idle, Terry Jones, Michael Palin. *Cast*: Michael Palin (Chaplain), John Cleese (Humphrey Williams)

> CHAPLAIN
>
> Let us praise God. O Lord...
>
> CONGREGATION
>
> O Lord...
>
> CHAPLAIN
>
> ... Ooh, You are so big...

CONGREGATION

... ooh, You are so big...

CHAPLAIN

... So absolutely huge.

CONGREGATION

... So absolutely huge.

CHAPLAIN

Gosh, we're all really impressed down here, I can tell You.

CONGREGATION

Gosh, we're all really impressed down here, I can tell You.

CHAPLAIN

Forgive us, O Lord, for this, our dreadful toadying, and...

CONGREGATION

And barefaced flattery.

CHAPLAIN

But You are so strong and, well, just so super.

CONGREGATION

Fantastic.

HUMPHREY

Amen.

CONGREGATION

Amen.

The Python team refused to show the studio a script on the basis that 'If we couldn't work out how to make a Monty Python film, they couldn't tell us.' Instead they submitted an outline budget and a poem:

There's everything in this movie,
Everything that fits.
From the Meaning of Life in the universe,
To girls with great big tits.
We've got movie stars and foreign cars,
Explosions and the lot
Filmed as only we know how,
On the budget that we've got.
We spent a fortune on locations
And quite a bit on drink
And there's even the odd philosophical joke,
Just to make you buggers think.
Yet some parts are as serious
And as deep as you could wish
But largely it's all tits and ass
And quite a bit of fish.
Other bits are fairly childish
And some are frankly rude
But at least we've got a lot of nice girls
All banging around in the nude.
So take your seats, enjoy yourselves
And let's just hope it's funny
Because it's not only done to make you laugh
But to make us lots of money.
So sit back and have a good time
With your boyfriend or your wife
Relax and just enjoy yourself
For this is the Meaning of Life.

THE LAST EMPEROR
1987

Dir: Bernardo Bertolucci. *Scr*: Mark Peploe, Bernardo Bertolucci. *Cast*: Peter O'Toole (Reginald Johnston), John Lone (Pu Yi)

The fifteen-year-old Emperor of China quizzes his Scottish tutor about conditions outside the palace.

> PU YI
>
> Is it true, Mr Johnston, that many people out there have had their heads cut off?

> JOHNSTON
>
> It is true, your Majesty. Many heads have been chopped off. It does stop them thinking.

The logistics for the epic production were breathtaking. The Internet Movie Database cites the following statistics:

- 19,000 extras were used over the course of the film;

- Hairdresser Giancarlo De Leonardis imported 2,200 pounds of human hair to make the elaborate wigs needed for the court. For the coronation scenes, his staff spent ten days training fifty Chinese to pin wigs and plaits onto 2,000 extras in under two hours;

- An Italian chef was brought in to cook for the international cast. He brought with him 22,000 bottles of Italian mineral water, 450 pounds of Italian coffee, 250 gallons of olive oil and 4,500 pounds of pasta;

- The Buddhist lamas who appear in the film could not be touched by women, so extra male wardrobe helpers were hired to dress them;

- Security was so tight around the shoot that when, one day, Peter O'Toole forgot his pass, he was denied entrance to the set.

Dir: Oliver Stone. *Scr*: Oliver Stone, Stanley Weiser. *Cast*: Michael Douglas (Gordon Gekko)

Shareholder and corporate raider Gordon Gekko explains his decision to buy an ailing paper company.

> GEKKO
>
> Teldar Paper, Mr Cromwell, Teldar Paper has thirty-three different vice presidents each earning over 200,000 dollars a year. Now, I have spent the last two months analysing what all these guys do, and I still can't figure it out. One thing I do know is that our paper company lost 110 million dollars last year, and I'll bet that half of that was spent in all the paperwork going back and forth between all these vice presidents. The new law of evolution in corporate America seems to be survival of the unfittest. Well, in my book you either do it right or you get eliminated. In the last seven deals that I've been involved with, there were 2.5 million stockholders who have made a pretax profit of 12 billion dollars. Thank you. I am not a destroyer of companies. I am a liberator of them! The point is, ladies and gentlemen, that greed, for lack of a better word, is good. Greed is right, greed works. Greed clarifies, cuts through, and captures the essence of the evolutionary spirit. Greed, in all of its forms; greed for life, for money, for love, knowledge has marked the upward surge of mankind. And greed, you mark my words, will not only save Teldar Paper, but that other malfunctioning corporation called the USA.

GLENGARRY GLEN ROSS   1992

Dir: James Foley. *Scr*: David Mamet, based on his play. *Cast*: Alec Baldwin (Blake)

The employees in a real estate office are encouraged to be ruthless.

> BLAKE
> We're adding a little something to this month's
> sales contest. As you all know, first prize is a
> Cadillac Eldorado . . . Second prize is a set of
> steak knives. Third prize is you're fired.

PHILADELPHIA   1993

Dir: Jonathan Demme. *Scr*: Ron Nyswaner. *Cast*: Charles Napier (Judge Garnett),
Denzel Washington (Joe Miller)

Lawyer Joe Miller reminds a trial judge we live in an imperfect world.

> JUDGE GARNETT
> In this courtroom, Mr Miller, justice is blind
> to matters of race, creed, colour, religion, and
> sexual orientation.

> JOE
> With all due respect, your honour, we don't live
> in this courtroom, do we?

COLOR OF NIGHT   1994

Dir: Richard Rush. *Scr*: Matthew Chapman, Billy Ray. *Cast*: Bruce Willis (Dr
Bill Capa), Rubén Blades (Detective Hector Martinez)

A psychiatrist is questioned after one of his patients commits suicide.

> DR CAPA
> Do I need a lawyer?

> DETECTIVE MARTINEZ
> You're in LA. Everybody needs a lawyer.

DISCLOSURE

Dir: Barry Levinson. *Scr*: Paul Attanasio. Based on a novel by Michael Crichton. *Cast*: Roma Maffia (Catherine Alvarez)

A lawyer tries to dissuade her client from taking action after he has been sexually harassed by his female boss.

> CATHERINE
>
> If you sue, you'll never get another job in the computer business; if you don't sue they'll bury you in Austin. If you sue it's news; if you don't it's gossip. If you sue nobody will believe you; if you don't, your wife won't. They will make your life into a living hell for the next three years until this case goes to trial. And for that privilege, it's going to cost you a minimum of a hundred thousand dollars. Do you not think it's a game, Mr Sanders? It's a game to them. How do you feel about losing?

DEAD MAN WALKING

Dir: Tim Robbins. *Scr*: Tim Robbins. Based on a book by Helen Prejean. *Cast*: Susan Sarandon (Sister Helen Prejean), Unknown (Prison Guard)

A guard supervising an inmate on death row is surprised by the compassion shown by a visitor.

> SISTER PREJEAN
>
> I just don't see the sense of killing people to say that killing people's wrong.

> PRISON GUARD
>
> You know what the Bible says, 'An eye for an eye'.

> SISTER PREJEAN
>
> You know what else the Bible asks for death

as a punishment? For adultery, prostitution,
homosexuality, trespass upon sacred grounds,
profaning a sabbath and contempt to parents.

PRISON GUARD
I ain't gonna get in no Bible quoting with no
nun, 'cause I'm gonna lose.

Director Tim Robbins cast his wife in the Oscar-winning lead role
and used his parents, sons and sister in various scenes. His brother
David wrote the soundtrack.

SCHIZOPOLIS   1996
Dir: Steven Soderbergh. *Scr*: Steven Soderbergh. *Cast*: Margaret Lawhon (TV
Newscaster)

In a baffling, dystopian world even the news broadcasts are surreal.

TV NEWSCASTER
A New Mexico woman was named Final Arbiter of
Taste and Justice today, ending God's lengthy
search for someone to straighten this country
out. Eileen Harriet Palglace will have final say
on every known subject, including who should be
put to death, what clothes everyone should wear,
what movies suck, and whether bald men who grow
ponytails should still get laid.

SWINGERS   1996
Dir: Doug Liman. *Scr*: Jon Favreau. *Cast*: Vince Vaughn (Trent Walker)

Trent tries to persuade some girls at a nightclub that his friend is a
man to be reckoned with.

TRENT
This is the guy behind the guy behind the guy.

Dir: Woody Allen. *Scr*: Woody Allen. *Cast*: Caroline Aaron (Doris), Woody Allen (Harry Block)

Doris despairs of author Harry's lifestyle and preoccupations.

        DORIS
You have no values. With you it's all nihilism,
cynicism, sarcasm, and orgasm.

        HARRY
Hey, in France I could run for office with that
slogan and win.

'IF MY FILMS DON'T SHOW A PROFIT, I KNOW I'M DOING SOMETHING RIGHT'

Enduringly known for his curmudgeonly New York Jewish wisecracks, his controversial love life and his refusal to attend award ceremonies, Woody Allen (b. 1935) has been writing, acting and directing for six decades and shows little sign of slowing. To date he has won four Oscars, two for *Annie Hall* (directing and screenplay, 1978) and one each for *Hannah and Her Sisters* (screenplay, 1987) and *Midnight in Paris* (screenplay, 2012). Although the hits have been interspersed with less successful endeavours, his inventiveness has rarely wavered and his focus on character ensures his projects attract the biggest screen stars as well as perennial collaborators.

Relying largely on regular producing partners and crew, he keeps his budgets modest and retains the right to 'final cut', ensuring his films have a unique authorial voice; even his interviews, stand-up routines and short-story collections carry the familiar Allen stamp.

From *Getting Even* (1971), a collection of short stories:

- Can we actually 'know' the universe? My God, it's hard enough finding your way around in Chinatown.

- I don't believe in an afterlife, although I am bringing a change of underwear.

- Eternal nothingness is OK if you're dressed for it.

- Not only is there no God, but try getting a plumber on weekends.

From *Without Feathers* (1975), another collection of short stories:

- As the poet said, 'Only God can make a tree' – probably because it's so hard to figure out how to get the bark on.

- Money is better than poverty, if only for financial reasons.

- What a wonderful thing, to be conscious! I wonder what the people in New Jersey do.

- Why does man kill? He kills for food. And not only food: frequently there must be a beverage.

- It's not that I'm afraid to die, I just don't want to be there when it happens.

- The lion and the calf shall lie down together but the calf won't get much sleep.

As a stand-up comic:

- I was in analysis. I was suicidal. As a matter of fact, I would have killed myself, but I was in analysis with a strict Freudian and if you kill yourself they make you pay for the sessions you miss.

- I feel sex is a beautiful thing between two people. Between five, it's fantastic.

- I was involved in an extremely good example of oral contraception two weeks ago. I asked a girl to go to bed with me, she said 'no'.

- I was thrown out of college for cheating on the metaphysics exam; I looked into the soul of the boy sitting next to me.

- When I was kidnapped, my parents snapped into action. They rented out my room.

- Interestingly, according to modern astronomers, space is finite. This is a very comforting thought – particularly for people who can never remember where they have left things.

From interviews between 1985 and 2011:

- It figures you've got to hate yourself if you've got any integrity at all.

- If my films make one more person miserable, I'll feel I have done my job.

- Life doesn't imitate art, it imitates bad television.

- My relationship with death remains the same – I'm strongly against it.

- Someone once asked me if my dream was to live on in the hearts of people, and I said I would prefer to live on in my apartment.

- For some reason I'm more appreciated in France than I am back home. The subtitles must be incredibly good.

- I think universal harmony is a pipe dream and it may be more productive to focus on more modest goals, like a ban on yodelling.

- I do feel that [life] is a grim, painful, nightmarish, meaningless experience, and that the only way that you can be happy is if you tell yourself some lies and deceive yourself.

- The two biggest myths about me are that I'm an intellectual, because I wear these glasses, and that I'm an artist because my films lose money.

- I'm not an actor. I can't play Chekhov, I can't play Shakespeare or Strindberg. I can do that thing that I do. There's a few different kinds of things I can act credibly. I can play an intellectual or a low-life.

THE ICE STORM   1997

Dir: Ang Lee. *Scr*: James Schamus. Based on a novel by Rick Moody. *Cast*: Christina Ricci (Wendy Hood)

A disaffected teenager is invited to say grace at supper with her family.

>   WENDY
> Dear Lord, thank you for this Thanksgiving
> holiday. And for all the material possessions we
> have and enjoy. And for letting us white people
> kill all the Indians and steal their tribal
> lands. And stuff ourselves like pigs, even though
> children in Asia are being napalmed.

Rick Moody, author of the novel, was so pleased with the film he sobbed through the end credits.

MAGNOLIA   1999

Dir: Paul Thomas Anderson. *Scr*: Paul Thomas Anderson. *Cast*: Philip Baker Hall
(Jimmy Gator)

A police officer tries to balance compassion with justice.

> JIMMY
>
> Sometimes people need a little help. Sometimes
> people need to be forgiven. And sometimes they
> need to go to jail.

Paul Thomas Anderson initially approached George C. Scott to play
the role of Earl Partridge, a man dying from cancer. Scott threw the
script across the room, saying 'This is the worst fucking thing I've
ever read.' Anderson then took the project to Jason Robards, who
revealed he had actually been diagnosed with the disease. When
he told Anderson 'I don't know if I can do it – I'm on oxygen', the
director cheerfully replied: 'Bring it along, it'll save me on props.'

TRAFFIC   2000

Dir: Steven Soderbergh. *Scr*: Stephen Gaghan. *Cast*: Michael Douglas (Robert
Wakefield)

An Ohio judge appointed as head of the Office of National Drug
Control describes his new job.

> ROBERT
>
> What's Washington like? Well, it's like Calcutta
> — surrounded by beggars. The only difference is
> the beggars in Washington wear 1,500-dollar suits
> and they don't say please or thank you.

On the first day of shooting *Sex, Lies, and Videotape* Soderbergh's
producers sent him a joking telegram saying he 'couldn't direct
traffic', let alone a feature film. Twelve years later he won an Oscar
for directing *Traffic*.

As with telephone numbers in films, which are frequently composed with the structure 555-xxxx to ensure no viewer might dial and achieve a successful connection to a random subscriber, vehicle plates follow a format which means they have no actual bearing on established registrations. One of the characters' cars has the plate 2GAT123: the same California ID – on different vehicles – also appears in *Beverly Hills Cop II, L.A. Story, Go, Pay It Forward, Mulholland Drive, Crazy/Beautiful, Two and a Half Men*, and *S.W.A.T.*

BOILER ROOM   2000

Dir: Ben Younger. *Scr*: Ben Younger. *Cast*: Ben Affleck (Jim Young)

Ambitious stockbroker Jim addresses a new intake of recruits to his company.

> JIM
>
> There's an important phrase that we use here, and I think it's time that you all learned it. Act as if. You understand what that means? Act as if you are the fucking President of this firm. Act as if you got a nine-inch cock. Okay? Act as if.

THE LORD OF THE RINGS:
THE FELLOWSHIP OF THE RING   2001

Dir: Peter Jackson. *Scr*: Peter Jackson, Fran Walsh, Philippa Boyens. Based on a book by J. R. R. Tolkien. *Cast*: Ian McKellen (Gandalf)

> GANDALF
>
> One Ring to rule them all,
> One Ring to find them,
> One Ring to bring them all
> And in the darkness bind them.

CRASH   2004

Dir: Paul Haggis. *Scr*: Paul Haggis, Robert Moresco. *Cast*: Chris 'Ludacris' Bridges (Anthony), Larenz Tate (Peter Waters)

A woman crosses the street to avoid two black men in her middle-class neighbourhood.

                    ANTHONY
Wait, wait, wait. See what that woman just did?
You see that? She got colder the minute she saw
us. Man, look around you, man. You couldn't
find a whiter, safer or better-lit part of the
city right now. But yet this white woman sees
two black guys who look like UCLA students
strolling down the sidewalk, and her reaction
is blind fear? I mean, look at us, dawg, are
we dressed like gang-bangers? Huh? No. Do we
look threatening? No. Fact: If anyone should
be scared around here, it's us! We're the only
two black faces surrounded by a sea of over-
caffeinated white people patrolled by the
trigger happy LAPD. So you tell me. Why aren't
we scared?

                    PETER
Because we have guns?

                    ANTHONY
You could be right.

SYRIANA   2005

Dir: Stephen Gaghan. *Scr*: Stephen Gaghan. Based on a book by Robert Baer. *Cast*: Tim Blake Nelson (Danny Dalton)

An oil executive dismisses warnings that his business practices are illegal.

                    DANNY

Corruption is our protection. Corruption keeps
us safe and warm. Corruption is why you and I
are prancing around in here instead of fighting
over scraps of meat out in the streets.
Corruption is why we win.

'Syriana' is a term used by US political think tanks to describe their vision of a newly structured Middle East. Writer/director Gaghan did extensive research into the global oil industry before he began work on the script, visiting Washington DC, the French Riviera, Lebanon, Syria and Dubai.

He met businessmen, lobbyists, arms dealers and oil traders as well as members of Hezbollah including on one occasion – when he was blindfolded for security reasons – Sheik Mohammed Hussein Fadlallah.

THERE WILL BE BLOOD   2007

Dir: Paul Thomas Anderson. *Scr*: Paul Thomas Anderson. Based on a novel by Upton Sinclair. *Cast*: Daniel Day-Lewis (Daniel Plainview), Paul Dano (Eli Sunday)

Plainview explains how he no longer needs to buy Eli's land because he has already drilled beneath it to steal his oil.

                  PLAINVIEW

Stop crying, you snivelling ass! Stop your
nonsense. You're just afterbirth, Eli—

                    ELI

No...

                  PLAINVIEW

 slithering out of your mother's filth.

                    ELI

No . . .

                    PLAINVIEW

They should have put you in a glass jar on
the mantlepiece. Where were you when Paul was
suckling at his mother's teat? Where were you?
Who was nursing you, poor Eli? One of Bandy's
sows? That land has been had. Nothing you can
do about it. It's gone. It's had. You lose.

                    ELI

If you would just take this lease, Daniel—

Plainview screams like a madman.

                    PLAINVIEW

Drainage! Drainage, Eli, you boy. Drained dry!

Plainview calms himself.

                    PLAINVIEW

I'm so sorry. Here, if you have a milkshake, and
I have a milkshake, and I have a straw — there
it is, that's a straw, you see? You watching?
And my straw reaches *acrooooooosss* the room, and
starts to drink your milkshake. I . . . drink . . .
your . . . milkshake! I drink it up!

Paul Thomas Anderson claimed he watched *The Treasure of the Sierra Madre* (1948) for inspiration every night while shooting. That film – about gold prospectors in Mexico – was directed by John Huston, on whom Day-Lewis based Plainview's voice and physical manner; he also studied oral histories of the period to shape his speech patterns.

THE JUDGE   2014

Dir: David Dobkin. *Scr:* Nick Schenk, Bill Dubuque. *Cast:* Robert Downey Jr. (Hank Palmer)

A shady lawyer persuades his principled client that only tricky skills can win a tricky case.

> HANK
>
> Everyone wants Atticus Finch until there's a dead hooker in the bathtub.

THREE BILLBOARDS OUTSIDE EBBING, MISSOURI   2017

Dir: Martin McDonagh. *Scr:* Martin McDonagh. *Cast:* Frances McDormand (Mildred)

> MILDRED
>
> Wow. When you can't trust the lawyers and the advertising men, what the hell's America coming to, huh?

WAR

ALL QUIET ON THE WESTERN FRONT   1930

Dir: Lewis Milestone. *Scr*: George Abbott, Maxwell Anderson, Erich Maria Remarque. Based on a book by Erich Maria Remarque. *Cast*: Edwin Maxwell (Herr Bäumer)

BÄUMER

You still think it's beautiful to die for your country. The first bombardment taught us better. When it comes to dying for your country, it's better not to die at all.

Germany was still sensitive about her defeat in the First World War and hard-core patriots tried to disrupt screenings by shouting slogans and releasing rats into theatres. When the Nazi party came to power, the film was banned and those who wanted to see it had to take special tours to neighbouring Switzerland and France where it played to full houses.

MRS MINIVER   1942

Dir: William Wyler. *Scr*: Arthur Wimperis, George Froeschel, James Hilton, Claudine West. Based on a novel by Jan Struther. *Cast*: Henry Wilcoxon (Vicar)

A vicar laments the parishioners his village has lost to the war.

VICAR

We, in this quiet corner of England, have suffered the loss of friends very dear to us — some close to this church: George West, choir boy; James Bellard, station master and bell ringer and a proud winner, only one hour before his death, of the Belding Cup for his beautiful Miniver rose; and our hearts go out in sympathy to the two families who share the cruel loss of a young girl who was married at this altar only two weeks ago. The homes of many of us have been destroyed, and the lives of young and old have been taken. There is scarcely a household that hasn't been struck to the heart. And why? Surely you must have asked yourself this question. Why in all conscience should these be the ones to suffer? Children, old people, a young girl at the height of her loveliness. Why these? Are these our soldiers? Are these our fighters? Why should they be sacrificed? I shall tell you why. Because this is not only a war of soldiers in uniform. It is a war of the people, of all the people, and it must be fought not only on the battlefield, but in the cities and in the villages, in the factories and on the farms, in the home, and in the heart of every man, woman and child who loves freedom. Well, we have buried our dead, but we shall not forget them. Instead they will inspire us with an unbreakable determination to free ourselves and those who come after us from the tyranny and terror that threaten to strike us down. This is the people's war! It is our war! We are the fighters! Fight it then! Fight it with all that is in us, and may God defend the right.

The wartime film was made at a bleak time for the Allies and director William Wyler repeatedly rewrote this speech, acutely aware of its importance for morale. President Roosevelt recognized its power and the text was the basis for much subsequent propaganda.

When Greer Garson won the Oscar for Best Actress, she delivered a speech lasting five and a half minutes, prompting the Academy to impose a forty-five-second time limit thereafter.

Dir: Ernst Lubitsch. *Scr*: Edwin Justus Mayer. Based on a story by Melchior Lengyel. *Cast*: Jack Benny (Joseph Tura), Sig Ruman (Colonel Ehrhardt)

German Colonel Ehrhardt unwittingly insults actor Josef Tura, who has disguised himself as a Nazi sympathizer.

> TURA
>
> Her husband is that great, great Polish actor
> Josef Tura. You've probably heard of him.

> COLONEL EHRHARDT
>
> Oh, yes. As a matter of fact I saw him on the
> stage when I was in Warsaw once before the war.

> TURA
>
> Really?

> COLONEL EHRHARDT
>
> What he did to Shakespeare, we are doing now to
> Poland.

SCRIPT DOCTORS

Polish: to fix minor problems in an otherwise completed script.

Punch up: to give key scenes and dialogue extra energy.

The single most dreaded phrase in the film business is 'it died at the box office'. Nobody has yet devised a way to take out health insurance for a picture, but producers are willing to spend fortunes on script doctors. As with all specialists, their fees are steep and membership of their guild hard-won and exclusive. When a project has been given the green light – that is to say, that finances have been committed – the pressure to 'lock' the script becomes immense; once the actors are cast, the locations are fixed and the crew is on the clock, it is too late to tinker under the hood.

So where is the original writer in all this? By the time she has handed in dozens of drafts, rewrites and polishes, she may have lost her way, become burnt out or simply fallen victim to the infighting of executive factions. There may have been others involved, all of whom are vying to maintain their contractual, financial and credit positions. As the first day of principal photography approaches and directors and producers are mired in the innumerable day-to-day issues leading up to the shoot, a quick fix from a trusted expert is increasingly desirable. So, as they say in *Ghostbusters*, 'Who you gonna call?'

If you're worried about *Indiana Jones and the Last Crusade* (1989), *Sleepy Hollow* (1999) or *The Bourne Ultimatum* (2007), you need playwright Tomáš Straussler (better known as Sir Tom Stoppard, OM, CBE, FRSL). Although he has plenty of Tonys and an Oscar to his name for credited works including *Brazil* (1985), *Shakespeare in Love* (1998) and *Enigma* (2001), he is regularly hired on anonymous rewrites: 'The second reason for doing it is that you get to work with people you admire. The first reason, of course, is that it's overpaid.'

One day, while in the shower, he received a call from Steven Spielberg, an old friend. The director was shooting *Schindler's List* (1993) and was having trouble getting a scene written by Steven Zaillian to work on camera. Still dripping wet, Stoppard improvised a solution on the spot while the crew waited on location in Poland. Like most in his trade, Stoppard has huge respect for the writers whose work he is summoned to 'fix', but accepts it as an unavoidable part of the way the business works. 'I [urged] him just to film Zaillian's script. But Steven, like a lot of other people in movies, tends to think one more opinion can't hurt.'

Zaillian was almost certainly untroubled by contributions from others as he retained sole credit when the film won the Best Adapted Screenplay Oscar. The Screenwriters Guild of America has strict rules about how much of a filmed work must have been written by any individual to qualify for a shared credit: for original work 50 per cent, and for adapted material 33 per cent. Without a credit, there will be no residuals (royalties) or any chance of nomination for awards, so script doctors accept anonymity in return for a fee that may run to $300,000 a week.

As far back as the 1930s Ben Hecht (*Scarface, Notorious, Wuthering Heights*) was in demand for his uncredited assistance on such hits as *Gone with the Wind, Foreign Correspondent* and *Mutiny on the Bounty*. Today the hottest names include David Koepp (*Jurassic Park*), Scott Frank (*Minority Report*), Aaron Sorkin (*The Social Network*) and Susannah Grant (*Erin Brockovich*). Most studios have their favourite writers on speed-dial for last-minute fixes, even as late as post-production when the editing process sometimes reveals weaknesses in the story line and re-shoots are hurriedly ordered. Even actors have their preferred saviours: Vince Vaughn uses Dana Fox (*Couples Retreat*), Will Smith asks for Akiva Goldsman (*The Da Vinci Code*) and Matt Damon counts on George Nolfi (*The Bourne Ultimatum*).

Despite the hefty cheques they write, studio executives remain reluctant to discuss the prevalence of these last-minute fixes – and are ambivalent about their benefits. Two anonymous LA sources highlight the dilemma: 'Once a movie is green-lit, you're no longer spending development dollars, so it's not speculative spending. You're now making an investment on making this the best movie it can be. And at that point in the process, that last 10 per cent of the script is the most important.' Even so, 'Sometimes you have to spend even more money to fix the problem created by the script doctor you just hired. It's a crapshoot.'

HAIL THE CONQUERING HERO   1944

Dir: Preston Sturges. *Scr*: Preston Sturges. *Cast*: Elizabeth Patterson (Martha, Libby's Aunt)

                    LIBBY'S AUNT
Well, that's the war for you. It's always hard
on women. Either they take your men away and
never send them back at all, or they send them
back unexpectedly just to embarrass you. No
consideration at all.

CROSSFIRE   1947

Dir: Edward Dmytryk. *Scr*: John Paxton. Based on a novel by Richard Brooks. *Cast*: Robert Young (Captain Finlay)

                    CAPTAIN FINLAY
My grandfather was killed just because he was an
Irish Catholic. Hating is always the same, always
senseless. One day it kills Irish Catholics, the
next day Jews, the next day Protestants, the next
day Quakers. It's hard to stop. It can end up
killing people who wear striped neckties.

THE BRIDGE ON THE RIVER KWAI   1957

Dir: David Lean. *Scr*: Carl Foreman, Michael Wilson. Based on a novel by Pierre Boulle. *Cast*: Sessue Hayakawa (Colonel Saito), Alec Guinness (Lieutenant Colonel Nicholson)

The Japanese commander of a POW camp discusses with the commander of his Allied prisoners the importance of the railway bridge they have been forced to build.

                    COLONEL SAITO
Do you know what will happen to me if the bridge
is not built on time?

> **LT. COL. NICHOLSON**
> I haven't the foggiest.

> **COLONEL SAITO**
> I'll have to kill myself. What would you do if
> you were me?

> **LT. COL. NICHOLSON**
> I suppose if I were you . . . I'd have to kill
> myself.

Pierre Boulle's novel was a bestseller and producer Sam Spiegel bought a copy to read on his flight from Paris to London. By the time he arrived in England he was so determined to make a film of it that he got on the next flight back and demanded a meeting with the author, who promptly agreed to sell him the rights.

THE MAGNIFICENT SEVEN   1960

Dir: John Sturges. *Scr*: William Roberts. Based on a film by Akira Kurosawa. *Cast*: Steve McQueen (Vin Tanner)

> **VIN**
> We deal in lead, friend.

DR STRANGELOVE   1964

Dir: Stanley Kubrick. *Scr*: Stanley Kubrick, Terry Southern, Peter George. Based on a novel by Peter George. *Cast*: Peter Sellers (President Muffley)

Faced with a nuclear crisis, the President tries to quell uproar among his military staff.

> **PRESIDENT MUFFLEY**
> Gentlemen, you can't fight in here! This is the
> War Room.

Peter Sellers was paid $1 million [$8.5 million], over half the film's budget, for playing the parts of President Merkin Muffley, Group Captain Lionel Mandrake and Dr Strangelove; Stanley Kubrick famously quipped: 'I got three for the price of six.' International paranoia about nuclear war was running so high at the time the film was made that a camera crew shooting aerial footage near a US base in Greenland was forced down and accused of being Soviet spies.

ZULU   1964

Dir: Cy Endfield. *Scr*: John Prebble, Cy Endfield. *Cast*: Nigel Green (Colour Sergeant Frank Bourne), Stanley Baker (Lieutenant John Chard)

Outnumbered British soldiers do battle with Zulu warriors at Rorke's Drift, 1879.

```
          SERGEANT BOURNE
    It's a miracle.


          LIEUTENANT CHARD
    If it's a miracle, Colour Sergeant, it's a short-
    chamber Boxer Henry .45 calibre miracle.


          SERGEANT BOURNE
    And a bayonet, sir, with some guts behind.
```

Racial tensions had not eased in the century that passed between the historical events and their portrayal on film. Cast and crew on location in South Africa were warned not to fraternize with the topless tribal dancers as the penalty for inter-racial sex at the time was seven years' hard labour.

South Africa's Minister of Native Affairs refused to allow black citizens to see the film because 'it might incite them to rise up in revolt.'

THE BATTLE OF ALGIERS / *La battaglia di Algeri*   1966

Dir: Gillo Pontecorvo. *Scr*: Gillo Pontecorvo, Franco Solinas. Based on a book by Saadi Yacef. *Cast*: Uncredited

---

> JOURNALIST
>
> M. Ben M'Hidi, don't you think it's a bit cowardly to use women's baskets and handbags to carry explosive devices that kill so many innocent people?
>
> BEN M'HIDI
>
> And doesn't it seem to you even more cowardly to drop napalm bombs on defenceless villages, so that there are a thousand times more innocent victims? Of course, if we had your airplanes it would be a lot easier for us. Give us your bombers, and you can have our baskets.

The film was commissioned by the Algerian government to portray the 1954 revolution in an even-handed way. In 2003 the *New York Times* reported that the Pentagon screened the film for senior troops involved in the Iraq conflict. The invitation read: 'How to win a battle against terrorism and lose the war of ideas.'

BATTLE OF BRITAIN   1969

Dir: Guy Hamilton. *Scr*: James Kennaway, Wilfred Greatorex. Based on a novel by Derek Dempster, Derek Wood. *Cast*: Hein Riess (Reichsmarschall Hermann Göring), Unknown (Airman)

A German pilot shocks the commander of the Luftwaffe by speaking the truth.

> GÖRING
>
> I'm here to help. Is there anything I can do for you?

AIRMAN

Yes, Reichsmarschall. Give me a squadron of
Spitfires.

PATTON   1970

Dir: Franklin J. Schaffner. *Scr*: Francis Ford Coppola, Edmund H. North. Based
on a book by Ladislas Farago, Omar Bradley. *Cast*: George C. Scott (General
Patton)

General Patton addresses his troops.

GENERAL PATTON
Be seated. Now I want you to remember that no
bastard ever won a war by dying for his country.
He won it by making the other poor dumb bastard
die for *his* country.

The quote above comes from a long speech by Patton at the very start
of the film and has become so well known that it is now frequently
cited as an actual remark by the general. Scott won an Oscar for
his performance but refused to accept it because he disapproved of
competitive awards for acting.

CROMWELL   1970

Dir: Ken Hughes. *Scr*: Ken Hughes. *Cast*: Richard Harris (Oliver Cromwell)

CROMWELL
Every man who wages war believes God is on
his side. I'll warrant God should often wonder
who is on His.

Richard Harris said he had a nervous breakdown during filming,
and actually woke up one day thinking they were going to execute
the actor playing King Charles I (Alec Guinness).

APOCALYPSE NOW   1979

Dir: Francis Ford Coppola. *Scr*: John Milius, Francis Ford Coppola, Michael Herr. Based on a novella by Joseph Conrad. *Cast*: Robert Duvall (Lieutenant Colonel Bill Kilgore), Sam Bottoms (Lance B. Johnson)

An air cavalry commander relishes the destruction his regiment has wrought.

> LT. COL. KILGORE
>
> Smell that? You smell that?

> LANCE
>
> What?

> LT. COL. KILGORE
>
> Napalm, son. Nothing else in the world smells like that.

He kneels, savouring it.

> LT. COL. KILGORE
>
> I love the smell of napalm in the morning. You know, one time we had a hill bombed for twelve hours. When it was all over, I walked up. We didn't find one of 'em, not one stinkin' dink body. The smell, you know that gasoline smell, the whole hill. Smelled like...

He scents the air.

> LT. COL. KILGORE
>
> ... victory.

'IT'S NOT ABOUT VIETNAM. IT *IS* VIETNAM'

The making of Francis Ford Coppola's magisterial *Apocalypse Now* mirrors the end result as an epic, barely credible adventure; the schedule on location in the Philippines went from five to seventeen months, the budget from $12 million to $31 million [$42 million to $108 million], the director himself contemplated suicide on several occasions and by the end of the shoot he had lost nearly 50kg.

Based on Conrad's short novel *Heart of Darkness* (1899), the film moves the story from colonial Congo to Vietnam where Willard, a US captain, is sent to kill Kurtz, a Green Beret general driven mad by the wilderness and by his own power. The war and the jungle itself become characters in an exploration of morality and civilization; Coppola identified increasingly closely with Kurtz and introduced the film at its Cannes début by saying:

> 'My film is not a movie; it is not about Vietnam. It *is* Vietnam. It's what it was really like; it was crazy. And the way we made it was very much like the way the Americans were in Vietnam. We were in the jungle, there were too many of us, we had access to too much money, too much equipment, and little by little we went insane.'

The original adaptation was by John Milius but later drafts grew to incorporate much documentary material about the war from Michael Herr's Vietnam war memoir *Dispatches* (1977). As a result of the diverse inspirations, wayward actors and extraordinary upheavals during production, Coppola ended up rewriting a huge amount as he went along. Several weeks into shooting he replaced Harvey Keitel (as Willard) with Martin Sheen and was forced to begin the movie again.

When Sheen filmed the opening scenes, he was so drunk

he punched his reflection in a mirror, slicing his hand open; Coppola just told the camera to keep rolling and filmed the ensuing mayhem as he yelled improvised directions at the actor. During hugely expensive battle sequences, the helicopters the production had borrowed from President Marcos were recalled to fight a real war. Tropical storms destroyed several large sets, causing a hiatus of eight weeks. Despite full-time security guards, the crew's payroll was stolen.

By this stage Coppola had mortgaged everything he owned to cover the budget overages; when filming resumed, Sheen (aged thirty-six) had a heart attack. Although Coppola's prime concern was the actor's safety, he was terrified the studios would shut him down if they discovered the truth, saying: '[Even] if Marty dies I want to hear that everything's okay until I say Marty is dead.'

When Marlon Brando, the film's principal star, arrived for a month's work, he was grotesquely overweight and extremely sensitive about how he would be filmed; Coppola sidestepped the issue by shooting him largely in half-lit close-ups. Despite being paid $3.5 million [$12 million] for a month's work, Brando also declared he had not read the script – and when he did so, refused to play it.

Realizing he could not force his star to perform, Coppola decided to 'just shoot for the next three weeks irrationally'. After Brando ended one crucial scene by saying 'I can't think of any more dialogue today', Coppola bared his heart to his wife's documentary camera:

> '[I'm] feeling like an idiot for having set in motion stuff that doesn't make any sense, that doesn't match [other scenes], and yet I'm doing it and the reason that I'm doing it is out of desperation because I have no rational way to do it. What I have to do is to admit that I don't know what I'm doing.'

Both Captain Willard and Colonel Kurtz deliver speeches which reflect Coppola's mindset:

CAPTAIN WILLARD: How many people had I already killed? There were those six that I knew about for sure. Close enough to blow their last breath in my face. But this time, it was an American and an officer. That wasn't supposed to make any difference to me, but it did. Shit. . . charging a man with murder in this place was like handing out speeding tickets in the Indy 500.

COLONEL KURTZ: I remember when I was with Special Forces. Seems a thousand centuries ago. We went into a camp to inoculate some children. We'd left the camp after we had inoculated the children for polio. And this old man came running after us, and he was crying. He couldn't see. We went back there, and they had come and hacked off every inoculated arm. There they were, in a pile — a pile of little arms. And I remember, I . . . I . . . I cried. I wept like some grandmother. I wanted to tear my teeth out. I didn't know what I wanted to do. And I want to remember it. I never want to forget it. I never want to forget. And then I realized — like I was shot, like I was shot with a diamond, a diamond bullet right through my forehead. And I thought, 'My God, the genius of that. The genius.' The will to do that. Perfect, genuine, complete, crystalline, pure! And then I realized, they were stronger than me

> because they could stand it. These were not
> monsters. These were men — trained cadres.
> These men who fought with their hearts
> who have families, who have children, who
> are filled with love — that they had the
> strength, the strength to do that. If I had
> ten divisions of those men, then our troubles
> here would be over very quickly.

Shooting was eventually completed in May 1977, but the editing took a further two years. Initially released to mixed reviews, it was recut on several occasions and quickly recouped its costs; today it stands close to the top of every significant poll for the greatest film of the past one hundred years.

THE GREAT SANTINI   1979

Dir:. Lewis John Carlino. *Scr*: Lewis John Carlino, Herman Raucher. Based on a novel by Pat Conroy. *Cast*: Robert Duvall (Lieutenant Colonel Wilbur 'Bull' Meechum)

LT. COL. 'BULL' MEECHUM

Now, I don't want you to consider me as just your
commanding officer. I want you to look on me
like I was, well — God. If I say something, you
pretend it's coming from the burning bush. Now,
we're members of the proudest, most elite group of
fighting men in the history of the world. We are
Marines! Marines Corps fighter pilots! We have no
other function. That is our mission and you are
either gonna hack it or pack it. Do you read me?
Within thirty days, I am gonna lead the toughest,
flyingest sons-of-bitches in the world. The 312
Werewolf Squadron will make history, or it will

die trying. Now, you're flying with Bull Meecham
now and I kid you not, this is the eye of the
storm. Welcome aboard.

THE BIG RED ONE   1980

Dir: Samuel Fuller. *Scr*: Samuel Fuller. *Cast*: Kelly Ward (Private Johnson), Lee
Marvin (The Sergeant)

During the Second World War, an American platoon in Europe
passes a war memorial.

> PRIVATE JOHNSON
> Would you look at how fast they put the names of
> all our guys who got killed?

> SERGEANT
> That's a World War One memorial.

> PRIVATE JOHNSON
> But the names are the same.

> SERGEANT
> They always are.

PLATOON   1986

Dir: Oliver Stone. *Scr*: Oliver Stone. *Cast*: Kevin Dillon (Bunny), Reggie Johnson
(Junior)

Bunny has made his peace with his tour of Vietnam in a way that
unsettles his platoon mate Junior.

> BUNNY
> You know, Junior, some of the things we done,
> man . . . I don't feel like we done something
> wrong. But sometimes, man, I get this bad

```
feeling. I told the Padre the truth, man. I
like it here. You get to do what you want.
Nobody fucks with you. The only worry you got
is dying. And if that happens, you won't know
about it anyway. So, what the fuck, man.

                    JUNIOR
Shit, I got to be in this hole with you, man?
I just know I shouldn't have come.
```

FULL METAL JACKET   1987

Dir: Stanley Kubrick. *Scr*: Stanley Kubrick, Michael Herr, Gustav Hasford. Based on a novel by Gustav Hasford. *Cast*: R. Lee Ermey (Gunnery Sergeant Hartman)

A drill sergeant welcomes a batch of new recruits to the US Marines.

```
                    HARTMAN
Today . . . is Christmas! There will be a magic
show at zero-nine-thirty! Chaplain Charlie will
tell you about how the free world will conquer
Communism with the aid of God and a few Marines!
God has a hard-on for Marines because we kill
everything we see! He plays His games, we play
ours! To show our appreciation for so much power,
we keep heaven packed with fresh souls! God was
here before the Marine Corps! So you can give
your heart to Jesus, but your ass belongs to
the Corps! Do you ladies understand?
```

R. Lee Ermey had been a Marine instructor during the Vietnam War; Kubrick hired him as a technical adviser but Ermey wanted to play the role written for Hartman, the drill sergeant. To persuade the director he was right for the part, Ermey filmed an audition in which he improvised a torrent of expletives and insults while being bombarded by tennis balls. After he won the part, Ermey gave Kubrick 150 pages of suggested dialogue and was eventually permitted to improvise most of his own lines.

A FEW GOOD MEN   1992

Dir: Rob Reiner. *Scr*: Aaron Sorkin. *Cast*: Tom Cruise (Lieutenant Daniel Kaffee), J. A. Preston (Judge Randolph), Jack Nicholson (Colonel Nathan Jessep)

US Marine Colonel Jessep challenges a liberal lawyer to weigh the value of one life against many. 'Code Red' is a military term for punishment by one's peers.

> LIEUTENANT KAFFEE
>
> Colonel Jessep, did you order the Code Red?
>
> JUDGE RANDOLPH
>
> You don't have to answer that question!
>
> COLONEL JESSEP
>
> I'll answer the question! You want answers?
>
> LIEUTENANT KAFFEE
>
> I think I'm entitled to.
>
> COLONEL JESSEP
>
> You want answers?
>
> LIEUTENANT KAFFEE
>
> I want the truth!
>
> COLONEL JESSEP
>
> You can't handle the truth! Son, we live in a
> world that has walls, and those walls have to
> be guarded by men with guns. Who's gonna do it?
> You? You, Lieutenant Weinburg? I have a greater
> responsibility than you could possibly fathom.
> You weep for Santiago, and you curse the Marines.
> You have that luxury. You have the luxury of not

knowing what I know. That Santiago's death, while tragic, probably saved lives. And my existence, while grotesque and incomprehensible to you, saves lives. You don't want the truth because deep down in places you don't talk about at parties, you want me on that wall, you need me on that wall. We use words like honour, code, loyalty. We use these words as the backbone of a life spent defending something. You use them as a punchline. I have neither the time nor the inclination to explain myself to a man who rises and sleeps under the blanket of the very freedom that I provide, and then questions the manner in which I provide it. I would rather you just said thank you, and went on your way. Otherwise, I suggest you pick up a weapon, and stand a post. Either way, I don't give a damn what you think you are entitled to.

LIEUTENANT KAFFEE
Did you order the Code Red?

COLONEL JESSEP
I did the job I...

LIEUTENANT KAFFEE
Did you order the Code Red?

COLONEL JESSEP
You're goddamn right I did!

JACKIE BROWN   1997

Dir: Quentin Tarantino. *Scr*: Quentin Tarantino. Based on a novel by Elmore Leonard. *Cast*: Samuel L. Jackson (Ordell Robbie)

Arms dealer Ordell has perfected his own particular sales patter.

```
                    ORDELL
AK-47. The very best there is. When you
absolutely, positively got to kill every
motherfucker in the room, accept no substitutes.
```

Despite the fact that Samuel L. Jackson's character sells guns for a living the film contains the least violence and the lowest body count of any of Tarantino's films; nine shots are fired, and only four deaths result.

FADE IN . . .

'If I really considered myself a writer, I wouldn't be writing screenplays. I'd be writing novels.'

Quentin Tarantino

Why is a screenplay not just a book with lazy punctuation and a clunky typeface? A good novel is an artefact as well as an inspiration, lying comfortably in the hand and stored carefully on a shelf among other favourites waiting to be revisited. It unlocks a different world for each reader, provoking and enlarging their imagination. It is a perpetual beginning, and an end in itself. A screenplay, really just a handbook detailing action and dialogue, is as likely to be used as a wedge for an unsteady video monitor as a notepad for taking orders for the make-up department's lunch requests. Pages are torn out as sequences are completed and scenes are annotated with timings, continuity requirements and lens data. At the end of the shoot most will be thrown away.

A script, for all the love and attention the screenwriter has given it, is a tool. It will never be seen by its intended audience; what lies within exists to be shaped by directors, spoken by actors and visualized by cinematographers. Computer graphics departments may provide mountains, space ships, explosions and tears, and each will have a reality the audience is not invited to imagine for themselves. The editor will tell us when to look at our hero – and when to look away – and the composer will let us know whether we should laugh or cry.

Although the crew hope to do justice to the power and vision of the script, their primary task is to deliver around ninety minutes of material to a precise set of technical standards while dealing with changeable weather, cold-ridden actors, dogs barking nearby and tricky props. The writer may have spent whole days perfecting the closing dialogue but at the moment it will be spoken aloud the camera department is likely be more concerned with reframing a shot to exclude a traffic light in the distance or laying sandbags on the pavement to ensure the actor can stop at the correct point for the focus-puller.

Generally, writers find life on set either disappointingly slow or maddeningly complex. Although some have a close relationship with directors, it is usually because they are familiar with these realities and willing to view writing as a wider process which accommodates egos, rainstorms and tea breaks. Those who fight for the honour of every last word on the page are usually given a brief introduction to the cast and then hastily driven home.

Stories abound of writers being banished from the sets of 'their' movies; with production costs running into hundreds of thousands of dollars a day, a disagreement with the director about the kind of car the actor would drive can cost as much as the car itself. Since everyone on the set is keen to avoid expense and delay, the typical writer's contract will read as follows:

OWNERSHIP OF THE WORK: Writer hereby assigns to Producer the sole and exclusive ownership throughout the world and in perpetuity of all rights, title and interest

SAVING PRIVATE RYAN   1998

Dir: Steven Spielberg. *Scr*: Robert Rodat. *Cast*: Tom Hanks (Captain John Miller)

A team of US soldiers is sent behind enemy lines to rescue a paratrooper whose four brothers have been lost in combat.

> CAPTAIN MILLER
> He better be worth it. He better go home and cure a disease, or invent a longer-lasting light bulb.

All the lead actors were made to undergo exhaustive military training with the exception of Matt Damon, playing Private Ryan, since director Spielberg wanted the other soldiers to feel a genuine resentment towards him.

GLADIATOR   2000

Dir: Ridley Scott. *Scr*: David Franzoni, John Logan, William Nicholson. *Cast*: Russell Crowe (Maximus Decimus Meridius), Richard Harris (Marcus Aurelius)

> MAXIMUS
> Five thousand of my men are out there in the freezing mud. Three thousand of them are bloodied and cleaved. Two thousand will never leave this place. I will not believe that they fought and died for nothing.

MARCUS AURELIUS
And what would you believe?

MAXIMUS
They fought for you and for Rome.

MARCUS AURELIUS
And what is Rome, Maximus?

MAXIMUS
I've seen much of the rest of the world. It is brutal and cruel and dark. Rome is the light.

MARCUS AURELIUS
Yet you have never been there. You have not seen what it has become. I am dying, Maximus. When a man sees his end, he wants to know there was some purpose to his life. How will the world speak my name in years to come? Will I be known as the philosopher? The warrior? The tyrant? Or will I be the emperor who gave Rome back her true self? There was once a dream that was Rome. You could only whisper it. Anything more than a whisper and it would vanish, it was so fragile. And I fear that it will not survive the winter.

The two horses depicted on Maximus's breastplate are named Argento and Scarto – Silver and Trigger (literally, Lever) – a *hommage* to the equine stars of famous Westerns.

RULES OF ENGAGEMENT   2000
Dir: William Friedkin. *Scr*: Stephen Gaghan, James Webb. *Cast*: Tommy Lee Jones (Colonel Hayes 'Hodge' Hodges), Guy Pearce (Major Mark Biggs)

Hodges – now a lawyer – tries to convey what life was really like as a young marine.

COLONEL HODGES

I'll make you a deal. If you can tell me right
now what the life expectancy was for a second
lieutenant dropped into a hot landing zone in
Vietnam in 1968, I'll tell you everything I
remember about Ca Lu.

MAJOR BIGGS

One week.

COLONEL HODGES

Negative. Sixteen minutes. Sixteen fucking
minutes. That's all I remember about Ca Lu.

BLACK HAWK DOWN   2001

Dir: Ridley Scott. *Scr*: Ken Nolan. Based on a book by Mark Bowden. *Cast*: Eric
Bana (Special Forces Sergeant Norm 'Hoot' Gibson)

A Special Forces sergeant explains the fierce camaraderie of
combat.

HOOT

When I get home people will ask me, 'Hey, Hoot,
why do you do it, man? Why? You some war junkie?'
You know what I'll say? I won't say a goddamn
word. Why? They won't understand. They won't
understand why we do it. They won't understand
that it's about the men next to you, and that's
it. That's all it is.

The film was scrupulous in its attention to detail and factual
accuracy, even including some authentic satellite imagery and radio
transmissions from the battle. Director Ridley Scott only betrayed
the realism by insisting that soldiers had their names painted on
their helmets as he worried that audiences would be unable to
distinguish between actors in otherwise identical uniforms.

TROY 2004

Dir: Wolfgang Petersen. *Scr*: David Benioff. *Cast*: Sean Bean (Odysseus)

Odysseus, King of Ithaca, is under no illusion how the Greek battle for Troy will unfold.

> ODYSSEUS
>
> War is young men dying and old men talking.

INGLOURIOUS BASTERDS 2009

Dir: Quentin Tarantino. *Scr*: Quentin Tarantino. *Cast*: Christoph Waltz (Colonel Hans Landa), Denis Ménochet (M. LaPadite)

An SS Colonel suspects a French farmer of sheltering a Jewish family.

> COLONEL LANDA
>
> So, Monsieur LaPadite, let me purpose a
> question. In this time of war, what is your
> number one duty? Is it to fight the Germans
> in the name of France to your last breath?
> Or is it to harass the occupying army to the
> best of your ability? Or is it to protect the
> poor unfortunate victims of warfare who cannot
> protect themselves? Or is your number one duty
> in this time of bloodshed to protect those very
> beautiful women who constitute your family?

The Colonel waits.

> COLONEL LANDA
>
> That was a question, Monsieur LaPadite. In this
> time of war, what do you consider your number one
> duty?

> LAPADITE
>
> To protect my family.

COLONEL LANDA

Now, my job dictates that I must have my men enter your home and conduct a thorough search before I can officially cross your family's name off my list. And if there are any irregularities to be found, rest assured, they will be.

He pauses.

COLONEL LANDA

That is, unless you have something to tell me that will make the conducting of a search unnecessary. I might add also that any information that makes the performing of my duty easier will not be met with punishment. Actually, quite the contrary; it will be met with reward. And that reward will be that your family will cease to be harassed in any way by the German military during the rest of our occupation of your country.

The farmer stares across the table at his German opponent.

COLONEL LANDA

You are sheltering enemies of the state, are you not?

Ashamed, the farmer knows he is beaten.

LAPADITE

Yes.

COLONEL LANDA

You're sheltering them underneath your floorboards, aren't you?

LaPadite is crying silently now.

LAPADITE

Yes.

COLONEL LANDA

Point out to me the areas where they're hiding.

Slowly, the farmer stands and indicates.

COLONEL LANDA

Since I haven't heard any disturbance, I assume
that while they're listening they don't speak
English?

LAPADITE

Yes.

COLONEL LANDA

I'm going to switch back to French now, and
I want you to follow my masquerade. Is that
clear?

LAPADITE

Yes.

*Colonel Landa stands up from the table. He speaks
in French now:*

COLONEL LANDA

Monsieur LaPadite, I thank you for milk and
your hospitality. I do believe our business
here is done.

*He opens the front door and waves for his troops to
approach the house.*

COLONEL LANDA

Mademoiselle LaPadite, I thank you for your
time. We shan't be bothering your family any
longer.

The LaPadite women watch the Nazi soldiers, machine guns at the ready, enter the house. Colonel Landa silently points out the area of the floor the farmer showed him.

COLONEL LANDA
So, Monsieur and Madame LaPadite, I bid you adieu.

He motions to the soldiers with his index finger. They tear up the wood floor with machine-gun fire.

SICARIO: DAY OF THE SOLDADO   2018

Dir: Stefano Sollima. *Scr*: Taylor Sheridan. *Cast*: Josh Brolin (Matt Graver), Benicio del Toro (Alejandro)

In the war against drugs in Mexico, allegiances are fickle.

MATT
You gonna help us start a war.

ALEJANDRO
With who?

MATT
Everyone.

HEROES

THE THIN MAN   1934

Dir: W. S. Van Dyke. *Scr*: Albert Hackett, Frances Goodrich. Based on a novel by Dashiell Hammett. *Cast*: William Powell (Nick Charles), Myrna Loy (Nora Charles)

Nick and Nora have successfully solved a murder mystery.

            NICK
    I'm a hero. I was shot twice in the *Tribune*.

            NORA
    I read you were shot five times in the tabloids.

            NICK
    It's not true. He didn't come anywhere near my
    tabloids.

MR DEEDS GOES TO TOWN   1936

Dir: Frank Capra. *Scr*: Robert Riskin, Clarence Budington Kelland. *Cast*: Gary Cooper (Longfellow Deeds)

Longfellow Deeds hopes to use his fortune to protect those less fortunate than himself.

            DEEDS
    From what I can see, no matter what system of
    government we have, there will always be leaders
    and always be followers. It's like the road out
    in front of my house. It's on a steep hill.
    Every day I watch the cars climbing up. Some go
    lickety-split up that hill on high, some have
    to shift into second, and some sputter and shake
    and slip back to the bottom again. Same cars,
    same gasoline, yet some make it and some don't.
    And I say the fellas who can make the hill on
    high should stop once in a while and help those

who can't. That's all I'm trying to do with this
money. Help the fellas who can't make the hill
on high.

Capra, famous for his warm-hearted but intelligent films during the
1930s and 1940s, said in an interview towards the end of his life: 'I
made mistakes in drama. I thought drama was when actors cried.
But drama is when the audience cries.'

Harry Cohn, who produced the film, always kept a keen eye on
costs and insisted his directors only be allowed to print one shot per
set-up. Capra circumvented the rule by keeping the cameras rolling
at the end of each take; instead of calling 'cut', he would just tell the
actors and crew to 'do it again'.

MR SMITH GOES TO WASHINGTON   1939

Dir: Frank Capra. *Scr*: Sidney Buchman, Myles Connolly. *Cast*: James Stewart
(Jefferson Smith)

Junior senator Jefferson Smith may be new to politics but he is
determined to uphold his beliefs.

                    SMITH
    Liberty's too precious a thing to be buried in
    books, Miss Saunders. Men should hold it up in
    front of them every single day of their lives
    and say: I'm free to think and to speak. My
    ancestors couldn't, I can, and my children will.
    Boys ought to grow up remembering that.

THE GRAPES OF WRATH   1940

Dir: John Ford. *Scr*: Nunnally Johnson. Based on a novel by John Steinbeck. *Cast*:
Henry Fonda (Tom Joad)

Tom Joad promises to be a tireless champion of the oppressed.

I'll be all around in the dark — I'll be
everywhere. Wherever you can look — wherever
there's a fight, so hungry people can eat, I'll
be there. Wherever there's a cop beatin' up a
guy, I'll be there. I'll be in the way guys
yell when they're mad. I'll be in the way kids
laugh when they're hungry and they know supper's
ready, and when the people are eatin' the stuff
they raise and livin' in the houses they build —
I'll be there, too.

Darryl F. Zanuck paid $100,000 [$1.8 million] for the rights to
John Steinbeck's novel, a huge amount of money for the time.
Steinbeck insisted the film-makers treat the book – and its subject,
the plight of the working man during the Great Depression – with
due respect; when he saw the result he was delighted and said Henry
Fonda's performance as Tom Joad made him 'believe my own words'.
Before production started, Zanuck sent undercover investigators to
the migrant camps to see if Steinbeck had exaggerated the appalling
conditions, but discovered the reality was even more shocking than
the book had suggested.

IT'S A WONDERFUL LIFE   1946

Dir: Frank Capra. *Scr*: Frances Goodrich, Albert Hackett, Frank Capra. Based on
a short story by Philip Van Doren Stern. *Cast*: Henry Travers (Clarence)

An angel shows a suicidal man what the world would be like without
him.

CLARENCE

Strange, isn't it? Each man's life touches so
many other lives. When he isn't around he leaves
an awful hole, doesn't he?

Dir: Howard Hawks. *Scr*: William Faulkner, Leigh Brackett, Jules Furthman. Based on a novel by Raymond Chandler. *Cast*: Martha Vickers (Carmen Sternwood), Humphrey Bogart (Philip Marlowe)

The wayward Carmen resents private investigator Marlowe's intrusion into her family's life.

> CARMEN
> You're not very tall, are you?

> MARLOWE
> Well, I, uh, I try to be.

'MY GOD, THE HERO IS A BEE!'

Hollywood has always enjoyed the lustre of a famous name, so when the talkies took off and screenplays began to require dialogue as well as spectacle, producers sought the best talent money could buy. So many contemporary novelists were happy to work for the inflated fees offered that when the *Film Daily* Product Guide published a 'List of Available Writers' in 1937, the names for hire included three Nobel prize nominees (Theodore Dreiser, Upton Sinclair and Thornton Wilder) and one future winner, William Faulkner (he received the award in 1950).

The rest of the bunch included such literary luminaries as James M. Cain, F. Scott Fitzgerald, Anita Loos, Mary McCarthy, Ogden Nash, Dorothy Parker, S. J. Perelman, J. B. Priestley, Ayn Rand, Damon Runyon, James Thurber, Evelyn Waugh, Rebecca West, P. G. Wodehouse, Thomas Wolfe, Alexander Woollcott, Stefan Zweig and, astonishingly, the experimental writer and poet Gertrude Stein.

Perhaps unsurprisingly, producers entranced by literary fame were not always fully aware of their protégés' oeuvre. Belgian author Maurice Maeterlinck had won the Nobel prize in 1911 largely for a play about fairies, *The Blue Bird*, and in 1919 Samuel Goldwyn lured him to Los Angeles with a contract worth $100,000 [$1.4 million]. He installed the great man in a hilltop villa and left him alone to adapt some of his earlier works. Each day a translator would take away the scant pages and translate them; after three months a script took shape. Goldwyn read it at once in his office but is said to have burst out immediately, waving the papers in astonishment: 'My God, the hero is a bee!'

Not all producers were so lavish in their inducements: after signing Faulkner to work for him, Jack Warner once crowed to another screenwriter that 'I've got America's best writer for $300 [$4,400] a week.'

Noted authors hired to adapt their own work for the screen or to contribute to other films include:

- Arnold Bennett (*Piccadilly*, 1929)
- John Steinbeck (*The Red Pony*, 1949)
- Somerset Maugham (*Trio*, 1955)
- Vladimir Nabokov (*Lolita*, 1962)
- Roald Dahl (*You Only Live Twice*, 1967)
- Anthony Burgess (*A Clockwork Orange*, 1971)
- Mario Puzo (*The Godfather*, 1972)
- Martin Amis (*Saturn 3*, 1980)
- William Boyd (*Chaplin*, 1992)
- Gabriel Garcia Márquez (*Love in the Time of Cholera*, 1997)
- Harold Pinter (*Sleuth*, 1997)
- John Irving (*The Cider House Rules*, 1999)

- Frederic Raphael (*Eyes Wide Shut*, 1999)
- Bret Easton Ellis (*American Psycho*, 2000)
- Ian McEwan (*Atonement*, 2007)
- Dave Eggers (*Where the Wild Things Are*, 2009)
- Robert Harris (*The Ghost*, 2010)

One of the most bizarre encounters between the highbrow and the lowbrow occurred in 1957 when United Pictures of America approached Aldous Huxley, author of *Brave New World*, to devise a screenplay for a full-length Mr Magoo cartoon. The story was to have been based on Cervantes' *Don Quixote* but the project was abandoned after the studio encountered a small hitch: Mr Magoo is comically short-sighted, and none of the executives had had the courage to tell Huxley (who was virtually blind himself) this key fact.

HIGH NOON   1952
Dir: Fred Zinnemann. *Scr*: Carl Foreman. Based on a story by John W. Cunningham. *Cast*: Lon Chaney Jr (Martin Howe)

Retired sheriff Martin Howe explains why he refuses to help the new lawman in town.

<pre>
                    MARTIN
It's a great life. You risk your skin catchin'
killers and the juries turn 'em loose so they
can come back and shoot at ya again. If you're
honest, you're poor your whole life, and in the
end you wind up dyin' all alone on some dirty
street. For what? For nothin'. For a tin star.
</pre>

The classic film is often described as 'a western for people who don't like westerns'.

JOHNNY GUITAR   **1954**

Dir: Nicholas Ray. *Scr*: Philip Yordan. Based on a novel by Roy Chanslor. *Cast*: John Carradine (Old Tom)

A mysterious gunslinger enters town.

> OLD TOM
>
> That's a lot of man you're carrying in those boots, stranger.

LAWRENCE OF ARABIA   **1962**

Dir: David Lean. *Scr*: Robert Bolt, Michael Wilson. *Cast*: Harry Fowler (William Potter), Peter O'Toole (T. E. Lawrence)

Lawrence puts out a lit match between his thumb and forefinger. Corporal Potter watches and tries to copy him.

> POTTER
>
> It damn well hurts!

> LAWRENCE
>
> Certainly it hurts.

> POTTER
>
> What's the trick then?

> LAWRENCE
>
> The trick, William Potter, is not minding that it hurts.

The film was based on T. E. Lawrence's military memoirs *Seven Pillars of Wisdom* (1926); he turned down several offers to film the story during his lifetime. In 1960 Michael Wilson wrote a screen version explicitly to persuade Lawrence's literary executors that a worthy adaptation could be made, and the rights were granted to producer Sam Spiegel. Robert Bolt received sole credit for the final script until the Writers Guild of America reinstated Wilson's name in 1995.

David Lean shot the entire film favouring movement from left to right across the screen to emphasize the sense of a journey. When Technicolor released a subsequent master print, they inadvertently flipped one of the reels and the error persisted through the film's release on video. Lean had to wait until the material was restored and reissued in 1989 to correct the mistake. Although the original version is over three and a half hours long, it contains not a single line spoken by a woman.

A FISTFUL OF DOLLARS   1964

Dir: Sergio Leone. *Scr*: Victor Andrés Catena, Jaime Comas Gil, Sergio Leone.
Cast: Marianne Koch (Marisol), Clint Eastwood (Joe)

A Wild West drifter risks his life to free a family from their violent captors.

> MARISOL
> Why do you do it for us?

> JOE
> Why? I knew someone like you once. There was no one there to help. Now, get moving.

LORD JIM   1965

Dir: Richard Brooks. *Scr*: Richard Brooks. Based on a novel by Joseph Conrad.
Cast: Peter O'Toole (Lord Jim)

Lord Jim, a sailor ashamed of having abandoned his ship with passengers still aboard, tries to come to terms with his past.

> LORD JIM
> I've been a so-called coward and a so-called hero and there's not the thickness of a sheet of

paper between them. Maybe cowards and heroes are just ordinary men who, for a split second, do something out of the ordinary. That's all.

Joseph Conrad – originally Józef Teodor Konrad Korzeniowski – was a Polish author who wrote in English after becoming a British subject in 1886. Although his most famous story is almost certainly *Heart of Darkness*, films have also been made of his other works including *Lord Jim*, *Almayer's Folly*, *An Outcast of the Islands*, *Nostromo*, *The Secret Agent*, *The Duel*, *Victory*, *The Shadow Line* and *The Boxer*.

DIRTY HARRY   1971

Dir: Don Siegel. *Scr*: Harry Julian Fink, Rita M. Fink, Dean Riesner. *Cast*: Clint Eastwood (Harry Callahan)

Policeman Harry Callahan is forced to adopt the tactics of the criminal he is pursuing.

> HARRY
>
> I know what you're thinking. 'Did he fire six shots or only five?' Well, to tell you the truth, in all this excitement I kind of lost track myself. But being as this is a .44 Magnum, the most powerful handgun in the world, and would blow your head clean off, you've got to ask yourself one question: Do I feel lucky? Well, do ya, punk?

Andrew Robinson, who plays the 'Scorpio' killer, is a sworn pacifist and deeply uncomfortable around guns. He would visibly flinch whenever he pulled a trigger, so director Don Siegel had to shut down the production while he was sent to a training range to gain confidence. In some shots in the finished film he can still be seen to blink as he fires.

Dir: Steven Spielberg. *Scr*: Carl Gottlieb. Based on a novel by Peter Benchley.
Cast: Roy Scheider (Martin Brody)

Police chief Brody warns bounty hunters they have underestimated
the size of the shark that threatens their beaches.

> BRODY
> You're gonna need a bigger boat.

According to principal writer Carl Gottlieb, this line was not
scripted but improvised by Roy Scheider.

I SHALL NOT RETURN

Based on Peter Benchley's bestselling book, *Jaws* was the first
film to gross $100 million [$475 million] in its theatrical
release: over the summer of 1975, sixty-seven million Americans
bought a ticket to see it and it recouped its production costs
within two weeks. Although it is still hailed as one of the young
Spielberg's finest films, many have lamented that it paved the
way for the dominance of the blockbuster, encouraging the
industry to focus on the massive marketing campaigns and
merchandising tie-ins still favoured today.

The making of the film, however, gave little reassurance that
its release would be such a hit. The producers paid Benchley
$175,000 [$825,000] for the rights before the book had even
been published, but rejected his first three attempts at a script.
When Spielberg – after some hesitation – was hired to direct,
he wrote his own version before turning to Howard Sackler,
whom he credited with the structural changes necessary for a
screen version.

Spielberg then asked Carl Gottlieb, better known as a sitcom
writer, to come on board for a week to 'polish' the script and

prevent it from feeling too dark. Gottlieb stayed on, only completing the task after the production had already been underway for nine weeks; scenes were often delivered the night before they were scheduled to be shot. Just as Roy Scheider had come up with the much-quoted line 'You're gonna need a bigger boat', Robert Shaw (Quint) rewrote the famous scene about his survival after the torpedoing of the USS *Indianapolis* by the Japanese in July 1945.

QUINT: Japanese submarine slammed two
torpedoes into our side, Chief. We was comin'
back from the island of Tinian to Leyte...
just delivered the bomb. The Hiroshima bomb.
Eleven hundred men went into the water. Vessel
went down in twelve minutes. Didn't see the
first shark for about a half an hour. Tiger.
Thirteen-footer. You know how you know that
when you're in the water, Chief? You tell by
looking from the dorsal to the tail fin. What
we didn't know, was our bomb mission had been
so secret, no distress signal had been sent.
They didn't even list us overdue for a week.
Very first light, Chief, sharks come cruisin',
so we formed ourselves into tight groups. You
know, it was kinda like old squares in the
battle like you see in the calendar named
'The Battle of Waterloo', and the idea was:
shark comes to the nearest man, that man he
starts poundin' and hollerin' and screamin'
and sometimes the shark will go away...
but sometimes he wouldn't go away. Sometimes
that shark he looks right into ya. Right into
your eyes. And, you know, the thing about a

shark . . . he's got lifeless eyes. Black eyes.
Like a doll's eyes. When he comes at ya,
doesn't seem to be living . . . until he bites
ya, and those black eyes roll over white and
then . . . ah, then you hear that terrible high-
pitched screamin'. The ocean turns red, and
despite all the poundin' and the hollerin',
they all come in and they . . . rip you to
pieces. You know by the end of that first
dawn, lost a hundred men. I don't know how
many sharks, maybe a thousand. I know how many
men, they averaged six an hour. On Thursday
morning, Chief, I bumped into a friend of
mine, Herbie Robinson from Cleveland. Baseball
player. Boatswain's mate. I thought he was
asleep. I reached over to wake him up. He
bobbed up, down in the water just like a
kinda top. Upended. Well, he'd been bitten in
half below the waist. Noon, the fifth day, Mr
Hooper, a Lockheed Ventura saw us. He swung in
low and he saw us . . . he was a young pilot,
a lot younger than Mr Hooper. Anyway, he saw
us and he come in low and three hours later
a big fat PBY comes down and starts to pick
us up. You know that was the time I was most
frightened . . . waitin' for my turn. I'll never
put on a lifejacket again. So, 1,100 men went
in the water; 316 men come out and the sharks
took the rest, June the 29th, 1945. Anyway, we
delivered the bomb.

Principal photography was originally estimated at fifty-
two days but lasted nearly six months as a result of technical
delays, bad weather and the inevitable complications of staging

complex drama and special effects with real boats as camera platforms. The mechanical shark – nicknamed Bruce, after Spielberg's lawyer – suffered repeated mechanical failures, trapping George Lucas's head in its mouth during testing and sinking to the ocean floor on its first outing. Desperate to keep to the schedule during Bruce's frequent trips to the repair shop, Spielberg resorted to filming several sequences with a moving underwater camera suggesting the predator's point-of-view. This stop-gap measure eventually contributed hugely to the film's atmosphere.

On dry land, things were just as fraught. Robert Shaw, cast only days before shooting started, was in trouble with the US tax authorities and had to be flown to Canada on his days off. Shaw and Richard Dreyfuss (playing Matt Hooper) had frequent disagreements on set – and occasional actual fights – although their animosity benefited the story. Peter Benchley disliked the ending Spielberg had devised and objected so vehemently he was barred from the set.

By the end of the gruelling production period, the crew were at the end of their tether. Carl Gottlieb recalls how on the last day Spielberg, sensing he would be the focus of their wrath, wore his most expensive clothes in the hope he might avoid being thrown overboard. When the final shot was approved, he leaped into a waiting speedboat and raced away, shouting: 'I shall not return!'

When composer John Williams first played the ominous opening theme for the director, Spielberg is reported to have thought it was a joke. The score went on to win an Oscar, although the film suffered one final setback: Williams was conducting the orchestra for the ceremony when the result was announced, and had to run up on stage to collect his statuette before returning to his duties in the pit.

NETWORK

Dir: Sidney Lumet. *Scr*: Paddy Chayefsky. *Cast*: Peter Finch (Howard Beale)

On live TV, a news presenter controversially encourages his viewers to become more involved in the world around them.

> **HOWARD**
>
> We know things are bad — worse than bad. They're crazy. It's like everything everywhere is going crazy, so we don't go out any more. We sit in the house, and slowly the world we're living in is getting smaller, and all we say is: 'Please, at least leave us alone in our living rooms. Let me have my toaster and my TV and my steel-belted radials and I won't say anything. Just leave us alone.' Well, I'm not gonna leave you alone. I want you to get MAD! I don't want you to protest. I don't want you to riot — I don't want you to write to your congressman, because I wouldn't know what to tell you to write. I don't know what to do about the depression and the inflation and the Russians and the crime in the street. All I know is that first you've got to get mad.

He begins to shout at the camera:

> **HOWARD**
>
> You've got to say: 'I'm a human being, goddammit! My life has value!' So, I want you to get up now. I want all of you to get up out of your chairs. I want you to get up right now and go to the window. Open it, and stick your head out, and yell: 'I'm as mad as hell, and I'm not gonna take this any more!'

ROCKY 1976

Dir: John G. Avildsen. *Scr*: Sylvester Stallone. *Cast*: Talia Shire (Adrian Pennino), Burt Young (Paulie Pennino)

Two friends wonder whether underdog boxer Rocky has what it takes to win.

> ADRIAN
> Einstein flunked out of school, twice.

> PAULIE
> Is that so?

> ADRIAN
> Yeah. Beethoven was deaf. Helen Keller was blind.
> I think Rocky's got a good chance.

Stallone wrote his first draft in three days. When he sold it to the producers for $350,000 [$1.7 million], he had $106 [$520] in the bank, no car, and was trying to sell his dog because he couldn't afford to feed it.

THE SHOOTIST 1976

Dir: Don Siegel. *Scr*: Miles Hood Swarthout, Scott Hale. Based on a novel by Glendon Swarthout. *Cast*: John Wayne (J. B. Books)

An ageing gunfighter tries to live his last days with the dignity and integrity of his youth.

> BOOKS
> I won't be wronged. I won't be insulted. I won't
> be laid a hand on. I don't do these things to
> other people, and I require the same from them.

Sequences in the story showing Books as a young man were taken directly from Wayne's earlier films, including *Red River*, *Rio Bravo* and *El Dorado*.

STAR WARS   1977

Dir: George Lucas. *Scr*: George Lucas. *Cast*: Harrison Ford (Han Solo)

> **HAN SOLO**
> Hokey religions and ancient weapons are no match
> for a good blaster by your side, kid.

Director George Lucas based the character of Han Solo on his
friend Francis Ford Coppola, modestly admitting: 'Before I met
[Francis] I couldn't write a word, and now I'm the King of Wooden
Dialogue.' Lucas himself was surprised by the film's extraordinary
success, saying afterwards: 'I thought [*Star Wars*] was too wacky for
the general public.'

SUPERMAN   1978

Dir: Richard Donner. *Scr:* Mario Puzo, David Newman, Leslie Newman, Robert
Benton. Based on characters created by Jerry Siegel, Joe Shuster. *Cast:* Christopher
Reeve (Superman/Clark Kent), Margot Kidder (Lois Lane)

Superman carries Lois Lane to safety high above Metropolis.

> **SUPERMAN**
> Easy, Miss, I've got you.

> **LOIS LANE**
> You've got me? Who's got you?

LIFE OF BRIAN   1979

Dir: Terry Jones. *Scr*: Terry Jones, John Cleese, Graham Chapman, Terry Gilliam,
Eric Idle, Michael Palin. *Cast*: Graham Chapman (Brian Cohen), John Cleese
(Arthur)

Brian of Nazareth is tired of being mistaken for his neighbour Jesus.

> **BRIAN**
> I'm not the Messiah! Will you please listen? I am
> not the Messiah, do you understand? Honestly!

GIRL
Only the true Messiah denies His divinity.

BRIAN
What? Well, what sort of chance does that give me?
All right! I am the Messiah!

FOLLOWERS
He is! He is the Messiah!

BRIAN
Now fuck off!

Silence.

ARTHUR
How shall we fuck off, O Lord?

The film also contains the memorable put-down from Brian's mother: 'He's not the Messiah, he's a very naughty boy.' After the team finished *Monty Python and the Holy Grail,* they grew tired of journalists endlessly asking what their next project would be – until Eric Idle answered as a joke: 'Jesus Christ: The Lust For Glory.' The first scene they dreamed up was to show Jesus, a professional carpenter, complaining about the shoddy construction of the cross used to crucify him.

THE RIGHT STUFF 1983

Dir: Philip Kaufman. *Scr*: Philip Kaufman. Based on a book by Tom Wolfe. *Cast*: O-Lan Shepard (Girl), Kim Stanley (Pancho Barnes)

Pancho's Bar is the only place local Air Force test pilots can drink, and it attracts plenty of groupies.

GIRL
I just noticed that a fancy pilot like Slick over
there doesn't have his picture on your wall. What

do you have to do to get your picture up there
anyway?

> PANCHO BARNES
> You have to die, sweetie.

THE UNTOUCHABLES 1987

Dir: Brian De Palma. *Scr*: David Mamet. Based on the book by Oscar Fraley, Eliot Ness. *Cast*: Steven Goldstein (Scoop), Kevin Costner (Eliot Ness)

Federal Agent Eliot Ness has finally arrested Chicago's most notorious mobster. A journalist pursues him.

> SCOOP
> Mr Ness! Any comment for the record? 'The man who
> put Al Capone on the spot.'

> NESS
> I just happened to be there when the wheel went
> round.

> SCOOP
> Word is they're going to repeal Prohibition.
> What'll you do then?

> NESS
> I think I'll have a drink.

DIE HARD 1988

Dir: John McTiernan. *Scr*: Steven E. de Souza, Jeb Stuart. Based on a novel by Roderick Thorp. *Cast*: Alan Rickman (Hans Gruber), Bruce Willis (John McClane)

A terrorist talks to his unknown adversary on a walkie-talkie.

> GRUBER
> Mr Mystery Guest? Are you still there?

MCCLANE

Yeah, I'm still here. Unless you wanna open the front door for me.

GRUBER

No, I'm afraid not. But you have me at a loss. You know my name, but who are you? Just another American who saw too many movies as a child? Another orphan of a bankrupt culture who thinks he's John Wayne? Rambo? Marshal Dillon?

MCCLANE

I was always kinda partial to Roy Rogers, actually. I really like those sequined shirts.

GRUBER

Do you really think you have a chance against us, Mr Cowboy?

MCCLANE

Yippee-ki-yay, motherfucker.

'SLUG IN A DITCH!'

As with many movies, *Die Hard* was considered too rollicking for younger audiences watching the film on television. In order to create an acceptable family viewing experience, the frequent swear-words were overdubbed – with varying degrees of success. As the story unfolded, the results became increasingly surreal:

Yippee-ki-yay, my friend!

Yippee-ki-yay, melon farmer!

Yippee-ki-yay, Mr Falcon!

This last is especially intriguing since nobody in the film is actually called Falcon.

These days Hollywood favours 'fricking' to cover the most popular expletive, and a direct version of the insult can be softened by re-recording it as 'thank you'. Not content to play that game, the Coen brothers enjoy a dig at TV prudishness by replacing the offensive word with 'froozing'.

Here are a few more mealy-mouthed examples. In most cases the original dialogue is clear enough, but translations follow the more truly inventive:

```
Your mother sews socks that smell, Karras, you
faithless slime. (Your mother sucks cocks in
Hell, Karras, you faithless slime.)
```
The Exorcist (1973)

```
Scum buzzard. (Sonofabitch.)
```
Smokey and the Bandit (1977)

```
Man, who do I look like, Christopher Columbo?
(Fuck yo mama!)
```
National Lampoon's Vacation (1983)

```
This town is like a great big chicken just
waiting to get plucked. (This town is like a
great big pussy just waiting to get fucked.)
```
Scarface (1983)

```
Slug in a ditch!
```
Repo Man (1984)

```
Did you slip her the hot wild affection? (Did
you slip her the hot beef injection?)
```
The Breakfast Club (1985)

Pardon my French, but you're an aardvark.
Ferris Bueller's Day Off (1986)

We bury the funsters!
Lethal Weapon (1987)

You're gonna be a bad mothercrusher!
Robocop (1987)

Mickey Fickey!
Do the Right Thing (1989)

We were going to ask Ty Cobb to play, but
none of us could stand that son of a squid.
Field of Dreams (1989)

Go feel your mother!
Goodfellas (1990)

Come back here, you steroid!
Total Recall (1990)

I popped your wife, and later I'm gonna pop
her again.
The Last Boy Scout (1991)

Hand me the keys, you fuzzy sock-sucker.
The Usual Suspects (1994)

Give me the keys, you fairy godmother!
The Usual Suspects (1994)

Jesus, how much did you smoke? All it took was
a phat karate punch. (All it took was a phat
chronic blunt.)
Mallrats (1995)

Forget me? Forget you, you mother forgetter!
Casino (1995)

Get out of my freshly vacuumed house.
Fargo (1996)

I gave simple fruitful instructions.
Fargo (1996)

This is what happens when you find a stranger
in the Alps! (This is what happens when you
fuck a stranger in the ass!)
The Big Lebowski (1998)

I've had it with these monkey-fightin' snakes
on this Monday-to-Friday plane.
Snakes on a Plane (2006)

NAKED   1993

Dir: Mike Leigh. *Scr*: Mike Leigh. *Cast*: David Thewlis (Johnny)

A disturbed young man rails against the unthinking culture that
surrounds us.

                          JOHNNY
Was I bored? No, I wasn't fuckin' bored. I'm
never bored. That's the trouble with everybody —
you're all so bored. You've had nature explained
to you and you're bored with it, you've had the
living body explained to you and you're bored
with it, you've had the universe explained to
you and you're bored with it, so now you want
cheap thrills and, like, plenty of them, and it
doesn't matter how tawdry or vacuous they are

```
as long as it's new . . . as long as it's new as
long as it flashes and fuckin' bleeps in forty
fuckin' different colours. So whatever else you
can say about me, I'm not fuckin' bored.
```

Mike Leigh's technique for shaping a story is the opposite of the traditional process. On this project the cast rehearsed for three months to refine their improvisations and the actual shooting 'script' was only two dozen pages long.

FARGO   1996

Dir: Joel Coen, Ethan Coen. *Scr*: Ethan Coen, Joel Coen. *Cast*: Frances McDormand (Marge Gunderson)

An imperturbable small-town police officer arrests a murderer at the scene of the crime.

```
                    MARGE
So that was Mrs Lundegaard on the floor in
there. And I guess that was your accomplice
in the wood chipper. And those three people in
Brainerd. And for what? For a little bit of
money. There's more to life than a little money,
you know. Don'tcha know that? And here ya are,
and it's a beautiful day. Well, I just don't
understand it.
```

The film states that its events are based on a true story but the Coen brothers later admitted they only added the disclaimer to make the unusual narrative seem more plausible; they once referred to Minnesota as 'Siberia with family restaurants'.

The wood chipper used in the movie is now on display at the Fargo-Moorhead Visitors' Center.

THE PEOPLE VS. LARRY FLYNT   1996

Dir: Miloš Forman. *Scr*: Scott Alexander, Larry Karaszewski. *Cast*: Woody Harrelson (Larry Flynt)

A pornography tycoon asks the court to consider society's hypocrisy.

> FLYNT
> I think the real obscenity comes from raising
> our youth to believe that sex is bad and ugly and
> dirty, and yet it is heroic to go spill guts and
> blood in the most ghastly manner in the name of
> humanity. With all the taboos attached to sex,
> it's no wonder we have the problems we have. It's
> no wonder we're angry and violent and genocidal.
> But ask yourself the question: what is more
> obscene? Sex or war?

THE ROCK   1996

Dir: Michael Bay. *Scr*: Douglas S. Cook, David Weisberg, Mark Rosner. *Cast*: Sean Connery (John Mason), Nicolas Cage (Stanley Goodspeed)

A veteran agent mistrusts his young accomplice.

> MASON
> Are you sure you're ready for this?

> GOODSPEED
> I'll do my best.

> MASON
> Your best! Losers always whine about their best.
> Winners go home and fuck the prom queen.

> GOODSPEED
> Carla *was* the prom queen.

THE BIG LEBOWSKI   1998

Dir: Joel Coen, Ethan Coen. *Scr*: Joel Coen, Ethan Coen. *Cast*: Jeff Bridges (The
Dude)

Jeff Lebowski may be laid back but he has strong views about how
he should be addressed.

> THE DUDE
>
> Let me explain something to you. Um, I am not
> 'Mr Lebowski'. You're Mr Lebowski. I'm the Dude.
> So that's what you call me. You know, that or,
> uh, His Dudeness, or uh, Duder, or El Duderino
> if you're not into the whole brevity thing.

Several key scenes are set in a bowling alley. The film-makers
might be delighted to know that in Norway posters and VHS
covers carried the endorsement '*anbefales av norsk bowling forbund*'
('recommended by the Norwegian Bowling Association').

ERIN BROCKOVICH   2000

Dir: Steven Soderbergh. *Scr*: Susannah Grant. *Cast*: Julia Roberts (Erin Brockovich)

Erin Brockovich represents the people of Hinkley, California, in a
class-action suit against a company accused of poisoning the town's
water.

> ERIN
>
> These people don't dream about being rich. They
> dream about being able to watch their kids swim
> in a pool without worrying that they'll have to
> have a hysterectomy at the age of twenty. Like
> Rosa Diaz, a client of ours. Or have their spine
> deteriorate, like Stan Blume, another client of
> ours. So before you come back here with another
> lame-ass offer, I want you to think real hard

about what your spine is worth, Mr Walker. Or
what you might expect someone to pay you for
your uterus, Ms Sanchez? Then you take out your
calculator and you multiply that number by a
hundred. Anything less than that is a waste of
our time. By the way, we had that water brought
in special for you folks. It came from a well
in Hinkley.

GLADIATOR   2000

Dir: Ridley Scott. *Scr*: David Franzoni, John Logan, William Nicholson. *Cast*:
Russell Crowe (Maximus)

MAXIMUS
My name is Maximus Decimus Meridius, commander
of the Armies of the North, General of the
Felix Legions, loyal servant to the true emperor
Marcus Aurelius. Father to a murdered son,
husband to a murdered wife. And I will have my
vengeance, in this life or the next.

THUMBS DOWN

The making of *Gladiator* was almost as huge an undertaking
as the events it portrayed. The wardrobe department was
required to provide more than 10,000 costumes, the props
department built twenty-four full-size functional chariots and
most of the larger animals in the Rabat zoo were borrowed for
the sequences shot in Morocco. The Germania battle scenes
took twenty days to complete; they were shot in Surrey where
an area had already been earmarked for deforestation, so the
local council were delighted when the production designer told
them they wanted to burn the woodland to the ground.

Any script which deals with historic events must tread a careful line between what is factually accurate and what is dramatically desirable and credible. For *Gladiator*, the production team carried out plenty of research but found that not everything they discovered could be used in the final film. The documented fact that gladiators endorsed commercial products in the arena was dropped because they felt the audience would believe it a crass anachronism. When Ridley Scott and his production designer visited the Colosseum, they deemed it too small for cinematic spectacle and built a partial, expanded version in Malta. It was so large and detailed that when the shoot was over the producers offered it to the local authorities as the basis for a theme park.

Scott originally came on board after two producers showed him a painting, *Pollice Verso* (*Thumbs Down*), of a gladiator turning to the crowd for their verdict on whether or not he should kill the man he has just defeated. Scott said: 'That image spoke to me of the Roman Empire in all its glory and wickedness. I knew right then and there I was hooked.' Many scholars now doubt this was standard procedure in the arena but the film-makers decided not to deny their audience such a familiar visual gesture. The most egregious bending of the truth is the story itself, which portrays Commodus (Joaquin Phoenix) as a vain, insecure tyrant who kills his father Marcus Aurelius (Richard Harris) in desperation to secure his appointment as emperor. In reality, father and son ruled together for several years and many historians now suspect Marcus Aurelius died of the plague.

Commodus was the only emperor known to have fought as a gladiator and there is some evidence his opponents would have been disabled with stiletto wounds before the fights in order to ensure his victory. In reality this underhand practice was kept from Commodus in order to flatter him, although the screenwriters portray him stabbing Maximus (Russell Crowe) in the back before they confront each other in the arena. Historically Maximus (an entirely fictional creation) did not kill Commodus; the emperor was strangled in his dressing room by his wrestling partner Narcissus.

The film had several writers. The first, David Franzoni, had been inspired by a book about gladiatorial combat (*Those About To Die*) although one source suggests the early script is 'different in almost every detail from the finished movie'. John Logan was then brought on board, followed by William Nicholson who subsequently reinstated many of the scenes Logan had cut from Franzoni's drafts. Eventually Franzoni was brought back as a co-producer to supervise the rewrites, and thanks to his new role shared that year's Best Picture Oscar.

According to Nicholson, Russell Crowe was never fully satisfied with the script and frequently refused to appear if changes he demanded were not made. He disliked the crucial speech 'in this life or the next, I will have my vengeance', telling the writer: 'Your lines are garbage, but I'm the greatest actor in the world and I can make even garbage sound good.' Even so, Crowe's commitment to realism was impressive – many of the cuts and stitches in the battle sequences were real, and in filming the gladiatorial fights he broke bones in his foot and hip.

As if Crowe's behaviour were not trying enough for the writers, Richard Harris disliked learning new lines when changes were made and would frequently just speak the dialogue he had already memorized. Oliver Reed, a famously wayward performer, accepted the role of Proximo because he liked the idea of a 'free trip to London to see a couple of shows'; his only demand was that he never work past five in the evening. Supporting the film's narrative, if not the film-makers themselves, Crowe and Harris became friends on set but Reed disliked Crowe and on one occasion challenged him to a fight.

Reed suffered a fatal heart attack in Malta with much of his key material still to be shot. As his role was vital, the insurance company faced a claim estimated at $25 million [$36 million] to reshoot a large proportion of the footage with a new actor. After nearly six months of shooting, Scott and his crew were already exhausted so the director decided to complete Reed's scenes using a mix of body doubles and CGI (computer-generated imagery); the decision saved the insurers $22 million [$32 million].

The film, dedicated to Oliver Reed's memory, recouped its costs within weeks of its release and went on to win five Oscars.

24 HOUR PARTY PEOPLE   2002

Dir: Michael Winterbottom. *Scr*: Frank Cottrell Boyce. *Cast*: Steve Coogan (Tony Wilson)

Real-life music legend Tony Wilson tries to justify a disastrous turnout for the opening night of his new Hacienda club.

> TONY
> The smaller the attendance the bigger the history.
> There were twelve people at the Last Supper. Half
> a dozen at Kitty Hawk. Archimedes was on his own
> in the bath.

Not everyone represented in the story appreciated the way they were portrayed. Peter Hook, New Order's bassist, described the result as 'a film about the biggest cunt in Manchester, played by the second biggest'.

TAKEN 2008

Dir: Pierre Morel. *Scr*: Luc Besson, Robert Mark Kamen. *Cast*: Liam Neeson
(Bryan Mills)

A retired CIA agent speaks with the man who has kidnapped his
daughter.

> BRYAN
>
> I don't know who you are. I don't know what you
> want. If you are looking for ransom, I can tell
> you I don't have money. But what I do have are
> a very particular set of skills; skills I have
> acquired over a very long career. Skills that
> make me a nightmare for people like you. If you
> let my daughter go now, that'll be the end of
> it. I will not look for you, I will not pursue
> you. But if you don't, I will look for you, I
> will find you, and I will kill you.

ZEROES

LA GRANDE ILLUSION   1937

Dir: Jean Renoir. *Scr*: Jean Renoir, Charles Spaak. *Cast*: Jean Gabin (Lieutenant Maréchal)

Lieutenant Maréchal is a man of simple pleasures.

>   LIEUTENANT MARÉCHAL
>   The theatre is too deep for me. I prefer
>   bicycling.

SULLIVAN'S TRAVELS   1941

Dir: Preston Sturges. *Scr*: Preston Sturges. *Cast*: Robert Warwick (Mr LeBrand), Porter Hall (Mr Hadrian), Joel McCrea (John Lloyd Sullivan)

LeBrand and Hadrian discuss Sullivan's previous film – a flop.

>   LEBRAND
>   It died in Pittsburgh.
>
>   HADRIAN
>   Like a dog!
>
>   SULLIVAN
>   Aw, what do they know in Pittsburgh.
>
>   HADRIAN
>   They know what they like.
>
>   SULLIVAN
>   If they knew what they liked, they wouldn't live
>   in Pittsburgh!

Sturges got the idea for the movie from John Garfield's account of his travels as a hobo during the 1930s. Apparently without irony, the secretary of the National Association for the Advancement of Colored People wrote a letter to the director congratulating him on his 'dignified and decent treatment of Negroes' in the film.

THE LADY FROM SHANGHAI   1947

Dir: Orson Welles. *Scr*: Orson Welles. Based on a novel by Sherwood King. *Cast*:
Orson Welles (Michael O'Hara)

A lawyer is caught up in an increasingly complex plot to fake a man's
death.

> **MICHAEL**
> Some people can smell danger. Not me.

KIND HEARTS AND CORONETS   1949

Dir: Robert Hamer. *Scr*: Robert Hamer, John Dighton. Based on a novel by
Roy Horniman. *Cast*: Joan Greenwood (Sibella Holland), Dennis Price (Louis
Mazzini)

Murderer Louis Mazzini tracks a D'Ascoyne family member.

> **SIBELLA**
> He says he wants to go to Europe to expand his
> mind.

> **LOUIS**
> He certainly has room to do so.

ACE IN THE HOLE   1951

Dir: Billy Wilder. *Scr*: Billy Wilder, Lesser Samuels, Walter Newman. *Cast*: Kirk
Douglas (Chuck Tatum)

A newsman always gets his story – even if he has to make it up.

> **CHUCK**
> I can handle big news and little news. And if
> there's no news, I'll go out and bite a dog.

Wilder's wife Audrey Young suggested another wonderful line: 'I
don't go to church. Kneeling bags my nylons.'

A FACE IN THE CROWD   1957

Dir: Elia Kazan. *Scr*: Budd Schulberg. *Cast*: Patricia Neal (Marcia Jeffries), Walter Matthau (Mel Miller)

Mel disparages the brash television star he and Marcia work for.

> MARCIA
>
> Got his introduction ready?
>
> MEL
>
> Home town boy, not only making good, but making everybody.
>
> MARCIA
>
> For a mild man, you sound vicious.
>
> MEL
>
> Didn't you know? All mild men are vicious. They hate themselves for being mild, and they hate the windy extroverts whose violence seems to have a strange attraction for nice girls... who should know better.

NORTH BY NORTHWEST   1959

Dir: Alfred Hitchcock. *Scr*: Ernest Lehman. *Cast*: Cary Grant (Roger O. Thornhill)

An innocent businessman is pursued by a gang who believe he is a government spy; the authorities try to persuade him he is not in danger.

> ROGER
>
> Now you listen to me, I'm an advertising man, not a red herring. I've got a job, a secretary, a mother, two ex-wives and several bartenders that depend upon me, and I don't intend to disappoint them all by getting myself 'slightly' killed.

The famously dapper Grant was profiled in *Esquire* magazine in 1960: 'Although Grant, who is fifty-six, favours such abominations as large tie knots and claims to have originated the square-style breast-pocket handkerchief, he is so extraordinarily attractive that he looks good in practically anything. He insists upon tight armholes in his suit jackets [and] finds the most comfortable of all underwear to be women's nylon panties.'

THE MAN WHO SNEEZED IN LINCOLN'S NOSE

The creation of *North by Northwest* (1959) is a fine example of the collaboration between writer and director on a wholly original screenplay. Alfred Hitchcock was planning to adapt Hammond Innes's novel *The Wreck of the Mary Deare* and his composer friend Bernard Hermann suggested he hire Ernest Lehman (*Sabrina*, *Sweet Smell of Success*, *West Side Story*) to write it. After several weeks, Lehman claimed he couldn't find a way to make the book play on screen, but the two men enjoyed each other's company so much they resolved to put their energies into a different project. When Hermann said he wanted to write 'the Hitchcock picture to end all Hitchcock pictures', the director confessed he had always wanted to shoot a chase on Mount Rushmore, a vast carving in the Black Hills of South Dakota featuring the faces of four American presidents.

The way they developed the plot was almost the exact opposite of the traditional process for a narrative work. Starting only with this brief visual sequence, they devised several other scenarios as building blocks: a murder at the United Nations, a dead body in a car on an automobile production line, a tornado and a grand finale in Alaska. Hitchcock suggested a narrative focusing on a protagonist mistaken for a spy by a criminal gang and the result did indeed deliver one of the director's most perfect creations: Lehman was nominated for an Oscar, and the film remains as popular with critics as it was with the public.

Not all the initial scenarios made it into the final draft: Alaska was abandoned in favour of the Mount Rushmore chase, and Hitchcock was eventually persuaded that a scene where Thornhill hid in one of Lincoln's nostrils only to suffer a sneezing fit was undignified. The sequence where Thornhill finds himself alone on the vast Indiana plains pursued by a tornado was rejected by Lehman on the basis that the cyclone is certainly dangerous but could hardly be blamed on the criminals. Hitchcock capitulated, and the famous biplane sequence ('That's funny, that plane's dustin' crops where there ain't no crops') was devised.

The result is seamlessly crafted and contains many outstanding cinematic moments; screenwriter William Goldman suggests the ending is one of the greatest ever examples of filmic storytelling. In his memoir *Adventures in the Screen Trade* (1983), he writes:

'Near the conclusion of *North by Northwest*, Cary Grant finds himself in something of a pickle.

His true love, Eva Marie Saint, is dangling helplessly in space on the face of Mount Rushmore. If she falls, splat. The reason she has not fallen is that Grant is holding her with one hand while with the other he grabs a rock ledge. Not easy. Watching all this is Martin Landau, the sub-villain, who stands a few feet away, holding the precious statuette that contains valuable microfilm inside, said microfilm being of great danger to America should it fall into enemy hands. Grant, desperate, looks up at Landau and asks for help.

Landau walks over to Grant and, instead of bending down and aiding him, puts his foot on Grant's fingers and begins pressing down. He grinds his shoe down as hard as he can.

That's the pickle.

Now, between that moment and the end of this superb Ernest Lehman–Alfred Hitchcock collaboration, the following occurs.

(a) Landau is made to cease and desist.

(b) Grant saves himself.

(c) Grant also saves Eva Marie Saint.

(d) The two of them get married.

(e) The microfilm is saved for America.

(f) James Mason, the chief villain, is captured and handed over to the authorities.

(g) Grant and Saint take a train ride back east.

That's a lot of narrative to be successfully tied up. And I would like you to guess how long it takes in terms of screentime for it to be accomplished. Got your guess? Here's the answer – forty-three seconds.

Here's how they do it, from the moment where Landau is crunching Grant's hand. The camera's in close-up on the shoe and the fingers. A shot rings out. The shoe begins to slide away from the fingers. Next, a cut of the statuette falling safely to the ground and cracking, revealing the microfilm inside. Now Landau falls to his death off Mount Rushmore. Now another part of Mount Rushmore, where Leo G. Carroll, a good guy, thanks a police officer who is holding a rifle. Behind Carroll is

Mason, flanked by more officers. Now back to Grant and Eva Marie, him saying you can do it, her saying I can't, back and forth, quick cuts between them, and then a really brilliant shot of Grant pulling her up, only now he's not on Mount Rushmore, he's in the upper berth of a train, and he brings her to him, calls her 'Mrs Thornhill' – Thornhill being his last name, so we know they're married now – and as they embrace, a final shot of the train roaring into a tunnel as 'The End' flashes on the screen.

I don't know a more adroit ending to a film.'

THE APARTMENT   1960

Dir: Billy Wilder. *Scr*: Billy Wilder, I. A. L. Diamond. *Cast*: Jack Lemmon (C.C. 'Bud' Baxter)

Mild-mannered Baxter has a keen eye for detail.

C. C. BAXTER

On November 1st, 1959, the population of New York City was 8,042,783. If you laid all these people end to end, figuring an average height of five feet six and a half inches, they would reach from Times Square to the outskirts of Karachi, Pakistan. I know facts like this because I work for an insurance company — Consolidated Life of New York. We're one of the top five companies in the country. Our home office has 31,259 employees, which is more than the entire population of uhh . . . Natchez, Mississippi. I work on the 19th floor. Ordinary Policy Department, Premium Accounting Division, Section W, desk number 861.

THE SOUND OF MUSIC   1965

Dir: Robert Wise. *Scr*: Ernest Lehman. *Cast*: Richard Haydn (Max Detweiler),
Christopher Plummer (Captain Von Trapp)

As Germany threatens to annex Austria, the cowardly Max
reluctantly agrees to help the von Trapp family escape.

> MAX
>
> I hope you appreciate the sacrifice I'm making.

> CAPTAIN VON TRAPP
>
> You have no choice.

> MAX
>
> I know... That's why I'm making it.

Christopher Plummer hated his role in the hugely successful film,
referring to it in subsequent interviews as 'The Sound of Mucus'.
He also said of Julie Andrews (a rising star after the release of *Mary
Poppins* the previous year) that 'working with her is like being hit
over the head by a Valentine's Day card'.

THE SPY WHO CAME IN FROM THE COLD   1965

Dir: Martin Ritt. *Scr*: Paul Dehn, Guy Trosper. Based on a novel by John le Carré.
Cast: Richard Burton (Alec Leamas)

British secret agent Leamas finds himself disgusted by the hypocrisy
of his trade.

> LEAMAS
>
> What the hell do you think spies are? Moral
> philosophers measuring everything they do
> against the word of God or Karl Marx? They're
> not! They're just a bunch of seedy, squalid
> bastards like me: little men, drunkards, queers,
> hen-pecked husbands, civil servants playing

```
cowboys and Indians to brighten their rotten
little lives. Do you think they sit like monks
in a cell, balancing right against wrong?
```

Le Carré originally felt Richard Burton was too famous and too glamorous for the part of Alec Leamas, but Burton's dedicated, understated performance won him over.

ONCE UPON A TIME IN THE WEST   1968
Dir: Sergio Leone. *Scr*: Sergio Leone, Sergio Donati. *Cast*: Henry Fonda (Frank)

A brutal gunslinger puts a member of his gang in his place.

```
        FRANK
How can you trust a man who wears both a belt
and suspenders? The man can't even trust his
own pants.
```

Sergio Leone was delighted to learn that one cinema in Paris ran the film for two years. When he finally visited the theatre he was greeted by fans who wanted his autograph – as well as by the projectionist, who was less welcoming. The technician yelled at the director: 'I kill you! The same movie over and over again for two years! And it's so SLOW!'

THE PRODUCERS   1968
Dir: Mel Brooks. *Scr*: Mel Brooks. *Cast*: Zero Mostel (Max Bialystock)

A desperate producer tries to impress his new partner.

```
        BIALYSTOCK
You know who I used to be?
```

A PRODUCER'S HEART

While directors turn their attention to the physical creation of a film, producers are more interested in the waiting public. Without tickets sold there can be no movie at all – or, to be more accurate, no next movie. For an artist, acclaim is success. For a financier, success is success.

Once a producer has decided what kind of story he wants to see and hired a team to deliver it, he has to imagine an audience and take an educated guess as to how many of them will actually make the journey to the cinema. His job title may sound glamorous but its nature is complex: from raising finance to securing distribution, shepherding wayward talent and finessing promises into contracts, every step of the journey is fraught. As the old saying goes, 'you're not making a movie until the camera is rolling'. Where many of the cast and crew breathe a sigh of relief that the process is finally under way and they now have a chance to do what they love best, a producer begins to sweat: this is the point where the money is going out – and it may never come back in.

With this level of risk as well as the huge investment of time involved, it is no wonder that financiers keep their eye on the bottom line while they wield a firm hand in the running of the show. But with so many egos under their command, we should not be surprised either that rivalries appear:

> You can take all the sincerity in Hollywood, place it in the navel of a firefly and still have room enough for three caraway seeds and a producer's heart.

> *Fred Allen*

Producers are men who will keep their heads in the noisy presence of writers and directors and not be carried away by art in any of its subversive guises. Their task is to guard against the unusual. They are the trusted loyalists of cliché.

Ben Hecht

If producers suffer such familiar complaints, it is largely because those who may have reason to gripe about them – the actors, writers and directors – have easy access to the press. The challenges of getting a project off the ground can seem a thankless task, although when a project is a hit gratitude is rarely needed; prizes and profit points are perfectly sufficient. When the golden envelopes are opened and *Variety* publishes the weekly takings, producers leap into the limelight claiming, often rightly, that the movie was their personal dream and that it could never have seen the light of day without their persistence.

If no producer, no movie.

Dino De Laurentiis

The Oscar for Best Picture is always awarded to the producer, even though in the eyes of the public the film's kudos is associated with the director; in 1972 Albert Ruddy took home a statuette for *The Godfather* while Francis Ford Coppola lost out to Bob Fosse with *Cabaret*. After that, Coppola made sure he also took a producer's role on *The Godfather: Part II*.

In the heyday of the studio system – from the dawn of the talkies to the 1950s – the heads of MGM, Universal or Fox could green-light their favourite projects with a simple memo, choosing among their tightly controlled empire of stars, directors and writers to create an instant team. Many of their contracted artists resented this control:

I discovered early in my movie work that a movie is never any better than the stupidest man connected with it. There are times when this distinction may be given to the writer or director. Most often it belongs to the producer... Ninety per cent of the producers I have known were not bright. They were as slow-witted and unprofessional toward making up a story as stockbrokers might be, or bus drivers.

Ben Hecht

By 1950, two changes had begun to be felt: the Supreme Court had ended the studios' monopoly over cinema distribution, and television had given artists greater freedom to work on their own terms. Even so, working outside the framework of Hollywood's fiefdoms, film-makers still needed financiers and ambassadors for their projects. Thus began the rise of the independent producer. Sam Spiegel (*Lawrence of Arabia*, 1962), Robert Evans (*Chinatown*, 1974) and Joseph E. Levine (*A Bridge Too Far*, 1977) were some of the first in the industry to gain a reputation for power, integrity and intelligence. Not surprisingly, such men took care to protect themselves when they hired the rest of the talent:

Hollywood has always been full of bartenders and waiters who want to be directors. Trouble is, most of them have achieved their ambition.

Sam Spiegel

When a director hires a producer, you're in deep shit. A director needs a boss, not a yes man.

Robert Evans

The ultimate sign of success for a producer is when his own name helps sell the film to the public, or when he can be associated with a distinct style of production. Familiar names today include:

- Jerry Bruckheimer (*Pirates of the Caribbean, Armageddon*)
- Kathleen Kennedy (*Schindler's List, The Sixth Sense*)
- Ron Howard (*The Da Vinci Code, A Beautiful Mind*)
- Brian Grazer (*Apollo 13, Frost/Nixon*)
- Scott Rudin (*The Social Network, No Country for Old Men*).

THE ITALIAN JOB   1969

Dir: Peter Collinson. *Scr*: Troy Kennedy Martin. *Cast*: Michael Caine (Charlie Croker)

Charlie's henchmen use too much explosive when breaking into a car.

> CHARLIE
> You're only supposed to blow the bloody doors off!

Director Peter Collinson was raised by his grandparents before attending the Actors' Orphanage in Surrey. Noël Coward was President there and became Collinson's godfather, helping him find his way into the world of entertainment. When Collinson got his first big break on the film, he repaid the favour by casting Coward as Mr Bridger, the pampered criminal mastermind.

BADLANDS   1973

Dir: Terrence Malick. *Scr*: Terrence Malick. *Cast*: Sissy Spacek (Holly Sargis)

Two lovers flee after killing the girl's father.

> HOLLY
>
> I didn't feel shame or fear but just kind
> of . . . blah. Like when you're sitting there
> and all the water's run out of the bathtub.

THE PINK PANTHER STRIKES AGAIN   1976

Dir: Blake Edwards. *Scr*: Frank Waldman. *Cast*: Peter Sellers (Chief Inspector Clouseau), Harold Berens (Hotel Clerk)

A bumbling detective discovers that assumption is not the same as deduction.

> CLOUSEAU
>
> Does your dog bite?

> HOTEL CLERK
>
> No.

Clouseau pets the dog.

> CLOUSEAU
>
> Nice doggie.

The dog barks and bites Clouseau.

> CLOUSEAU
>
> I thought you said your dog did not bite!

> HOTEL CLERK
>
> That is not my dog.

Clouseau is painfully aware of his mistakes. In the same film he tries to suggest his frequent clumsiness is just part of a detective's technique: 'I see you are familiar with the falling-down-on-the-floor ploy.'

CADDYSHACK   1980

Dir: Harold Ramis. *Scr*: Harold Ramis, Douglas Kenney, Brian Doyle-Murray. *Cast*: Bill Murray (Carl Spackler), Sarah Holcomb (Maggie O'Hoolihan)

A golf caddy consoles himself over the lost opportunity of a tip.

> CARL
>
> So I jump ship in Hong Kong and I make my way over to Tibet, and I get on as a looper at a course over in the Himalayas.
>
> MAGGIE
>
> A looper?
>
> CARL
>
> A looper, you know, a caddy, a looper, a jock. So, I tell them I'm a pro jock, and who do you think they give me? The Dalai Lama himself. Twelfth son of the Lama. The flowing robes, the grace, bald. . . striking. So, I'm on the first tee with him. I give him the driver. He hauls off and whacks one — big hitter, the Lama — long, into a ten-thousand-foot crevasse, right at the base of this glacier. Do you know what the Lama says? Gunga galunga. . . gunga, gunga-lagunga. So we finish the eighteenth and he's gonna stiff me. And I say, 'Hey, Lama, hey, how about a little something, you know, for the effort, you know?' And he says, 'Oh. . . there won't be any money, but when you die, on your deathbed, you will receive total

consciousness.' So I got that going for me,
which is nice.

TOOTSIE 1982

Dir: Sydney Pollack. *Scr*: Larry Gelbart, Murray Schisgal, Don McGuire. *Cast*:
Dustin Hoffman (Michael Dorsey/Dorothy Michaels), Sydney Pollack (George
Fields)

An actor complains to his agent that he is not getting enough work.

> MICHAEL
>
> Are you saying that nobody in New York will
> work with me?

> GEORGE
>
> No, no, that's too limited . . . nobody in
> Hollywood wants to work with you either. I can't
> even set you up for a commercial. You played a
> tomato for thirty seconds — they went a half a
> day over schedule because you wouldn't sit down.

> MICHAEL
>
> Of course. It was illogical.

> GEORGE
>
> You were a tomato. A tomato doesn't have logic.
> A tomato can't move.

> MICHAEL
>
> That's what I said. So if he can't move, how's
> he gonna sit down, George? I was a stand-up
> tomato: a juicy, sexy, beefsteak tomato. Nobody
> does vegetables like me. I did an evening of
> vegetables off-Broadway. I did the best tomato,
> the best cucumber. I did an endive salad that
> knocked the critics on their ass.

KING OF COMEDY   1983

Dir: Martin Scorsese. *Scr*: Paul D. Zimmerman. *Cast*: Marta Heflin (Secretary),
Robert De Niro (Rupert Pupkin)

An embittered stand-up comedian forces a TV talk show host to put
him on his programme.

> **SECRETARY**
> Is Mr Langford expecting you?

> **RUPERT PUPKIN**
> Yes, I don't think he is.

THIS IS SPINAL TAP   1984

Dir: Rob Reiner. *Scr*: Christopher Guest, Michael McKean, Harry Shearer, Rob
Reiner. *Cast*: Rob Reiner (Marty DiBergi), Christopher Guest (Nigel Tufnel)

Marty, a documentary film-maker, interviews rock star Nigel as he
improvises at the piano.

> **MARTY**
> It's very pretty.

> **NIGEL**
> Yeah, I've been fooling around with it for a
> few months.

> **MARTY**
> It's a bit of a departure from what you
> normally play.

> **NIGEL**
> It's part of a trilogy, a musical trilogy I'm
> working on in D minor which is the saddest of
> all keys, I find. People weep instantly when
> they hear it, and I don't know why.

                    MARTY
It's very nice.

                    NIGEL
You know, just simple lines intertwining, very
much like — I'm really influenced by Mozart and
Bach, and it's sort of in between those, really.
It's like a 'Mach' piece, really. It's sort
of . . .

                    MARTY
What do you call this?

                    NIGEL
Well, this piece is called 'Lick My Love Pump'.

The film was improvised by all the performers, so lead actors Rob
Reiner, Christopher Guest, Michael McKean and Harry Shearer
went to the Writers' Guild hoping to give proper credit to everyone.
The Board of Directors voted fifteen to none that the credits should
stay as they were, listing only the four of them.

AMADEUS   1984

Dir: Miloš Forman. *Scr*: Peter Shaffer. *Cast*: F. Murray Abraham (Antonio Salieri)

Though a fierce rival, Salieri recognizes Mozart's genius.

                    SALIERI
I heard the music of true forgiveness filling
the theatre, conferring on all who sat there
perfect absolution. God was singing through
this little man to all the world, unstoppable,
making my defeat more bitter with every passing
bar.

Prague, where the film was shot, still contained so much of its original architecture that only four sets needed to be built. Sir Neville Marriner agreed to conduct the Academy of St Martin in the Fields for the soundtrack on condition that not a single note of Mozart's music be changed.

FERRIS BUELLER'S DAY OFF   1986

Dir: John Hughes. *Scr*: John Hughes. *Cast*: Matthew Broderick (Ferris Bueller)

A freewheeling high school student fears his best friend is too timid.

> FERRIS
> Cameron is so tight that if you stuck a lump
> of coal up his ass, in two weeks you'd have a
> diamond.

WITHNAIL AND I   1987

Dir: Bruce Robinson. *Scr*: Bruce Robinson. *Cast*: Paul McGann (Marwood, 'I'),
Ralph Brown (Danny), Richard E. Grant (Withnail)

Marwood and Withnail are startled by Danny's politics – and his narcotics.

> MARWOOD
> Give me a Valium, I'm getting the fear!

> DANNY
> You have done something to your brain. You have
> made it high. If I lay 10 mils of diazepam on
> you, it will do something else to your brain.
> You will make it low. Why trust one drug and not
> the other? That's politics, innit?

> MARWOOD
> I'm gonna eat some sugar.

He goes to the kitchen.

                    DANNY
        I recommend you smoke some more grass.

                    MARWOOD
        No way, no fucking way.

                    DANNY
        That is an unfortunate political decision.
        Reflecting these times.

                    WITHNAIL
        What are you talking about, Danny?

                    DANNY
        Politics, man. If you're hanging onto a rising
        balloon, you're presented with a difficult
        decision — let go before it's too late — or hang
        on and keep getting higher, posing the question:
        how long can you keep a grip on the rope?
        They're selling hippie wigs in Woolworth's,
        man. The greatest decade in the history of
        mankind is over. And as Presuming Ed here has
        so consistently pointed out, we have failed to
        paint it black.

WHITE MISCHIEF   1987

Dir: Michael Radford. *Scr*: Michael Radford, Jonathan Gems. Based on a novel
by James Fox. *Cast*: Sarah Miles (Alice de Janzé)

A jaded British expatriate opens her curtains to reveal the gorgeous
hills of Kenya.

                    ALICE
        Oh God — not another fucking beautiful day.

A FISH CALLED WANDA 1988

Dir: Charles Crichton, John Cleese (uncredited). *Scr*: John Cleese, Charles Crichton. *Cast*: Jamie Lee Curtis (Wanda Gershwitz)

A con artist finds her plans undermined by her idiotic partner-in-crime.

> WANDA
>
> Aristotle was not Belgian. The central message
> of Buddhism is not 'Every man for himself'.
> And the London Underground is not a political
> movement. Those are all mistakes, Otto. I looked
> them up.

The scenes in which Otto seduces Wanda in clumsy Italian had to be dubbed into Spanish for the Italian market. During the scene where a poodle is buried, the choirboys sing 'Miserere Dominus, canis mortuus est' ('Have mercy, Lord, the dog is dead').

John Cleese insisted the film was really directed by Crichton alone, and that Cleese had agreed to share the role solely because Crichton was seventy-seven and the financiers were nervous he might have lost his touch. Crichton was responsible for the Ealing comedies *The Lavender Hill Mob* (1951) and *The Titfield Thunderbolt* (1953).

COPYCAT 1995

Dir: Jon Amiel. *Scr*: Ann Biderman, David Madsen. *Cast*: William McNamara (Peter Foley)

A serial killer taunts one of his targets.

> PETER
>
> Don't you ever get tired... Of being a day
> late and a dollar short?

CASINO

Dir: Martin Scorsese. *Scr*: Nicholas Pileggi, Martin Scorsese. Based on a book by Nicholas Pileggi. *Cast*: Joe Pesci (Nicky Santoro)

Ferocious mobster Nicky Santoro does not suffer fools gladly.

> NICKY
> This guy could fuck up a cup of coffee.

The owners of the Riviera casino where the film was shot did not want the production to deter their real gambling clients, so scenes were scheduled in the brief slot between 1 a.m. and 4 a.m. Somewhat disingenuously, the casino owners boosted business by posting a large sign outside saying 'Robert De Niro, Sharon Stone, and Joe Pesci Filming the New Movie "Casino" Inside!'

'YOUR MOTHER WAS A HAMSTER'

An insult can be a finely honed stiletto or a sledgehammer, each effective according to adversary and circumstance. Screenwriters in the earlier part of the twentieth century were hamstrung by censors and public sensitivities but these constraints only served to focus their barbs. The following quotes, in chronological order, show how changing times can sharpen – or not – cinema's rapier wit.

You clinking clanking clattering collection of caliginous junk!
The Wizard of Oz (1939)

There's a name for you ladies, but it isn't used in high society . . . outside of a kennel.
The Women (1939)

UGARTE: You despise me, don't you?
RICK: If I gave you any thought, I probably
would.
Casablanca (1942)

I know you like a book, you little tramp. You'd
sell your own mother for a piece of fudge. But
you're smart with it. Smart enough to know when
to sell and when to sit tight. You've got a great
big dollar sign there where most women have a
heart.
The Killing (1956)

You're the son of a thousand fathers, all
bastards like you.
The Good, the Bad and the Ugly (1966)

Take your stinking paws off me, you damn dirty
ape.
Planet of the Apes (1968)

I call that bold talk for a one-eyed fat man.
True Grit (1969)

Well, if it isn't fat stinking billy goat Billy
Boy in poison! How art thou, thou globby bottle
of cheap, stinking chip oil? Come and get one in
the yarbles, if you have any yarbles, you eunuch
jelly thou!
A Clockwork Orange (1971)

You know, I'd almost forgotten what your eyes
looked like. Still the same. Pissholes in the
snow.
Get Carter (1971)

I don't wanna talk to you no more, you empty
headed, animal food trough wiper. I fart in your
general direction. Your mother was a hamster
and your father smelled of elderberries.
Monty Python and the Holy Grail (1975)

The day they lay you away, what I do on your
grave won't pass for flowers.
The Shootist (1976)

You punch like you take it up the ass!
Raging Bull (1980)

You're not too smart, are you? I like that in a man.
Body Heat (1981)

You're a neo maxi zoom dweebie.
The Breakfast Club (1985)

Did your parents have any children that lived?
Full Metal Jacket (1987)

You're in more dire need of a blow job than
any white man in history.
Good Morning Vietnam (1987)

You're one ugly motherfucker.
Predator (1987)

I'll use small words so that you'll be sure to
understand, you warthog faced buffoon.
The Princess Bride (1987)

[Soldier], you'd need three promotions to get to
be an asshole.
Biloxi Blues (1988)

She's got a heart like a twelve-minute egg.
Bright Lights, Big City (1988)

To call you stupid would be an insult to stupid
people. I've known sheep who could outwit you.
I've worn dresses with higher IQs.
A Fish Called Wanda (1988)

If my dog had a face like yours, I'd shave his
ass and teach him to walk backwards.
Gleaming the Cube (1989)

I wouldn't live with you if the world were
flooded with piss and you lived in a tree.
Parenthood (1989)

He was so crooked, he could eat soup with a
corkscrew.
The Grifters (1990)

You lewd, crude, rude, bag of pre-chewed food
dude.
Hook (1991)

Sit your five-dollar ass down before I make
change.
New Jack City (1991)

Mr Madison, what you've just said is one of
the most insanely idiotic things I have ever
heard. At no point in your rambling, incoherent
response were you even close to anything that
could be considered a rational thought. Everyone
in this room is now dumber for having listened

to it. I award you no points, and may God have mercy on your soul.
Billy Madison (1995)

Were you always this stupid, or did you take lessons?
The Long Kiss Goodnight (1996)

I don't give a tuppeny fuck about your moral conundrum, you meat-headed shit sack.
Gangs of New York (2002)

You cock-juggling thunder-cunt!
Blade: Trinity (2004)

Harry, let's face it. And I'm not being funny. I mean no disrespect, but you're a cunt. You're a cunt now, and you've always been a cunt. And the only thing that's going to change is that you're going to be an even bigger cunt.
In Bruges (2008)

Stop crying, you snivelling ass! Stop your nonsense. You're just an afterbirth, Eli. You slithered out of your mother's filth. They should have put you in a glass jar on the mantelpiece.
There Will Be Blood (2008)

GOOD WILL HUNTING   1997

Dir: Gus Van Sant. *Scr*: Matt Damon, Ben Affleck. *Cast*: Matt Damon (Will Hunting)

A talented but wayward college student criticizes a friend for being too conventional.

> WILL

You dropped a hundred and fifty grand on a
fucking education you coulda got for a dollar
fifty in late charges at the public library.

JACKIE BROWN   1997

Dir: Quentin Tarantino. *Scr*: Quentin Tarantino. Based on a novel by Elmore
Leonard. *Cast*: Samuel L. Jackson (Ordell Robbie), Bridget Fonda (Melanie
Ralston)

> ORDELL

You know you smoke too much of that shit, that
shit gonna rob you of your own ambition.

> MELANIE

Not if your ambition is to get high and watch
TV.

AMERICAN BEAUTY   1999

Dir: Sam Mendes. *Scr*: Alan Ball. *Cast*: Annette Bening (Carolyn Burnham),
Kevin Spacey (Lester Burnham)

> CAROLYN

Your father and I were just discussing his day at
work. Why don't you tell our daughter about it,
honey?

> LESTER

Janie, today I quit my job. And then I told my
boss to go fuck himself, and then I blackmailed
him for almost $60,000. Pass the asparagus.

> CAROLYN

Your father seems to think this kind of behaviour
is something to be proud of.

Outrun, outgunned… but never outdressed.

Romances, bromances and womances…

… great screen partnerships come in all forms.

Bogart and Bacall fell in love when they met on set…

… while Kidman and Cruise were already married.

If we can't love them…

… we can love to hate them.

The greatest stories speak for themselves.

>   LESTER
>
> And your mother seems to prefer that I go through
> life like a fucking prisoner while she keeps my
> dick in a mason jar under the sink.
>
>   CAROLYN
>
> How dare you speak to me that way in front of
> her. And I marvel that you can be so contemptuous
> of me, on the same day that you LOSE your job.
>
>   LESTER
>
> Lose it? I didn't lose it. It's not like,
> 'Whoops! Where'd my job go?' I *quit*. Someone pass
> the asparagus, please.

Earlier versions of the script contained one scene in which Lester does actually sleep with the underage Angela, and another where Ricky and Jane are arrested for Lester's murder.

O BROTHER, WHERE ART THOU? 2000

Dir: Joel Coen, Ethan Coen (uncredited). *Scr*: Ethan Coen, Joel Coen. Based on *The Odyssey* by Homer. *Cast*: George Clooney (Ulysses Everett McGill), Chris Thomas King (Tommy Johnson), Tim Blake Nelson (Delmar O'Donnell)

Three escaped convicts meet a travelling musician.

>   MCGILL
>
> What'd the devil give you for your soul, Tommy?
>
>   JOHNSON
>
> Well, he taught me to play this here guitar real
> good.
>
>   O'DONNELL
>
> Oh, son, for that you sold your everlasting soul?
>
>   JOHNSON
>
> Well, I wasn't usin' it.

Although set in 1930s Mississippi, the film is a loose adaptation of *The Odyssey*, an epic poem written during the eighth century BC.

WAKING LIFE   2001

Dir: Richard Linklater. *Scr*: Richard Linklater. *Cast*: Julie Delpy (Celine)

Celine is sceptical about past life experiences.

> CELINE
>
> Everybody says they've been the reincarnation
> of Cleopatra or Alexander the Great. I always
> want to tell them they were probably some dumb
> fuck like everybody else.

ZOOLANDER   2001

Dir: Ben Stiller. *Scr*: Ben Stiller, Drake Sather, John Hamburg. *Cast*: Ben Stiller (Derek Zoolander)

Male supermodel Derek Zoolander eulogises his late associates.

> ZOOLANDER
>
> Rufus, Brint and Meekus were like brothers to me.
> And when I say brother, I don't mean, like, an
> actual brother, but I mean it like the way black
> people use it. Which is more meaningful, I think.

He pauses to reflect.

> ZOOLANDER
>
> If there is anything that this horrible tragedy
> can teach us, it's that a male model's life is
> a precious, precious commodity. Just because
> we have chiselled abs and stunning features, it
> doesn't mean that we too can't die in a freak
> gasoline-fight accident.

Bret Easton Ellis wrote *Glamorama*, a novel about a moronic male supermodel who gets caught up in a fashion-related terrorist conspiracy, three years before *Zoolander* was released. He sued Ben Stiller for copyright infringement but the case was settled out of court. Although the story is a highly exaggerated satire on the modelling world, many of the industry's most successful faces admitted the details of the lifestyle were remarkably accurate.

SIDEWAYS   2004

Dir: Alexander Payne. *Scr*: Alexander Payne, Jim Taylor. Based on a novel by Rex Pickett. *Cast*: Paul Giamatti (Miles Raymond), Thomas Haden Church (Jack Cole)

Two middle-aged friends on a road trip contemplate their achievements.

>   MILES
> Half my life is over and I have nothing to show
> for it. Nothing. I'm a thumbprint on the window
> of a skyscraper. I'm a smudge of excrement on a
> tissue surging out to sea with a million tons of
> raw sewage.

>   JACK
> See? Right there. Just what you just said. That is
> beautiful. 'A smudge of excrement surging out to
> sea.'

>   MILES
> Yeah.

>   JACK
> I could never write that.

>   MILES
> Neither could I, actually. I think it's Bukowski.

Miles is a wine connoisseur and frequently cites his preferred grape variety as Pinot Noir. Following the release of the film, sales of this wine type rose by 20 per cent.

DODGEBALL: A TRUE UNDERDOG STORY 2004

Dir: Rawson Marshall Thurber. *Scr*: Rawson Marshall Thurber. *Cast*: Christine Taylor (Kate Veatch), Vince Vaughn (Peter La Fleur)

Kate despairs of her under-achieving boyfriend.

> **KATE**
> I'm curious — is it strictly apathy, or do you really not have a goal in life?

> **PETER**
> I found that if you have a goal you might not reach it. But if you don't have one, then you are never disappointed. And I gotta tell you... it feels phenomenal.

EAGLE VS SHARK 2007

Dir: Taika Waititi. *Scr*: Taika Waititi. *Cast*: Uncredited (Man on Phone), Jemaine Clement (Jarrod)

Jarrod attempts to place a threatening phone call to someone who – in the distant past – humiliated him at school. Jarrod's intended victim, however, is not at home.

> **MAN ON PHONE**
> Do you want to leave a message?

> **JARROD**
> Tell him that justice is waiting for him.

> **MAN ON PHONE**
> OK, Justin. Thank you. Bye bye.

He hangs up.

                    JARROD
    No! Justice. Justice!

SUPERBAD   2007

Dir: Greg Mottola. *Scr*: Seth Rogen, Evan Goldberg. *Cast*: Jonah Hill (Seth)

Two high school nerds decide to throw a party in the hope of boosting their love lives.

                    SETH
    You know when you hear girls say 'Ah man, I
    was so shit-faced last night, I shouldn't have
    fucked that guy'? We could be that mistake!

BAD TEACHER   2011

Dir: Jake Kasdan. *Scr*: Gene Stupnitsky, Lee Eisenberg. *Cast*: Cameron Diaz
(Elizabeth Halsey)

A red-hot high school teacher offers some dating advice.

                    ELIZABETH
    I tell you what I know. A kid who wears the same
    gymnastics sweatshirt three days a week isn't
    getting laid until he's twenty-nine. That's what
    I know.

DARKEST HOUR   2017

Dir: Joe Wright. *Scr*: Anthony McCarten. *Cast*: Gary Oldman (Winston
Churchill)

                    WINSTON CHURCHILL
    My father was like God. Busy elsewhere.

MEMORIES

Dir: Orson Welles. *Scr*: Orson Welles, Herman J. Mankiewicz. *Cast*: Everett
Sloane (Mr Bernstein)

BERNSTEIN

A fellow will remember a lot of things you
wouldn't think he'd remember. You take me. One
day, back in 1896, I was crossing over to Jersey
on the ferry, and as we pulled out there was
another ferry pulling in, and on it there was a
girl waiting to get off. A white dress she had
on. She was carrying a white parasol. I only saw
her for one second. She didn't see me at all,
but I'll bet a month hasn't gone by since that
I haven't thought of that girl.

This monologue was surely the inspiration for John Gage's speech in
Indecent Proposal (1993):

'I remember once when I was young, and I was coming
back from some place, a movie or something. I was on the
subway. And there was a girl sitting across from me, and
she was wearing this dress that was buttoned clear right
up to here. She was the most beautiful thing I'd ever seen.
And I was shy then, so when she would look at me, I would
look away. Then afterwards, when I would look back, she
would look away. Then I got to where I was gonna get off,
and got off. The doors closed. And as the train was pulling
away, she looked right at me and gave me the most incredible smile. It was awful. I wanted to tear the doors open.
I went back every night, same time for two weeks but she
never showed up. That was thirty years ago, and I don't
think that there's a day that goes by that I don't think
about her. I don't want that to happen again.'

NEVER GIVE A SUCKER AN EVEN BREAK   1941

Dir: Edward F. Cline. *Scr*: John T. Neville, Prescott Chaplin. *Cast*: W. C. Fields
(The Great Man)

              THE GREAT MAN
    I was in love with a beautiful blonde once, dear.
    She drove me to drink. 'Tis the one thing I'm
    indebted to her for.

OLD ACQUAINTANCE   1943

Dir: Vincent Sherman. *Scr*: John Van Druten, Lenore J. Coffee. *Cast*: Bette Davis
(Kit Marlowe)

              KIT
    There comes a time in every woman's life
    when the only thing that helps is a glass of
    champagne.

BEAT THE DEVIL   1953

Dir: John Huston. *Scr*: Truman Capote, John Huston. Based on a novel by James
Helvick (aka Claud Cockburn). *Cast*: Peter Lorre (Julius O'Hara)

A group of thieves kill time as they wait for their passage to
Africa.

              O'HARA
    What is time? Swiss manufacture it. French
    hoard it. Italians squander it. Americans say
    it's money. Hindus say it doesn't exist. Do you
    know what I say? I say time is a crook.

Humphrey Bogart was involved in a car accident during the shoot
and lost several teeth, compromising his recorded dialogue. Peter
Sellers, known at that time only as a capable mimic, overdubbed
the lines.

BY THE WAY, THE PRODUCER THINKS IT'S A GREAT IDEA

A screenwriter rarely creates a character with a particular actor in mind unless she knows her director or producer has good access to them. If she fills her script with enticingly tailored description ('his chiselled features and silver hair lend gravitas to his steely gaze as he surveys the dry plains before him, a cheroot in one hand and a Colt revolver in the other') then she will have a good deal of revision to do if Clint Eastwood passes on the project and the next available name is Daniel Radcliffe.

Canny writers prefer to paint an attractive one-size-fits-all portrait: 'sexy in an understated way, her elegant presence exudes a powerful wordless confidence'. If Anne Hathaway is not available but Julia Roberts likes it, the story still makes sense.

Once the lottery of casting is complete the writer can only hope that the actors will connect with her story and realize their roles sympathetically. If a big name is cast, she may dream of a smash hit but faces the possibility that the star will be powerful enough to demand fresh drafts.

Sometimes this is because they have a keen insight into her story's unseen potential; sometimes it is because they have always wanted to drive a Lamborghini, and feel a chase sequence will show that the college professor they have been hired to play is not just a two-dimensional, desk-bound, middle-aged academic. Oh, and also – the star's girlfriend has just graduated from drama school and feels that although the role of the history lecturer was written for a fifty-year-old whose grandparents died in the Holocaust, with a little tinkering it could be perfect for her.

By the way, the producer thinks it's a great idea.

THE SWIMMER   1968

Dir: Frank Perry. *Scr*: Eleanor Perry. Based on a story by John Cheever. *Cast*: Burt Lancaster (Ned Merrill), Janice Rule (Shirley Abbott)

Ned reminisces ruefully with a former lover.

> NED
>
> My mother gave me 25 cents for mowing the lawn
> around our house. Seems only a minute ago I
> could smell the grass... It's so fast. People
> grow up, and then they... We're all gonna die,
> Shirley. That doesn't make much sense, does it?

> SHIRLEY
>
> Sometimes it does... Sometimes at three o'clock
> in the morning.

MURDER BY DEATH   1976

Dir: Robert Moore. *Scr*: Neil Simon. *Cast*: Peter Falk (Sam Diamond)

A group of detectives summoned to solve a crime remain suspicious of one another.

> SAM
>
> The last time I trusted a dame was in Paris
> in 1940. She said she was going out to get a
> bottle of wine. Two hours later, the Germans
> marched into France.

HEAVEN'S GATE   1980

Dir: Michael Cimino. *Scr*: Michael Cimino. *Cast*: John Hurt (Billy Irvine), Kris Kristofferson (James Averill)

Rancher Billy Irvine and Marshal James Averill find their friendship tested as homesteaders settle in Wyoming.

> **BILLY**
> James, do you remember the good gone days?

> **JAMES**
> Clearer and better, every day I get older.

Director Michael Cimino leveraged his success with *The Deer Hunter* (1978) to make *Heaven's Gate* entirely on his own terms, leaving no aspect of the production untouched by his perfectionism. By the end of the fifth day's filming the crew were already four days behind schedule; one scene for which the stage direction says simply an actor 'walks past a cock-fight' took over two weeks to complete, and the main shoot lasted over a year. The budget was expanded from $7.5 million [$23 million] to $44 million [$134 million] but the US box office only recouped $3.5 million [$11 million] and the loss nearly bankrupted United Artists.

Vincent Canby of the *New York Times* wrote: 'it fails so completely that you might suspect Mr Cimino sold his soul to obtain the success of *The Deer Hunter* and the Devil has just come around to collect'.

MAD MAX II   1981

Dir: George Miller. *Scr*: Terry Hayes, George Miller, Brian Hannant. *Cast*: Harold Baigent (Narrator)

> **NARRATOR**
> My life fades, my vision dims. All that remains
> are memories. I remember a time of chaos,
> ruined dreams, this wasted land. Most of all,
> I remember the man we called Max, the road
> warrior. To understand who he was we have to
> go back to the other time. When the world was
> powered by the black fuel, and the desert sprung
> great cities of pipe and steel. Gone now, swept
> away. For reasons long forgotten, two mighty

warrior tribes went to war and touched off a
blaze which engulfed them all. Without fuel they
were nothing. They'd built a house of straw.
Suddenly their machines sputtered and stopped.
Their leaders talked and talked and talked,
but nothing could stem the avalanche. Their
world crumbled. Cities exploded. A whirlwind of
looting and a firestorm of fear. Men began to
feed on men.

THE TWO JAKES   1990

Dir: Jack Nicholson. *Scr*: Robert Towne. *Cast*: Jack Nicholson (J. J. 'Jake' Gittes)

Private investigator Jake Gittes reminisces about Los Angeles, his
life and his work.

          JAKE
Time changes things, like the fruit stand that
turns into a filling station. But the footprints
and signs from the past are everywhere. They've
been fighting over this land since the first
Spanish missionaries showed the Indians the
benefits of religion, horses and a few years
of forced labour. The Indians had it right all
along. They respected ghosts. You can't forget
the past any more than you can change it. Hearing
Katherine Mulwray's name started me thinking
about old secrets, family, property, and a guy
doin' his partner dirt. Memories are like that
— as unpredictable as nitro, and you never know
what's gonna set one off. Like the clues that
keep you on the right track are never where you
look for them. They fall out of the pocket of
somebody else's suit you pick up at the cleaners.

They're in the tune you can't stop humming, that
you never heard in your life. They're at the
other end of the wrong number you dial in the
middle of the night. The signs are in those old
familiar places you only think you've never been
before. But you get used to seeing them out of
the corner of your eye, and you end up tripping
over the ones that are right in front of you.

GROUNDHOG DAY   1993

Dir: Harold Ramis. *Scr*: Danny Rubin, Harold Ramis. *Cast*: Andie MacDowell
(Rita), Bill Murray (Phil Connors)

Phil is trapped in a time loop, reliving one single day forever – but
nobody believes him.

> RITA
> What about me, Phil? Do you know me too?

> PHIL
> I know all about you. You like producing, but
> you hope for more than Channel 9 Pittsburgh.

> RITA
> Well, everyone knows that!

> PHIL
> You like boats, but not the ocean. You go to
> a lake in the summer with your family up in
> the mountains. There's a long wooden dock and
> a boathouse with boards missing from the roof,
> and a place you used to crawl underneath to be
> alone. You're a sucker for French poetry and
> rhinestones. You're very generous. You're kind
> to strangers and children, and when you stand
> in the snow you look like an angel.

Rita is amazed.

> RITA
> How are you doing this?

> PHIL
> I told you. I wake up every day, right here,
> right in Punxsutawney, and it's always February
> 2nd, and there's nothing I can do about it.

No reason is given why Phil should find himself trapped in time, although earlier drafts suggested a disaffected ex-lover had cast a spell on him.

SHADOWLANDS   1993

Dir: Richard Attenborough. *Scr*: William Nicholson. *Cast*: Debra Winger (Joy Gresham)

A spirited poet inspires a passionless professor.

> JOY
> We can't have the happiness of yesterday
> without the pain of today. That's the deal.

AUSTIN POWERS: INTERNATIONAL MAN OF MYSTERY 1997

Dir: Jay Roach. *Scr*: Mike Myers. *Cast*: Mike Myers (Dr Evil)

> DR EVIL
> The details of my life are quite inconsequen-
> tial... Very well, where do I begin? My father
> was a relentlessly self-improving boulangerie
> owner from Belgium with low grade narcolepsy
> and a penchant for buggery. My mother was a
> fifteen-year-old French prostitute named Chloe
> with webbed feet. My father would womanize, he

would drink. He would make outrageous claims
like he invented the question mark. Sometimes,
he would accuse chestnuts of being lazy. The
sort of general malaise that only the genius
possess and the insane lament. My childhood
was typical. Summers in Rangoon, luge lessons.
In the spring, we'd make meat helmets. When I
was insolent, I was placed in a burlap bag and
beaten with reeds — pretty standard, really. At
the age of twelve, I received my first scribe.
At the age of fourteen, a Zoroastrian named
Vilma ritualistically shaved my testicles. There
really is nothing like a shorn scrotum. . . it's
breathtaking — I suggest you try it.

MEMENTO   2000

Dir: Christopher Nolan. *Scr*: Christopher Nolan. Based on a story by Jonathan
Nolan. *Cast*: Guy Pearce (Leonard Shelby), Carrie-Anne Moss (Natalie)

Leonard has lost his short-term memory and can only manage his
life by leaving himself written prompts.

> LEONARD
So you have information for me?

> NATALIE
Is that what your little note says?

> LEONARD
Yes.

> NATALIE
It must be hard living your life off a couple of
scraps of paper. You mix your laundry list with
your grocery list, you'll end up eating your
underwear for breakfast.

The entire opening scene is shown backwards but the sound effects were too disorienting in reverse so they were re-edited to match the altered cues.

AMÉLIE / *Le fabuleux destin d'Amélie Poulain* 2001

Dir: Jean-Pierre Jeunet. *Scr*: Guillaume Laurant, Jean-Pierre Jeunet. *Cast*: André Dussollier (Narrator)

> NARRATOR
> On September 3rd 1973, at 6:28pm and 32 seconds,
> a bluebottle fly capable of 14,670 wing beats
> a minute landed on Rue St Vincent, Montmartre.
> At the same moment, on a restaurant terrace
> nearby, the wind magically made two glasses
> dance unseen on a tablecloth. Meanwhile, in a
> fifth floor flat, 28 Avenue Trudaine, Paris 9,
> returning from his best friend's funeral, Eugène
> Colère erased his name from his address book. At
> the same moment, a sperm with one X chromosome,
> belonging to Raphaél Poulain, made a dash for
> an egg in his wife Amandine. Nine months later,
> Amélie Poulain was born.

ONE HOUR PHOTO 2002

Dir: Mark Romanek. *Scr*: Mark Romanek. *Cast*: Robin Williams (Seymour 'Sy' Parrish)

A photo technician becomes obsessed by a family whose prints he processes.

> SY
> No one ever takes a photograph of something they
> want to forget.

THE GREATEST STORY EVER SOLD

While the writers of Hollywood's golden age were peppering their screenplays with sparkling one-liners, their counterparts in the marketing departments seemed to be having a tougher time. The earliest attempts at poster captions are surprisingly flat-footed, relying almost without exception on lively punctuation to bolster sagging imaginations. Gradually, decade by decade, their techniques grew more sophisticated.

In the 1940s they seemed to feel audiences needed a talking point:

> The World's Greatest Dancers in the World's Greatest Musical Show!
> *Broadway Melody of 1940* (1940)

> Walt Disney's Technicolor FEATURE triumph!
> *Citizen Kane* (1941)

> EVERYBODY'S TALKING ABOUT IT! It's Terrific!
> *Fantasia* (1940)

> Millions Have Read This Great Novel… Millions more will see an even greater picture!
> *How Green Was My Valley* (1941)

> The Screen Dares To Open The Strange And Savage Pages Of A Shocking Best-Seller!
> *The Lost Weekend* (1945)

In the 1950s they seemed keen to make sure nobody missed the point of the film:

> It's all about women… and their men!
> *All About Eve* (1950)

The Bride gets the THRILLS! Father gets the BILLS!
Father of the Bride (1950)

The story of a blonde who wanted to go places, and a
brute who got her there – the hard way!
The Bad and the Beautiful (1952)

The story of a family's ugly secret and the stark moment
that thrust their private lives into public view!
Written on the Wind (1956)

A Man's Life in Their Hands...
12 Angry Men (1957)

Unspeakable Horrors From Outer Space Paralyse the
Living and Resurrect The Dead!
Plan 9 From Outer Space (1959)

In the 1960s they assumed audiences were smarter, and
favoured a more conversational tone:

Check in. Relax. Take a shower.
Psycho (1960)

How did they ever make a movie of Lolita?
Lolita (1962)

Remember, the next scream you hear may be your own!
The Birds (1963)

You are cordially invited to George and Martha's for an
evening of fun and games.
Who's Afraid of Virginia Woolf? (1966)

This is Benjamin. He's a little worried about his future.
The Graduate (1967)

Pray for Rosemary's Baby.
Rosemary's Baby (1968)

In the 1970s they realized that rhetoric and exclamation marks were for squares, and gave us laconic catchphrases instead:

Name Your Poison.
McCabe & Mrs Miller (1971)

Shaft's his name. Shaft's his game.
Shaft (1971)

Life is a Cabaret.
Cabaret (1972)

Don't go in the water.
Jaws (1975)

By the end of the 1970s, the decade in which the idea of the blockbuster and its associated saturation marketing was born, the discipline had finally come of age. A recent survey of advertising and branding professionals declared the following the greatest ever taglines:

We are not alone.
Close Encounters of the Third Kind (1977)

A long time ago in a galaxy far, far away…
Star Wars (1977)

Just when you thought it was safe to go back in the water.
Jaws 2 (1978)

In space no one can hear you scream.
Alien (1979)

Who ya gonna call?
Ghostbusters (1984)

Be afraid. Be very afraid.
The Fly (1986)

They're back.
Poltergeist II (1986)

The list is life.
Schindler's List (1993)

Houston, we have a problem.
Apollo 13 (1995)

Earth. It was fun while it lasted.
Armageddon (1998)

Proving that those who do not study the history of this arcane discipline are condemned to repeat it, the *Huffington Post* recently resurrected these ham-fisted examples:

Today the pond. Tomorrow the world.
Frogs (1972)

Unwittingly, he trained a dolphin to kill the President of the United States.
The Day of the Dolphin (1973)

Not to be confused with King Kong.
Ape (1976)

The Only Thing More Terrifying Than the Last 12 Minutes of This Film are the First 92.
Suspiria (1977)

Science Created Him. Now Chuck Norris Must Destroy Him.
Silent Rage (1982)

They came to Space Camp with the dream of becoming astronauts. Suddenly… Without warning… Before they were ready… They were launched into space.
SpaceCamp (1986)

Laugh. Cry. Share The Pants.
The Sisterhood of the Traveling Pants (2005)

He Was Dead… But He Got Better.
Crank (2006)

Titans Will Clash.
Clash of the Titans (2010)

THE BOURNE IDENTITY 2002

Dir: Doug Liman. *Scr*: Tony Gilroy, William Blake Herron. Based on a novel by Robert Ludlum. *Cast*: Matt Damon (Jason Bourne)

A secret agent saved from death has no memory of who – or what – he is.

> BOURNE
> I can tell you the license plate numbers of all six cars outside. I can tell you that our waitress is left-handed and the guy sitting up at the counter weighs 215 pounds and knows how to handle himself. I know the best place to look for a gun is the cab of the grey truck outside, and at this altitude I can run flat out for a half mile before

```
my hands start shaking. Now, why would I know
that? How can I know that and not know who I am?
```

MINORITY REPORT   2002

Dir: Steven Spielberg. *Scr*: Scott Frank, Jon Cohen. Based on a story by Philip K.
Dick. *Cast*: Tim Blake Nelson (Gideon)

A detective worries that his chief is getting out of his depth.

```
                    GIDEON
    Careful, Chief. Dig up the past, all you get is
    dirty.
```

Three years before production began, Spielberg assembled sixteen
'future experts' to sketch out how the year 2054 might look. The
team included Neil Gershenfeld, professor at MIT's Media Lab;
Shaun Jones, director of biomedical research at DARPA (Defense
Advanced Research Projects Agency); William Mitchell, dean of the
school of architecture at MIT; and Jaron Lanier, one of the inventors
of virtual reality technology.

GARDEN STATE   2004

Dir: Zach Braff. *Scr*: Zach Braff. *Cast*: Zach Braff (Andrew Largeman), Natalie
Portman (Sam)

Andrew and Sam look back on their New Jersey childhoods.

```
                    ANDREW
    There's a handful of normal kid things I kinda
    missed.

                    SAM
    There's a handful of normal kid things I kinda
    wish I had missed.
```

50 FIRST DATES   2004

Dir: Peter Segal. *Scr*: George Wing. *Cast*: Drew Barrymore (Lucy Whitmore)

Lucy suffers from short-term memory loss, so her lover Henry is forced to remind her every day that they are together.

> LUCY
>
> Can I have one last first kiss?

LET THE RIGHT ONE IN / *Låt den rätte komma in*   2008

Dir: Tomas Alfredson. *Scr*: John Ajvide Lindqvist, based on his novel. *Cast*: Kåre Hedebrant (Oskar), Lina Leandersson (Eli)

Schoolboy Oskar befriends his reclusive young neighbour.

> OSKAR
>
> Are you a vampire?

> ELI
>
> I live off blood... Yes.

> OSKAR
>
> Are you... dead?

> ELI
>
> No. Can't you tell?

> OSKAR
>
> But... Are you old?

> ELI
>
> I'm twelve. But I've been twelve for a long time.

The film contains several innovative sound effects. Puncturing a sausage was used to emulate biting into flesh, while drinking yogurt was used to sound like sucking blood. Blinking eyelids were dubbed with a recording of grape skins being pressed together.

CRAZY HEART   2009

Dir: Scott Cooper. *Scr*: Scott Cooper. Based on a novel by Thomas Cobb. *Cast*:
Jeff Bridges (Otis 'Bad' Blake)

A country and western singer finally manages to quit drinking.

> **'BAD' BLAKE**
> Ain't rememberin' wonderful?

Amazingly, the first draft sent to Jeff Bridges contained no music.

INCEPTION   2010

Dir: Christopher Nolan. *Scr*: Christopher Nolan. *Cast*: Leonardo DiCaprio
(Cobb), Ellen Page (Ariadne)

Cobb teaches his pupils how to create dreamscapes other people can
enter. Here, he experiences Ariadne's first attempt.

> **COBB**
> I know this bridge - this place is real. You
> didn't imagine it, you remembered it...

> **ARIADNE**
> I cross it every day on my way to the college.

> **COBB**
> Never recreate places from memory. Always imagine
> new places.

> **ARIADNE**
> You have to draw from what you know.

Cobb shakes his head.

> **COBB**
> Use pieces — a streetlamp, phone booths, a type of
> brick — not whole areas.

ARIADNE

Why not?

COBB

Because building dreams out of your own memories
is the surest way to lose your grip on what's
real and what's a dream.

BOYHOOD   2014

Dir: Richard Linklater. *Scr*: Richard Linklater. *Cast*: Jessi Mechler (Nicole)

NICOLE

You know how everyone's always saying seize the
moment? I don't know, I'm kind of thinking it's
the other way around. You know, like the moment
seizes us.

TEARS

I WALKED WITH A ZOMBIE   1943

Dir: Jacques Tourneur. *Scr*: Curt Siodmak, Ardel Wray. Based on an article by
Inez Wallace and on *Jane Eyre* by Charlotte Brontë. *Cast*: Tom Conway (Paul
Holland), Frances Dee (Betsy Connell)

Paul warns Betsy that life on the tropical island holds hidden terrors.

> PAUL
>
> It's easy enough to read the thoughts of a
> newcomer. Everything seems beautiful because
> you don't understand. Those flying fish, they're
> not leaping for joy, they're jumping in terror.
> Bigger fish want to eat them. That luminous
> water, it takes its gleam from millions of tiny
> dead bodies. The glitter of putrescence. There
> is no beauty here, only death and decay.

> BETSY
>
> You can't really believe that.

> PAUL
>
> Everything good dies here. Even the stars.

Perhaps missing the point of Tourneur's zombie metaphor, a
New York Times reviewer dismissed the film as 'a dull, disgusting
exaggeration of an unhealthy, abnormal concept of life'.

LIFEBOAT   1944

Dir: Alfred Hitchcock. *Scr*: Jo Swerling. Based on a story by John Steinbeck. *Cast*:
Walter Slezak (Willi), Tallulah Bankhead (Connie Porter)

Adrift at sea, German U-boat captain Willi and American citizen
Connie await rescue. To pass the time, Willi fixes Connie's diamond
bracelet.

> WILLI
>
> Looks like bits of ice.

                    CONNIE
I wish they were.

                    WILLI
They're really nothing but a few pieces of carbon
crystallized under high pressure at great heat.

                    CONNIE
Quite so, if you want to be scientific about it.

                    WILLI
I'm a great believer in science.

                    CONNIE
Like tears, for instance. They're nothing but H2O
with a trace of sodium chloride.

Even though most of the film was shot in a studio water tank, the entire cast suffered from seasickness at some point. When someone mentioned to Hitchcock that Tallulah Bankhead was not wearing underwear during one take, he replied: 'I don't know if this is a matter for the costume department, make-up, or hairdressing.'

WHERE'S ALFRED?

A 'cameo' role (named after a type of brooch which bears a bust or portrait) was originally a brief appearance by a real-life figure instantly recognizable to the audience. This usually meant that the person in question was playing themselves as opposed to a character in the story. In *The Lodger* (1927), Alfred Hitchcock cast himself in the insignificant role of a newsman on the telephone – facing away from the camera – and the term has now come to mean a member of the crew who has a part, however small, in the film itself.

Hitchcock amused himself – and us, once his mischievous appearances had become established as part of his house style – by taking cameos in thirty-nine of his fifty-two films. To begin with, the moments were innocuous enough: posting a letter, travelling on a bus, reading a newspaper. Before long, the appearances were more obvious: walking a horse across the screen or standing in front of a sign promoting 'Cut Rate Drugs'. In *Lifeboat* (1944), he is seen in the 'before' and 'after' pictures of a newspaper advertisement for 'Reduco Obesity Slayer', a fictitious weight-loss product (Hitchcock was almost comically portly).

The subtlest can be found in *Rope* (1948), where, apart from the opening credits, in which Hitchcock is glimpsed far away entering an apartment building, the entire story takes place in a single room with a cast of only nine. Fifty-five minutes into the film, in the skyline of New York seen through the windows, a distant red neon sign flashes: an image of the director's head appears once again above the logo for 'Reduco'.

Hitchcock briefly pursued a musical theme, appearing in various films carrying a violin, a cello, a trumpet, and in *Strangers on a Train* (1951) – magnificently – a double bass. The most unsettling sequence is surely in *Topaz* (1969), where the director is pushed through an airport terminal in a wheelchair, only to stand up, shake hands with a fellow traveller and walk out of the picture; the most brazen is the shot where Cary Grant travels on a bus and Hitchcock sits stony-faced and unmissable right beside him (*To Catch a Thief*, 1955).

NONE BUT THE LONELY HEART   1944

Dir: Clifford Odets. *Scr*: Clifford Odets. Based on a novel by Richard Llewellyn. *Cast*: Cary Grant (Ernie Mott)

A young ne'er-do-well tries to reform his life.

> **ERNIE**
> They say money talks . . . all it's ever said
> to me is goodbye.

BRIEF ENCOUNTER   1945

Dir: David Lean. *Scr*: David Lean. Based on a play by Noël Coward. *Cast*: Celia Johnson (Laura Jesson)

Married Laura feels guilty about the affair she is having.

> **LAURA**
> It's awfully easy to lie when you know that
> you're trusted implicitly. So very easy, and
> so very degrading.

One disgruntled viewer challenged Lean: 'Do you realise, Sir, that if Celia Johnson could contemplate being unfaithful to her husband, my wife could contemplate being unfaithful to me?'

OUT OF THE PAST   1947

Dir: Jacques Tourneur. *Scr*: Daniel Mainwaring, based on his novel (writing as Geoffrey Homes). *Cast*: Kirk Douglas (Whit Sterling)

Gangster Whit Sterling realizes he is still in love with a woman from his past.

> **WHIT**
> My feelings? About ten years ago, I hid them
> somewhere and haven't been able to find them.

SUNSET BOULEVARD 1950

Dir: Billy Wilder. *Scr*: Charles Brackett, Billy Wilder, D. M. Marshman Jr. *Cast*: Gloria Swanson (Norma Desmond)

A proud but ageing film star implores her favourite director to cast her just one more time.

> NORMA
>
> And I promise you I'll never desert you again because after *Salome* we'll make another picture and another picture. You see, this is my life! It always will be! Nothing else! Just us, the cameras, and those wonderful people out there in the dark. All right, Mr DeMille, I'm ready for my close-up.

Legendary studio head Louis B. Mayer felt the film painted an unfairly bleak portrait of the film business and told Wilder: 'You bastard! You have disgraced the industry that made and fed you. You should be tarred and feathered and run out of Hollywood.' Wilder, never usually lost for an elegant riposte, could only muster, 'Fuck you.'

THE LAVENDER HILL MOB 1951

Dir: Charles Crichton. *Scr*: T. E. B. Clarke. *Cast*: Stanley Holloway (Alfred 'Al' Pendlebury)

> PENDLEBURY
>
> Of all sad words of tongue or pen, the saddest are these — 'it might have been'.

The poignant words spoken by the crooked Pendlebury are from the poem 'Maud Muller' by John Greenleaf Whittier.

The Bank of England was consulted to find a plausible way to steal a million pounds, and their plan formed the basis for the plot.

The only reason the robbers fail in their mission at the end is that the British producers were aware US censorship rules regarding criminal behaviour would have meant the film could not be released in America.

ON THE WATERFRONT   1954

Dir: Elia Kazan. *Scr*: Budd Schulberg. *Cast*: Marlon Brando (Terry Malloy), Rod Steiger (Charley Malloy)

Boxer Terry Malloy is furious with his brother Charley for persuading him to participate in fixed bouts.

> TERRY
> It wasn't him, Charley, it was you. Remember
> that night in the Garden you came down to my
> dressing room and you said, 'Kid, this ain't your
> night. We're going for the price on Wilson.' You
> remember that? 'This ain't your night'! My night!
> I coulda taken Wilson apart! So what happens? He
> gets the title shot outdoors on the ballpark and
> what do I get? A one-way ticket to Palookaville!
> You was my brother, Charley, you shoulda looked
> out for me a little bit. You shoulda taken care
> of me just a little bit so I wouldn't have to
> take them dives for the short-end money.

> CHARLEY
> Oh, I had some bets down for you. You saw some
> money.

> TERRY
> You don't understand. I coulda had class. I
> coulda been a contender. I coulda been somebody,
> instead of a bum – which is what I am, let's
> face it. It was you, Charley.

Before sending the screenplay to Marlon Brando, producer Sam Spiegel slipped small pieces of paper between its pages so he could check in due course whether it had ever been opened. Brando turned the project down and the scraps were still in place when he returned the script; only after Spiegel approached Frank Sinatra for the role did Brando change his mind and ask to 're-read' it.

THE APARTMENT   1960

Dir: Billy Wilder. *Scr*: Billy Wilder, I. A. L. Diamond. *Cast*: Jack Lemmon (C. C. Baxter), Shirley MacLaine (Fran Kubelik)

Baxter discovers Fran's private life is less glamorous than he has imagined.

                    BAXTER
    The mirror... it's broken.

                    FRAN
    Yes, I know. I like it that way. Makes me look the
    way I feel.

'SHUT UP AND DEAL'

Billy Wilder had been impressed by Noël Coward and David Lean's *Brief Encounter* (1945), in which a character who never appears in the film lends the adulterous couple a key to his home so they can meet in secret. With *The Apartment* (1960), Wilder wanted to tell a story in which the owner of this vital venue takes centre-stage, but because the topic of marital infidelity was still controversial he had to wait several years until the Hays Production Code (see p.209) was relaxed.

When the film finally went ahead, Wilder set much of the action in the offices of a dull insurance company as a comic counterpoint to the sexual shenanigans the story describes. Marilyn Monroe –whom Wilder disliked after her difficult behaviour on *Some Like It Hot* (1959) – attended an early screening, but the risqué subject matter seems to have passed her by as she declared the picture 'a wonderful examination of the corporate world'.

Wilder and long-term collaborator I. A. L. Diamond wrote the script specifically with Jack Lemmon in mind as the hapless C. C. Baxter. When the director approached Shirley MacLaine for the part of Miss Kubelik, the elevator operator, he removed the last pages because he wanted her to play the lovelorn character with no idea she might eventually win Baxter's affections; MacLaine simply assumed Wilder had not yet figured out a suitable ending. She also claimed much of the film was written as the shoot progressed, and that the recurring gin rummy game came about because she was learning to play it with Frank Sinatra and Dean Martin during her lunch breaks.

The film contains plenty of classic Wilder and Diamond dialogue:

```
FRAN: I was jinxed from the word go. The first
time I was ever kissed was in a cemetery.
```

```
BAXTER: Mrs MacDougall, I think it is only
fair to warn you that you are now alone with a
notorious sexpot.
MARGIE: No kidding.
```

```
BAXTER: That's the way it crumbles, cookie-wise.
KIRKEBY: Premium-wise and billing-wise, we are
18 per cent ahead of last year, October-wise.
```

```
SHELDRAKE: Ya know, you see a girl a couple of
times a week, just for laughs, and right away
```

they think you're gonna divorce your wife. Now
I ask you, is that fair?
BAXTER: No, sir, it's very unfair... Especially
to your wife.

FRAN: What's a tennis racket doing in the
kitchen?
BAXTER: Tennis racket? Oh, I remember, I was
cooking myself an Italian dinner.

Even the closing lines were apparently written as the final scene
was being shot:

BAXTER: You hear what I said, Miss Kubelik?
I absolutely adore you.
FRAN: Shut up and deal.

FUNNY GIRL   1968

Dir: William Wyler. *Scr*: Isobel Lennart, based on her Broadway musical. *Cast*:
Barbra Streisand (Fanny Brice)

A comedienne laments her plain looks.

>   FANNY
> That's my problem — I'm a bagel on a plate full
> of onion rolls.

Cinematographer Vilmos Zsigmond – who would go on to win an
Oscar for *Close Encounters of the Third Kind* (1977) – was fired by
Streisand after three days because he ignored her stipulation that
her face should only ever be filmed from her preferred (left) side.

PLAY IT AGAIN, SAM   1972

Dir: Herbert Ross. *Scr*: Woody Allen, based on his play. *Cast*: Woody Allen (Allan Felix), Diana Davila (Museum Girl)

Allan approaches a pretty girl in an art gallery.

                    ALLAN
That's quite a lovely Jackson Pollock, isn't it?

                    MUSEUM GIRL
Yes, it is.

                    ALLAN
What does it say to you?

                    MUSEUM GIRL
It restates the negativeness of the universe.
The hideous lonely emptiness of existence.
Nothingness. The predicament of Man forced to
live in a barren, Godless eternity like a tiny
flame flickering in an immense void with nothing
but waste, horror and degradation, forming a
useless bleak straitjacket in a black absurd
cosmos.

                    ALLAN
What are you doing Saturday night?

                    MUSEUM GIRL
Committing suicide.

                    ALLAN
What about Friday night?

The film's title is a reference to the famous line from Casablanca (1942), although movie buffs will note that Humphrey Bogart actually says: 'Play it once, Sam. For old times' sake.'

TAXI DRIVER   1976

Dir: Martin Scorsese. *Scr*: Paul Schrader. *Cast*: Robert De Niro (Travis Bickle)

> TRAVIS
> Loneliness has followed me my whole life.
> Everywhere. In bars, in cars, sidewalks,
> stores, everywhere. There's no escape. I'm
> God's lonely man.

ANNIE HALL   1977

Dir: Woody Allen. *Scr*: Woody Allen, Marshall Brickman. *Cast*: Woody Allen (Alvy Singer)

> ALVY
> A relationship, I think, is like a shark.
> You know? It has to constantly move forward
> or it dies. And I think what we've got on our
> hands is a dead shark.

THE ELEPHANT MAN   1980

Dir: David Lynch. *Scr*: Christopher De Vore, Eric Bergren, David Lynch. Based on books by Sir Frederick Treves and Ashley Montagu. *Cast*: John Standing (Dr Fox), Anthony Hopkins (Dr Frederick Treves)

Two doctors assume a patient with a grotesquely disfigured face and body is also mentally subnormal.

> DR FOX
> Have you ever mentioned his mental state?

> DR FREDERICK TREVES
> Oh, he's an imbecile, probably from birth.
> Man's a complete idiot. Pray to God he's an
> idiot.

John Hurt's prosthetics took eight hours to apply each day and two hours to remove, so to prevent the actor from becoming exhausted he was only scheduled to work alternate days.

THE WHALES OF AUGUST   1987

Dir: Lindsay Anderson. *Scr*: David Berry, based on his play. *Cast*: Lillian Gish (Sarah Webber)

On the anniversary of her wedding, Sarah holds an imaginary conversation with the husband she lost in the Second World War.

<pre>
                  SARAH
  Forty-six years, Phillip. Forty-six red roses;
  forty-six white. White for truth, red for
  passion. That's what you always said: 'Passion
  and truth; that's all we need'. . . Oh, if only
  you were here, Phillip. Oh, Phillip, my corset
  has so many stays and so many ties. You said,
  'Too many, my love. The moon will set before I
  have you completely undone.' But I said, 'Never,
  my love. I won't be entirely undone — even by
  you. For what mystery would keep you with me if
  you unwrap them all?'
</pre>

STEEL MAGNOLIAS   1989

Dir: Herbert Ross. *Scr*: Robert Harling, based on his play. *Cast*: Dolly Parton (Truvy Jones)

Truvy chats with friends in her beauty salon.

<pre>
                  TRUVY
  Honey, time marches on and eventually you
  realize it's marching across your face.
</pre>

Disappointed by a poor take, director Herbert Ross unchivalrously asked singer Dolly Parton if she could actually act. Undeterred, she replied: 'No, but it's your job to make me look like I can.'

SECRETS & LIES   1996

Dir: Mike Leigh. *Scr*: Mike Leigh. *Cast*: Timothy Spall (Maurice Purley)

Maurice does his best to support and placate his fractious family.

```
            MAURICE
Secrets and lies! We're all in pain! Why can't
we share our pain? I've spent my entire life
trying to make people happy, and the three
people I love the most in the world hate each
other's guts and I'm in the middle! I can't
take it any more!
```

As with all Mike Leigh films, the script was improvised around a simple outline devised by the director. Leigh told each actor only as much as they would need to know at the beginning of the story and let them develop their own character from there; that way, the secrets revealed along the way would come as a genuine surprise as each scene was shot.

NOTTING HILL   1999

Dir: Roger Michell. *Scr*: Richard Curtis. *Cast*: Julia Roberts (Anna Scott)

Among friends, a film star laments the pressures of her career.

```
            ANNA
I've been on a diet every day since I was
nineteen, which basically means I've been hungry
for a decade. I've had a series of not nice
boyfriends, one of whom hit me, and every time
I get my heart broken the newspapers splash it
about as though it's entertainment. And it's
```

```
taken two rather painful operations to get me
looking like this . . . Really. And, one day
not long from now, my looks will go, they'll
discover I can't act and I'll become some sad
middle-aged woman who looks a bit like someone
who was famous for a while.
```

THE VIRGIN SUICIDES   1999

Dir: Sofia Coppola. *Scr*: Sofia Coppola. Based on a novel by Jeffrey Eugenides.
Cast: François Klanfer (Doctor), Hanna R. Hall (Cecilia Lisbon)

Cecilia is taken to hospital after cutting her wrists.

```
                    DOCTOR
What are you doing here, honey? You're not even
old enough to know how bad life gets.

                    CECILIA
Obviously, Doctor, you've never been a thirteen-
year-old girl.
```

LOST IN TRANSLATION   2003

Dir: Sofia Coppola. *Scr*: Sofia Coppola. *Cast*: Scarlett Johansson (Charlotte), Bill
Murray (Bob Harris)

A lonely wife and a famous actor fall to talking in a Tokyo bar.

```
                  CHARLOTTE
So, what are you doing here?

                    BOB
Uh, a couple of things. Taking a break from my
wife, forgetting my son's birthday. And getting
paid two million dollars to endorse a whiskey
when I could be doing a play somewhere.
```

CHARLOTTE
CHARLOTTE

Oh.

BOB

But the good news is, the whiskey works.

MILLION DOLLAR BABY   2004

Dir: Clint Eastwood. *Scr*: Paul Haggis. Based on short stories by F. X. Toole. *Cast*: Brian F. O'Byrne (Father Horvak)

A local priest wonders what is troubling one of his regular parishioners.

FATHER HORVAK

Frankie, I've seen you at Mass almost every
day for twenty-three years. The only person
comes to church that much is the kind who can't
forgive himself for something.

THE CONSEQUENCES OF LOVE /   2004
Le consequenze dell'amore

Dir: Paolo Sorrentino. *Scr*: Paolo Sorrentino. *Cast*: Toni Servillo (Titta di Girolamo)

A middle-aged mafia courier refuses to believe in fate.

TITTA

Bad luck doesn't exist. It is just an invention
of losers and poor people.

BROKEBACK MOUNTAIN   2005

Dir: Ang Lee. *Scr*: Larry McMurtry and Diana Ossana. Based on a novel by Annie Proulx. *Cast*: Jake Gyllenhaal (Jack), Heath Ledger (Ennis)

Two cowboys have been forced to hide their homosexual relationship from their families and community for too long.

JACK

Tell you what, we coulda had a good life
together! Fuckin' real good life! Had us a
place of our own. But you didn't want it, Ennis!
So what we got now is Brokeback Mountain!
Everything's built on that! That's all we got,
boy, fuckin' all. So I hope you know that,
even if you don't never know the rest! You
count the damn few times we have been together
in nearly twenty years and you measure the short
fucking leash you keep me on — and then you ask
me about Mexico and tell me you'll kill me for
needing somethin' I don't hardly never get. You
have no idea how bad it gets! I'm not you . . .
I can't make it on a coupla high-altitude fucks
once or twice a year! You are too much for me,
Ennis, you sonofawhoreson bitch! I wish I knew
how to quit you.

Ennis is crying now.

ENNIS

Well, why don't you? Why don't you just let
me be? It's because of you, Jack, that I'm like
this! I'm nothin' . . . I'm nowhere . . . Get the
fuck off me! I can't stand being like this no
more, Jack.

LITTLE MISS SUNSHINE   2006

Dir: Jonathan Dayton, Valerie Faris. *Scr*: Michael Arndt. *Cast*: Paul Dano
(Dwayne), Steve Carell (Frank Ginsberg)

Unhappy teenager Dwayne receives some unlikely encouragement
from his uncle.

                    DWAYNE

I wish I could just sleep until I was
eighteen and skip all this crap — high school
and everything — just skip it.

                    FRANK

Do you know who Marcel Proust is?

                    DWAYNE

He's the guy you teach.

                    FRANK

Yeah. French writer. Total loser. Never had
a real job. Unrequited love affairs. Gay.
Spent twenty years writing a book almost no
one reads. But he's also probably the greatest
writer since Shakespeare. Anyway, he uh. . .
he gets down to the end of his life, and he
looks back and decides that all those years he
suffered, those were the best years of his life
'cause they made him who he was. All those years
he was happy? You know, total waste. Didn't
learn a thing. So, if you sleep until you're
eighteen. . . Ah, think of the suffering you're
gonna miss. I mean, high school? High school —
those are your prime suffering years. You don't
get better suffering than that.

THE TREE OF LIFE   2011

Dir: Terrence Malick. *Scr*: Terrence Malick. *Cast*: Kelly Koonce (Father Haynes),
Jessica Chastain (Mrs O'Brien)

A grieving mother rejects the bland consolations of her priest.

                    FATHER HAYNES

He's in God's hands now.

He was in God's hands the whole time, wasn't he?

Terrence Malick has never been noted for his conventional narrative style. Even so, viewers in one Italian cinema may have thought the director had surpassed himself when *The Tree of Life* was shown for an entire week with the first two reels reversed. Until the projectionist spotted the error, nobody else noticed.

INCITING INCIDENTS AND PINCH POINTS

'Screenplays are structure.'

William Goldman

Some time around 335 BC the Greek philosopher Aristotle wrote his *Poetics*, a treatise on dramatic theory. Identifying six key elements – plot, character, theme, diction, music and spectacle – he attributed the greatest importance to plot (mythos). He also suggested that 'a whole is what has a beginning and middle and end', and this maxim has endured among playwrights down the centuries through the idea that narrative action should be divided into three parts.

Since then many others have attempted to anatomize the ingredients of a coherent and resonant story. The British writer and scholar Arthur Quiller-Couch suggested seven fundamental scenarios:

- Man against Man
- Man against Nature
- Man against God
- Man against Society
- Man in the Middle

- Man and Woman
- Man against Himself.

In 1916 the French writer George Polti proposed a mathematically pleasing thirty-six situations ranging from 'vengeance' and 'deliverance' to 'necessity of sacrificing loved ones' and 'fatal imprudence'. In 1946 Lajos Egri, widely recognized as 'the father of modern screenwriting gurus', published *The Art of Dramatic Writing*. Developing many of Aristotle's ideas, he established a logical method for setting out narrative structure. Within a matter of decades, the world of screenwriting was flooded with similar books analysing successful films, showing how their episodes conformed to such theories and thus seeming to prove that any script is fundamentally a set of rules for shepherding its characters from opening titles to credits.

Although today's largest productions have budgets upward of $200 million, studio executives – and their development staff – frequently test their investment with 'screenwriters' bibles' readily available from any good bookshop. 'Creative meetings' echo with reassuring buzz-phrases such as character arc, the call to adventure and threshold guardians.

Contemporary analysts have distilled their theories into a clear prescriptive outline. Joseph Campbell, borrowing the term 'monomyth' from James Joyce's *Finnegans Wake*, proposes seventeen heroic stages:

Departure

1.1 The Call to Adventure

1.2 Refusal of the Call

1.3 Supernatural Aid

1.4 The Crossing of the First Threshold

1.5 Belly of the Whale

Initiation

2.1 The Road of Trials

2.2 The Meeting with the Goddess

2.3 Woman as Temptress

2.4 Atonement with the Father

2.5 Apotheosis

2.6 The Ultimate Boon

Return

3.1 Refusal of the Return

3.2 The Magic Flight

3.3 Rescue from Without

3.4 The Crossing of the Return Threshold

3.5 Master of Two Worlds

3.6 Freedom to Live

Other well-known gurus today include Christopher Vogler, Syd Field and Robert McKee. McKee's former students include thirty-six Oscar winners and he has advised companies as diverse as Disney, MTV, Microsoft and NASA, although his own writing credits run to a modest five TV movies. Syd Field's last screenplay was for a documentary in 1967 but the *Hollywood Reporter* calls him 'the most sought-after screenwriting teacher in the world'. His books have been translated into nineteen languages and he has even recently released an iPhone app, *Script Launcher*.

12 YEARS A SLAVE   **2013**

Dir: Steve McQueen. *Scr*: John Ridley. Based on a book by Solomon Northup.
Cast: Chiwetel Ejiofor (Solomon Northup)

Shortly before the American Civil War, a free black man from New York is abducted and sold into slavery.

                        SOLOMON
    I don't want to survive, I want to live.

ENDINGS

A DAY AT THE RACES   1937

Dir: Sam Wood. *Scr*: Robert Pirosh, George Seaton, George Oppenheimer. *Cast*: Groucho Marx (Dr Hugo Z. Hackenbush)

Dr Hackenbush takes his patient's pulse.

DR HACKENBUSH
Either he's dead or my watch has stopped.

THE LADY VANISHES   1938

Dir: Alfred Hitchcock. *Scr*: Sidney Gilliat, Frank Launder. Based on a story by Ethel Lina White. *Cast*: Margaret Lockwood (Iris Henderson)

A young woman returns from a tour of Europe on the eve of her wedding.

IRIS
I've no regrets. I've been everywhere and
done everything. I've eaten caviar at Cannes,
sausage rolls at the dogs. I've played baccarat
at Biarritz and darts with the rural dean.
What is there left for me but marriage?

THE GRAPES OF WRATH   1940

Dir: John Ford. *Scr*: Nunnally Johnson. Based on a novel by John Steinbeck. *Cast*: Jane Darwell (Ma Joad)

The mother of a migrant family during the Great Depression remains convinced of the strength of the oppressed.

MA JOAD
That's what makes us tough. Rich fellas come
up an' they die an' their kids ain't no good,
an' they die out. But we keep a-comin'. We're
the people that live. They can't wipe us out.
They can't lick us. And we'll go on forever, Pa,
'cause . . . we're the people.

THE NAKED CITY   **1948**

Dir: Jules Dassin. *Scr*: Albert Maltz, Malvin Wald. *Cast*: Mark Hellinger
(Narrator)

A murder mystery unfolds against the backdrop of New York with
its myriad inhabitants.

> NARRATOR
>
> There are eight million stories in the naked
> city. This has been one of them.

Most unusually for the time, director Jules Dassin filmed a good
deal of the picture on location, often using hidden cameras to let
actors perform amid crowds without the need for unconvincing
background players. If he needed to control passers-by, he would
stage diversions, on one occasion hiring a juggler and on another
sending a crew member up a lamp post to wave a large American
flag.

THE THIRD MAN   **1949**

Dir: Carol Reed. *Scr*: Graham Greene. *Cast*: Orson Welles (Harry Lime)

Black marketeer Harry Lime tries to justify his criminal activities to
his friend Holly.

> HARRY
>
> Don't be so gloomy. After all, it's not
> that awful. Like the fellow says, in Italy
> for thirty years under the Borgias they had
> warfare, terror, murder and bloodshed but they
> produced Michelangelo, Leonardo da Vinci and the
> Renaissance. In Switzerland they had brotherly
> love: they had five hundred years of democracy
> and peace, and what did that produce? The cuckoo
> clock. So long, Holly.

'A DELICATE MATTER'

With its ambiguous encounters in echoing alleyways, *The Third Man* perfectly captures the atmosphere of a divided Vienna in the aftermath of war. Robert Krasker's chiaroscuro cinematography won an Oscar and his tilted camera angles were hugely influential on thrillers thereafter, but they were not to everyone's taste; director William Wyler sent Carol Reed a spirit level with a note saying, 'Carol, next time you make a picture, just put it on top of the camera, will you?'

Although Reed had proven his talent with two earlier productions – *Odd Man Out* (1947) and *The Fallen Idol* (1948), the latter also based on a story by Graham Greene – *The Third Man* was dogged by rumours that Orson Welles was its true director. Welles' performance as Harry Lime is a tour de force and he seemed to enjoy the idea that he might also have been secretly in charge. In later years he did little to settle the controversy, giving one interview in which he hinted that it was 'a delicate matter', but subsequently that it was indeed 'Carol's picture'. The latter is undoubtedly the case since Welles spent much of the time when he was supposed to be on set travelling around Europe and many of his non-speaking scenes had to be filmed with body doubles.

Reed's role can hardly be doubted: he insisted on running three production units simultaneously to get all the location footage they needed within the six weeks scheduled for Vienna. One crew covered the daytime shots, another the night and a third was responsible for the sewer scenes. By the end Reed was reportedly working twenty hours a day and was relying on Dexedrine (speed) to keep his energy levels up.

Other ambiguities linger: the famous speech at the top of the Ferris wheel does not appear in Greene's original treatment and was reputedly improvised by Welles, although he claimed it was inspired by an unnamed Hungarian play. Whoever did write it should have checked their facts: the Swiss have never been famous for making cuckoo clocks (their true home is Germany) and Switzerland itself was not neutral but a proud and feared military power during the Renaissance.

THE THING FROM ANOTHER WORLD   1951

Dir: Christian Nyby. *Scr*: Charles Lederer. Based on a story by John W. Campbell Jr. *Cast*: Douglas Spencer (Ned 'Scotty' Scott)

After narrowly defeating an alien invader who adopts human form, Scotty warns humanity never to drop its guard.

> SCOTTY
>
> I bring you a warning. Every one of you listening to my voice, tell the world, tell this to everybody wherever they are. Watch the skies. Everywhere. Keep looking. Keep watching the skies...

The producers asked the US Air Force for assistance with aircraft and locations but were refused because the government's official stance at the time was that UFOs did not exist.

THE TEAHOUSE OF THE AUGUST MOON   1956

Dir: Daniel Mann. *Scr*: John Patrick. Based on a novel by Vern J. Sneider. *Cast*: Marlon Brando (Sakini)

A wise Japanese translator defuses tensions between American occupiers and the inhabitants of Okinawa.

> SAKINI
>
> Little story now concluded. But history of world unfinished. Lovely ladies, kind gentlemen, go home to ponder. What was true at beginning

remains true. Pain make man think, thought make
man wise, and wisdom make life endurable. So,
may August moon bring gentle sleep. Sayonara.

Brando's performance as the Japanese Sakini was so convincing that
many viewers demanded their money back, believing that the actor
had not appeared in the film at all.

THE SEVENTH SEAL / *Det sjunde inseglet*   1957

Dir: Ingmar Bergman. *Scr*: Ingmar Bergman, based on his play. *Cast*: Bengt
Ekerot (Death), Max von Sydow (Antonius Block)

A wandering knight wagers his life on a game of chess.

DEATH

Are you ready?

ANTONIUS

My body is ready, but I am not.

THE INCREDIBLE SHRINKING MAN   1957

Dir: Jack Arnold. *Scr*: Richard Matheson, based on his novel. *Cast*: Grant
Williams (Scott Carey)

After being exposed to a radioactive cloud, a man condemned to
grow ever smaller makes peace with his destiny.

SCOTT

And I felt my body dwindling, melting, becoming
nothing. My fears locked away and in their
place came acceptance. All this vast majesty
of creation, it had to mean something. And then
I meant something, too. Yes, smaller than the
smallest, I meant something, too. To God there is
no zero. I still exist!

TOUCH OF EVIL   1958

Dir: Orson Welles. *Scr*: Orson Welles. Based on a novel by Whit Masterson. *Cast*:
Orson Welles (Captain Hank Quinlan), Marlene Dietrich (Tanya)

Corrupt police captain Quinlan realizes it cannot be long before
justice catches up with him.

>   QUINLAN
> Come on, read my future for me.

>   TANYA
> You haven't got any.

>   QUINLAN
> Hmm? What do you mean?

>   TANYA
> Your future's all used up.

Welles wanted Janet Leigh for one of the film's lead roles, but the fees
for the entire cast were constrained by an unusually tight budget;
Leigh's agent rejected the offer without even sending her the script.
When she found out, Leigh was furious, telling her representative
that being directed by Welles was far more important than any pay
check.

ON THE BEACH   1959

Dir: Stanley Kramer. *Scr*: John Paxton. Based on a novel by Nevil Shute. *Cast*:
Donna Anderson (Mary Holmes)

In a world dying from radiation poisoning after a nuclear war, a
survivor opts to take a lethal sedative.

>   MARY
> God, God forgive us, Peter. I think I'll have
> that cup of tea now.

'THE REST IS SILENCE'

If Shakespeare had handed in a draft of *Hamlet* to one of the Hollywood studios, he would have found himself swiftly summoned for a creative meeting. Executives might murmur that the Danish prince's speeches are meandering and his character arc lacks clarity. Worst of all, his final zinger – 'the rest is silence' – doesn't come as the credits roll.

Even if Sam Goldwyn or Louis B. Mayer hadn't demanded a rewrite, any decent star playing the prince would surely have asked the bard to lose the closing speeches by Horatio and Fortinbras in case they overshadowed his magnificent death scene.

Here are some examples of how a film should really end:

Oh, Auntie Em, there's no place like home!
The Wizard of Oz (1939)

Louis, I think this is the beginning of a
beautiful friendship.
Casablanca (1942)

Remember, honey, on your wedding day it's all
right to say yes.
Gentlemen Prefer Blondes (1953)

Well, nobody's perfect.
Some Like It Hot (1959)

Forget it, Jake. It's Chinatown.
Chinatown (1974)

The horror . . . the horror . . .
Apocalypse Now (1979)

Not everybody gets corrupted. You have to have
a little faith in people.
Manhattan (1979)

I'm the boss, I'm the boss, I'm the boss, I'm
the boss.
Raging Bull (1980)

I'll be right here.
E.T. the Extra Terrestrial (1982)

Let's just wait here awhile, see what happens.
The Thing (1982)

Well, ma'am, if I see him, I'll sure give him
the message.
Blood Simple (1984)

Roads? Where we're going, we don't need roads.
Back to the Future (1985)

I'm too old for this.
Lethal Weapon (1987)

Asshole!
A Fish Called Wanda (1988)

I find I am so excited I can barely sit still
or hold a thought in my head. I think it's the
excitement only a free man can feel, a free man
at the start of a long journey whose conclusion
is uncertain. I hope I can make it across the
border. I hope to see my friend and shake his
hand. I hope the Pacific is as blue as it has
been in my dreams. I hope.
The Shawshank Redemption (1994)

VINCENT: I think we should be leaving now.
JULES: Yeah, that's probably a good idea.
Pulp Fiction (1994)

You met me at a very strange time of my life.
Fight Club (1999)

I'm going to show them a world without you.
A world without rules and controls, without
borders or boundaries. A world where anything
is possible. Where we go from there is a choice
I leave to you.
The Matrix (1999)

Now, where was I?
Memento (2000)

ALFIE 1966

Dir: Lewis Gilbert. *Scr*: Bill Naughton, based on his novel and stage play. *Cast*: Michael Caine (Alfie Elkins)

Handsome but self-centred ladies' man Alfie begins to wonder what his string of conquests really adds up to.

        ALFIE
You know what? When I look back on my little life
and the birds I've known, and think of all the
things they've done for me and the little I've
done for them, you'd think I've had the best of
it along the line. But what have I got out of
it? I've got a bob or two, some decent clothes,
a car, I've got me health back and I ain't
attached. But I ain't got me peace of mind — and
if you ain't got that, you ain't got nothing.

I dunno. It seems to me if they ain't got you
one way, they've got you another. So what's the
answer? That's what I keep asking myself — what's
it all about? Know what I mean?

COOL HAND LUKE   1967

Dir: Stuart Rosenberg. *Scr*: Frank Pierson, Donn Pearce. Based on a novel by
Donn Pearce. *Cast*: George Kennedy (Dragline)

Dragline tells his fellow convicts how Cool Hand Luke kept his
dignity even as he was shot down by prison guards.

> DRAGLINE
> He was smiling. . . That's right. You know. . .
> that Luke smile of his. He had it on his face
> right to the very end. Hell, if they didn't know
> it 'fore, they could tell right then that they
> weren't gonna beat him. That old Luke smile. Oh,
> Luke. He was some boy. Cool Hand Luke. Hell,
> he's a natural-born world-shaker.

A complete prison set near Stockton, California, was constructed
for the shoot, including barracks, mess hall and warden's quarters.
Truckloads of Spanish moss were shipped from Louisiana and the
cast actually tarred a mile-long stretch of highway while filming.

CATCH-22   1970

Dir: Mike Nichols. *Scr*: Buck Henry. Based on a novel by Joseph Heller. *Cast*:
Alan Arkin (Captain John Yossarian), Olimpia Carlisi (Luciana)

The eccentric Yossarian tells his lover about a fellow soldier he saw
buried that day.

> YOSSARIAN
> He was very old.

LUCIANA
But he was a boy.

YOSSARIAN
Well, he died. You don't get any older than that.

CABARET   1972

Dir: Bob Fosse. *Scr*: Jay Presson Allen. Based on a play by John Van Druten and stories by Christopher Isherwood. *Cast*: Joel Grey (Master of Ceremonies)

MASTER OF CEREMONIES
Meine Damen und Herren, *Madames et Messieurs*,
Ladies and Gentlemen. Where are your troubles
now? Forgotten? I told you so. We have no
troubles here! Here, life is beautiful. The
girls are beautiful. Even the orchestra is
beautiful. *Auf Wiedersehen! A bientôt.*

Liza Minnelli worked with her own father, acclaimed musical director Vincente Minnelli, to design her hair and make-up. She said she could tell she was the star of the nightclub because she was the only performer with shaved armpits.

THE SHOOTIST   1976

Dir: Don Siegel. *Scr*: Miles Hood Swarthout, Scott Hale. Based on a novel by Glendon Swarthout. *Cast*: John Wayne (J. B. Books), James Stewart (Dr E. W. Hostetler)

An ageing gunfighter contemplates his mortality.

BOOKS
You told me I was strong as an ox.

DR HOSTETLER
Well, even an ox dies.

THE DEER HUNTER   1978

Dir: Michael Cimino. *Scr*: Deric Washburn. *Cast*: Robert De Niro (Michael 'Mike' Vronsky), Christopher Walken (Nikanor 'Nick' Chevotarevich)

A Vietnam veteran searches for an old friend in Saigon but is shocked to discover he has become a heroin addict.

> MICHAEL
>
> I came twelve thousand miles back here to get you. What's the matter with you? Don't you recognize me? Nicky, I love you, you're my friend. What are you doing? We don't have much time, Nick.

Nick holds a revolver to his own head. He pulls the trigger but it clicks on an empty chamber.

> MICHAEL
>
> Is this what you want? Is this what you want? I love you, Nick.

Michael pulls the trigger: another empty chamber.

> MICHAEL
>
> Come on, Nicky, come home. Just come home. Home. Talk to me.

He sees Nick's needle marks.

> MICHAEL
>
> What did you do to your arms?

He reminds Nick of their hunting days.

> MICHAEL
>
> Do you remember the trees? Do you remember all the different ways of the trees? Do you remember that? Do you remember? Huh? The mountains? Do you remember all that?

                    NICK
    One shot.

He smiles and laughs, remembering their old
catchphrase.

                    MICHAEL
    One shot, one shot.

Without warning, Nick pulls the trigger and
shoots himself.

                    MICHAEL
    Nicky, Nicky, don't, Nick, no!

De Niro suggested the gun used for this scene should contain real
bullets to heighten the tension. Only on the takes where the trigger
was pulled did the actors check there was no live round in the
chamber.

BLADE RUNNER   1982

Dir: Ridley Scott. *Scr*: Hampton Fancher, David Webb Peoples. Based on a novel
by Philip K. Dick. *Cast*: Rutger Hauer (Roy Batty)

An android fascinated by the possibility of his own humanity faces
death.

                    ROY
    Quite an experience to live in fear, isn't
    it? That's what it is to be a slave. I've seen
    things you people wouldn't believe. Attack
    ships on fire off the shoulder of Orion. I've
    watched C-beams glitter in the dark near the
    Tannhäuser Gate. All those moments will be lost
    in time, like tears in rain... Time to die.

Ridley Scott had been impressed by Rutger Hauer's performance in several films and cast him without ever having met him. In this project, Hauer was to play an icily murderous android (Batty), so for a joke he turned up on the first day wearing green sunglasses, pink satin trousers and a cuddly white sweater with animals on it. One production executive recalls that when Scott first saw him he 'literally turned white'.

'TEARS IN RAIN'

Blade Runner, Philip K. Dick and Ridley's Scott's provocative dystopian vision, polarized reactions on its first release and even if it is now widely agreed to be a masterpiece its ambiguities continue to intrigue. Rick Deckard (Harrison Ford) is a cop whose task it is to seek out and destroy escaped replicants – robot workers ostensibly indistinguishable from humans. The story, set in 2019, invites us to explore notions of consciousness and emotion. Director Ridley Scott believed Deckard himself was a replicant, producer Michael Deeley and Harrison Ford felt he must be human, while writer Hampton Fancher wanted the audience to decide for themselves.

The uncertainty worked in reverse, too. Rutger Hauer, playing replicant Roy Batty, was determined to make his character as human as possible and felt the scene of his death was a perfect opportunity to challenge Deckard's – and our – preconceptions about artificial intelligence. The lines he speaks in the film's various released versions differ from all the earlier scripts and Hampton Fancher's draft of 24 July 1980 contains no final speech at all apart from Batty taunting Deckard with the words:

```
Time to die.
```

Fancher's script with David Webb Peoples from December 1980 has:

> I've known adventures, seen places you
> people will never see, I've been Offworld
> and back... frontiers! I've stood on
> the back deck of a blinker bound for the
> Plutition Camps with sweat in my eyes
> watching the stars fight on the shoulder
> of Orion... I've felt wind in my hair,
> riding test boats off the black galaxies and
> seen an attack fleet burn like a match and
> disappear. I've seen it, felt it!

Fancher and Peoples' draft dated 23 February 1981 reads:

> I've seen things... seen things you
> little people wouldn't believe... Attack
> ships on fire off the shoulder of Orion
> bright as magnesium... I rode on the back
> decks of a blinker and watched C-beams
> glitter in the dark near the Tannhäuser
> Gate. All those moments... They'll be
> gone.

Hauer described the speech in the shooting script he was given as 'opera talk' and set about revising it the night before the cameras rolled; his amalgamation of scripted ideas and improvisation is frequently cited as the greatest dying speech on film.

MONTY PYTHON'S THE MEANING OF LIFE   1983

Dir: Terry Jones, Terry Gilliam. *Scr*: Graham Chapman, John Cleese, Terry Gilliam, Eric Idle, Terry Jones, Michael Palin. *Cast*: John Cleese (Grim Reaper), Graham Chapman (Host)

A group of friends at dinner receive an unexpected visitor.

> GRIM REAPER
> Silence! I have come for you — to take you
> away. That is my purpose. I am Death.

> HOST
> Well, that's cast rather a gloom over the
> evening, hasn't it?

BRAZIL   1985

Dir: Terry Gilliam. *Scr*: Terry Gilliam, Tom Stoppard, Charles McKeown. *Cast*: Ian Holm (Mr Kurtzmann), Jonathan Pryce (Sam Lowry)

Sam, a government employee in an Orwellian world, asks his boss Kurtzmann what has happened to a citizen named Buttle.

> KURTZMANN
> You see? The population census has got him down
> as 'dormanted'. The Central Collective Storehouse
> computer has got him down as 'deleted'.

> SAM
> Hang on.

Sam checks another computer terminal.

> KURTZMANN
> Information Retrieval has got him down as
> 'inoperative'. And there's another one — security
> has got him down as 'excised'. Administration
> has got him down as 'completed'.

ALIENS   1986

Dir: James Cameron. *Scr*: James Cameron. *Cast*: Carrie Henn (Rebecca 'Newt' Jorden), Sigourney Weaver (Ellen Ripley)

Ripley reassures Newt, the child she has rescued, that the alien threat is over as they prepare to return to Earth from deep space.

NEWT

Are we gonna sleep all the way home?

RIPLEY

All the way home.

NEWT

Can I dream?

RIPLEY

Yes, honey. I think we both can.

She tucks Newt in.

RIPLEY

Sleep tight.

NEWT

Affirmative.

Despite the apparently lavish budget, the film-makers had to cut corners wherever they could. The room with the hypersleep capsules was made to look larger with the use of mirrors; only six alien suits were used, constructed from a handful of latex appliances stuck on black leotards. The assault vehicle was a modified airport towing vehicle and Ripley's cabin bathroom is actually a British Airways toilet.

STAND BY ME   1986

Dir: Rob Reiner. *Scr*: Raynold Gideon, Bruce A. Evans. Based on a novel by Stephen King. *Cast*: Richard Dreyfuss (Gordie Lachance/Narrator)

The narrator recalls an unforgettable summer from his childhood.

>   NARRATOR
> I never had any friends later on like the ones I
> had when I was twelve. Jesus, does anyone?

CITY SLICKERS   1991

Dir: Ron Underwood. *Scr*: Lowell Ganz, Babaloo Mandel. *Cast*: Billy Crystal (Mitch Robbins)

Mitch attends Career Day at his son's school.

>   MITCH
> Value this time in your life, kids, because
> this is the time in your life when you still
> have your choices, and it goes by so fast.
> When you're a teenager, you think you can do
> anything, and you do. Your twenties are a blur.
> Thirties — you raise your family, you make a
> little money and you think to yourself: 'What
> happened to my twenties?' Forties — you grow
> a little potbelly, you grow another chin. The
> music starts to get too loud and one of your
> old girlfriends from high school becomes a
> grandmother. Fifties — you have a minor surgery.
> You'll call it a 'procedure', but it's a
> surgery. Sixties — you'll have a major surgery,
> the music is still loud but it doesn't matter
> because you can't hear it anyway. Seventies
> — you and the wife retire to Fort Lauderdale.
> You start eating dinner at two o'clock in the

afternoon, you have lunch around ten, breakfast
the night before. You spend most of your time
wandering around malls looking for the ultimate
soft yogurt and muttering: 'How come the kids
don't call?', 'How come the kids don't call?'
The eighties, you'll have a major stroke. You
end up babbling to some Jamaican nurse who your
wife can't stand but who you call mama. Any
questions?

THELMA & LOUISE   1991

Dir: Ridley Scott. *Scr*: Callie Khouri. *Cast*: Geena Davis (Thelma Dickinson),
Susan Sarandon (Louise Sawyer)

Two women on the run are surrounded by police but decide they
would rather die free than return to their former lives.

> THELMA
> OK, then listen — let's not get caught.

> LOUISE
> What're you talking about?

> THELMA
> Let's keep going!

> LOUISE
> What d'you mean?

Thelma nods at the sheer drop ahead of them.

> THELMA
> Go.

> LOUISE
> You sure?

THELMA
Yeah.

The car begins to gather speed...

THE SILENCE OF THE LAMBS   1991

Dir: Jonathan Demme. *Scr*: Ted Tally. Based on a novel by Thomas Harris. *Cast*:
Anthony Hopkins (Dr Hannibal Lecter)

A killer known for his cannibalistic tastes has escaped from prison.

LECTER
I do wish we could chat longer, but I'm having
an old friend for dinner.

UNFORGIVEN   1992

Dir: Clint Eastwood. *Scr*: David Webb Peoples. *Cast*: Clint Eastwood (Will
Munny), Jaimz Woolvett (The Schofield Kid)

A gunfighter consoles a young colleague who has shot an adversary.

WILL
It's a hell of a thing, killin' a man. You take
away all he's got and all he's ever gonna have.

SCHOFIELD KID
Yeah, well, I guess they had it comin'.

WILL
We all have it comin', kid.

The long-suffering David Webb Peoples wrote the script in 1976,
sixteen years before it was filmed. Eastwood resisted reading it for a
long time because his assistant didn't think it was any good; when
he finally did, he loved it but felt his character should be older – and
delayed production for a further ten years.

Dir: Robert Altman. *Scr*: Michael Tolkin, based on his novel. *Cast*: Tim Robbins (Griffin Mill), Greta Scacchi (June Gudmundsdottir)

A jaded Hollywood executive has rejected another unpromising screenplay.

> GRIFFIN
>
> It lacked certain elements that we need to market a film successfully.

> JUNE
>
> What elements?

> GRIFFIN
>
> Suspense, laughter, violence. Hope, heart, nudity, sex. Happy endings. Mainly happy endings.

To add realism, Altman called on many of his showbiz friends and acquaintances to play themselves in the film. The roll call included Bruce Willis, Anjelica Huston, Jack Lemmon, Susan Sarandon, Julia Roberts, John Cusack, Cher, James Coburn, Elliott Gould and Burt Reynolds. A trade paper estimated that if they had all charged their normal salaries the budget would have risen by $100 million [$180 million].

TINSELTOWN

No business in history can have been so widely associated with a landmark which cost a mere $21,000 [$310,000]. The sign, originally reading 'Hollywoodland', was put up in 1923 by property developers encouraging Los Angelenos to colonize the hills. In the 1940s it was damaged when its caretaker drove his Model A Ford into the letter 'H', and in 1949 the local Chamber of Commerce entered a contract to restore the sign on condition it was amended to say 'Hollywood'. By then the district was already a household name.

In its earliest years, American motion picture production was based on the East Coast where manufacturers of cameras and film stock were involved in bitter rivalry to establish supremacy through patents and rights agreements. When Thomas Edison began sending agents to impound unlicensed equipment, many film-makers headed west and in 1910 D. W. Griffith was the first director to complete a film (*In Old California*) shot entirely on location in the village of Hollywood, Los Angeles.

Since the slow photographic negatives of the time required a huge amount of illumination in order to yield a good image, and the crude artificial lighting then used was cumbersome and expensive, the wide open spaces and reliable sunshine of California proved a huge advantage. By 1915, Hollywood was established as the industry's movie capital.

'Industry' is often seen as a pejorative description by the writers, directors and actors who work within the system but its founders, such as the Warner brothers, Louis B. Mayer at MGM and Adolph Zukor at Paramount, were under no illusion that what they wanted to create were empires – personal fiefdoms, where the talent they hired was kept on a tight leash to ensure affordable, efficient delivery of product for their audiences. Despite this, the studios liked to imagine their productions carried the gloss of respectable creative endeavour and MGM's official slogan remains 'ars gratia artis' – art for art's sake.

Thus was born a long-running rivalry between employers and employed. The talent, bound by lucrative contracts, found solace in snide remarks, while the paymasters took consolation from their profits and smiled tightly. The *amour-propre* of the industry is such that even when hit movies such as *Sunset Boulevard*, *The Player* and *L.A. Confidential* portray Hollywood as corrupt, venal and philistine, their producers are all too happy to stand on the red carpet and share the glory.

This is merely a smattering of the insults that have been hurled at the industry over the years:

Those who do not study history are forced to get it from Hollywood.
Allen Barra

Half the people in Hollywood are dying to be discovered and the other half are afraid they will be.
Lionel Barrymore

There are only three ages for women in Hollywood - Babe, District Attorney, and Driving Miss Daisy.
Goldie Hawn

I'm a Hollywood writer, so I put on my sports jacket and take off my brain.
Ben Hecht

Every country gets the circus it deserves. Spain gets bullfights. Italy gets the Catholic Church. America gets Hollywood.
Erica Jong

Hollywood amuses me. Holier-than-thou for the public, and unholier-than-the-devil in reality.
Grace Kelly

I always thought the real violence in Hollywood isn't what's on the screen. It's what you have to do to raise the money.
David Mamet

Hollywood is a sewer with service from the Ritz Carlton.
Wilson Mizner

Hollywood is a place where they'll pay you a thousand dollars for a kiss and fifty cents for your soul.
Marilyn Monroe

The only -ism Hollywood believes in is plagiarism.
Dorothy Parker

Hollywood is a place that attracts people with massive holes in their souls.
Julia Phillips

In Europe an actor is an artist. In Hollywood, if he isn't working, he's a bum.
Anthony Quinn

In Hollywood the woods are full of people that learned to write but evidently can't read. If they could read their stuff, they'd stop writing.
Will Rogers

Agents are like tires on a car; in order to get anywhere at all, you need at least four of them, and they need to be rotated every 5,000 miles.
Billy Wilder

In Hollywood a marriage is a success if it outlasts milk.
Rita Rudner

Hollywood is loneliness beside the swimming pool.
Liv Ullmann

FOUR WEDDINGS AND A FUNERAL 1994

Dir: Mike Newell. *Scr*: Richard Curtis. *Cast*: Hugh Grant (Charles), Andie
MacDowell (Carrie)

Two old friends caught outside in a rain storm finally find the
courage to confess their feelings.

> CHARLES
>
> The truth of it is, I've loved you from the first
> second I met you.

Carrie tries to digest his words.

> CHARLES
>
> You're not suddenly going to go away again, are
> you?

> CARRIE
>
> No. I might drown. But otherwise, no.

> CHARLES
>
> OK, OK. We'll go in.

They head inside but Charles turns to her again:

> CHARLES
>
> But first, let me ask you one thing. Do you think
> — after we've dried off, after we've spent lots
> more time together — you might agree not to marry
> me? And do you think not being married to me
> might maybe be something you could consider doing
> for the rest of your life?

He waits for her answer.

> CHARLES
>
> Do you?

> CARRIE
>
> I do . . .

SE7EN   1995

Dir: David Fincher. *Scr*: Andrew Kevin Walker. *Cast*: Morgan Freeman (Detective Lieutenant William Somerset)

An ageing detective is left shocked by the brutality of the serial killer he has apprehended.

> SOMERSET
>
> Ernest Hemingway once wrote: 'The world is a fine place and worth fighting for.' I agree with the second part.

AMERICAN BEAUTY   1999

Dir: Sam Mendes. *Scr*: Alan Ball. *Cast*: Kevin Spacey (Lester Burnham)

A man fighting for joy and dignity narrates the story of his life – after he has died.

> LESTER
>
> I had always heard your entire life flashes in front of your eyes the second before you die. First of all, that one second isn't a second at all, it stretches on forever, like an ocean of time . . . For me, it was lying on my back at Boy Scout camp, watching falling stars . . . And yellow leaves, from the maple trees, that lined our street . . . Or my grandmother's hands, and the way her skin seemed like paper . . . And the first time I saw my cousin Tony's brand new Firebird . . . And Janie . . . And Janie . . . And . . . Carolyn. I guess I could be pretty pissed off about what happened to me . . . but it's hard to stay mad, when there's so much beauty in the world. Sometimes I feel like I'm seeing it all at once, and it's too much, my heart fills up

like a balloon that's about to burst . . . And
then I remember to relax, and stop trying to
hold on to it, and then it flows through me like
rain and I can't feel anything but gratitude for
every single moment of my stupid little life. . .
You have no idea what I'm talking about, I'm
sure. But don't worry . . . you will someday.

Writer Alan Ball claimed the film – originally intended as a play –
was inspired by his memory of watching a paper bag swirling in the
wind at the World Trade Center plaza.

EYES WIDE SHUT   1999

Dir: Stanley Kubrick. *Scr*: Stanley Kubrick, Frederic Raphael. Based on a novella
by Arthur Schnitzler. *Cast*: Sydney Pollack (Victor Ziegler)

Victor reassures a friend that the death of girl they knew was just an
unfortunate accident.

                    VICTOR
Life goes on. It always does: until it doesn't.

Director Kubrick hated travelling so the New York exteriors had to
be built in London. The film holds the record for the longest ever
continuous shooting schedule; on one occasion, Kubrick repeated
a shot of Tom Cruise walking through a door ninety times until he
felt it was right. Kubrick died four days after completing his edit, for
which he had the contractual right of final cut, so Warner Brothers
were bound to release the film exactly as it stood.

Among the various props in the movie can be seen a VHS copy
of *Rain Man*, a hit for Tom Cruise in 1988, and DVDs of several
Kubrick films including his previous production *Full Metal Jacket*
(1987).

FIGHT CLUB   1999

Dir: David Fincher. *Scr*: Jim Uhls. Based on a novel by Chuck Palahniuk. *Cast*:
Edward Norton (Narrator)

The leader of an anarchic self-help group warns his audience to seize
the day.

> NARRATOR
>
> This is your life and it's ending one minute
> at a time.

DANCER IN THE DARK   2000

Dir: Lars von Trier. *Scr*: Lars von Trier. *Cast*: Björk (Selma Ježková), David Morse
(Bill Houston)

Selma finds the fantasy world of cinema a comfort amid life's
challenges.

> SELMA
>
> You like the movies, don't you?

> BILL
>
> I love the movies. I just love the musicals.

> SELMA
>
> But isn't it annoying when they do the last song
> in the films?

> BILL
>
> Why?

> SELMA
>
> Because you just know when it goes really big...
> and the camera goes like out of the roof... and
> you just know it's going to end. I hate that. I
> would leave just after the next to last song...
> and the film would just go on forever.

PICTURE CREDITS

Plate section 1

Alfred Hitchcock on the set of *Psycho* © Kobal.
Scarlett Johansson in *Avengers – Age Of Ultron* © Shutterstock.
Sean Connery in *Diamonds are Forever* © Shutterstock.
James Stewart, Kim Novak in *Vertigo* © Shutterstock.
Will Smith, Margot Robbie in *Focus* © Shutterstock.
Sigourney Weaver in *Alien* © Shutterstock.
Daniel Day-Lewis in *Gangs of New York* © Kobal.
Colin Clive and Boris Karloff on the set of *The Bride of Frankenstein* © Kobal.

Plate section 2

Marilyn Monroe; 20th Century Fox/Frank Powolny/ Bottom left Bert Reisfeld
    © Kobal.
Liza Minnelli in *Cabaret*; ABC/Allied Artists © Kobal.
Brad Pitt in *Fight Club* © Kobal.
John Cleese in *A Fish Called Wanda* © Kobal.
Stanley Kubrick on the set of *2001: A Space Odyssey* © Kobal.
The set of *2001: A Space Odyssey* © Kobal.
Marlon Brando and Martin Sheen in *Apocalypse Now* © Kobal.
Frances McDormand in *Fargo* © Shutterstock.
Eddie Redmayne, Alicia Vikander in *The Danish Girl* © Shutterstock.
Steven Spielberg on the set of *Jaws* © Kobal.
Spielberg on the set of *Indiana Jones and The Kingdom Of The Crystal Skull*
    © Shutterstock.

Plate section 3

Cary Grant in *North by Northwest* © Kobal.
Clark Gable, Vivien Leigh in *Gone with the Wind* © Kobal.
Dan Aykroyd, John Belushi in *The Blues Brothers* © Kobal.
Anthony Hopkins in *The Silence of the Lambs* © Kobal.
Jack Lemmon, Tony Curtis in *Some Like it Hot* © Shutterstock.
John Travolta, Samuel L. Jackson in *Pulp Fiction* © Shutterstock.
Susan Sarandon, Geena Davis in *Thelma and Louise* © Shutterstock.

Lauren Bacall, Humphrey Bogart in *The Big Sleep* © Shutterstock.
Nicole Kidman, Tom Cruise in *Eyes Wide Shut* © Shutterstock.
Catherine Zeta-Jones in *Chicago* © Kobal.
Joan Crawford © Kobal.
Malcolm McDowell in *A Clockwork Orange* © Kobal.
Javier Bardem in *No Country for Old Men* © Kobal.
Orson Welles, Rita Hayworth in *The Lady from Shanghai* © Shutterstock.
Daniel Craig in *Spectre* © Shutterstock.

TEXT CREDITS

TITLES

CAST

Harris, Richard 49, 311, 323, 358, 359
Harvey, Laurence 94
Hauer, Rutger 452, 453,
Hawke, Ethan 115
Hayakawa, Sessue 307
Hayden, Sterling 39
Haydn, Richard 371
Hayworth, Rita 147, 159
Hedebrant, Kåre 414
Heflin, Marta 380
Hellinger, Mark 441
Helpmann, Robert 221
Henn, Carrie 411
Hepburn, Audrey 16, 95
Hepburn, Katharine 38, 43, 60, 61, 86, 276
Heston, Charlton 21, 272
Hill, Jonah 395
Hinds, Ciarán 205
Hitchcock, Patricia 270
Hoffman, Dustin 43, 44, 52, 219, 220, 221, 379
Holcomb, Sarah 378
Holden, William 1, 62, 63, 87,
Holliday, Judy 60
Holloway, Stanley 273, 422
Holm, Ian 23, 248, 455
Holmes, Taylor 15
Homolka, Oskar 160
Hopkins, Anthony 428, 453, 459
Howard, Leslie 122
Hudson, Kate 48
Hudson, Rock 88
Hull, Josephine 15
Hunter, Kim 124
Hurt, John 401, 429
Hurt, William 223, 224
Huston, John 280
Huston, Walter 85
Hyde-White, Wilfrid 273

Jackson, Samuel L. 107, 200, 320, 321, 390
Jaeckel, Richard 97
James, Clifton 275
James, Sid 91
Janssen, Famke 110
Johansson, Scarlett 431
Johnson, Celia 421
Johnson, Reggie 317
Jones, Gene 261
Jones, Terry 281
Jones, Tommy Lee 324

Karloff, Boris 38
Keaton, Diane 22, 134, 185, 222
Kelly, Gene 64, 215
Kennedy, George 449
Kidder, Margot 135, 347
King, Chris Thomas 391
Kinski, Klaus 136, 280
Klanfer, François 431
Kline, Kevin 110
Koch, Marianne 339
Koonce, Kelly 434
Korman, Harvey 188
Kotto, Yaphet 248
Kristofferson, Kris 98, 401

Lancaster, Burt 88, 401
Laughton, Charles 234
Lawhon, Margaret 290
Leandersson, Lina 414
Ledger, Heath 76, 264, 432
Lee, Spike 44
Leigh, Janet 237
Leigh, Vivien 9, 56, 156
Leitch, Donovan 25
Lemmon, Jack 89, 370, 424, 425, 460
Liotta, Ray 199
Ljunggren, Sten 49

Lockwood, Margaret 440
Lone, John 286
Lorre, Peter 399
Loy, Myrna 332
Lugosi, Bela 234,
Luna, Diego 230
Lynch, John Carroll 53

McCambridge, Mercedes 246
McCormack, Catherine 229
McCrea, Joel 364
McDormand, Frances 300, 354
MacDowell, Andie 404, 464
McDowell, Malcolm 133, 245, 246, 276
McGann, Paul 382
McGinley, John C. 73
McGregor, Ewan 30
McKellen, Ian 52, 296
McKern, Leo 274
McKinney, Bill 247
McLaglen, Victor 65
MacLaine, Shirley 52, 424, 425
McNamara, William 384
McQueen, Steve 41, 308, 440
Maffia, Roma 289
Maley, Peggy 183
Mara, Rooney 76
Marais, Jean 236
Martin, Steve 98, 138
Marvin, Lee 70, 317
Marx, Groucho 56, 211, 247
Matthau, Walter 366
Maxwell, Edwin 302
Mayo, Virginia 214
Melville, Jean-Pierre 18
Ménochet, Denis 326
Miles, Sarah 383

CREW